INDIANA UNIVERSITY OLYMPIANS

David Woods

INDIANA
UNIVERSITY
OLYMPIANS

FROM LEROY SAMSE TO LILLY KING

This book is a publication of

INDIANA UNIVERSITY PRESS
Office of Scholarly Publishing
Herman B Wells Library 350
1320 East 10th Street
Bloomington, Indiana 47405 USA

iupress.indiana.edu

© 2020 by David Woods
All rights reserved

No part of this book may be reproduced or utilized in any form or by any means, electronic or mechanical, including photocopying and recording, or by any information storage and retrieval system, without permission in writing from the publisher. The paper used in this publication meets the minimum requirements of the American National Standard for Information Sciences—Permanence of Paper for Printed Library Materials, ANSI Z39.48–1992.

*Manufactured in the
United States of America*

Cataloging information is available from the Library of Congress

ISBN 978-0-253-05007-6 (cloth)
ISBN 978-0-253-05009-0 (Web PDF)

1 2 3 4 5   25 24 23 22 21 20

CONTENTS

Preface ix

1 BASKETBALL 1

Steve Alford, 1984	5
Quinn Buckner and Scott May, 1976	15
Walt Bellamy, 1960	20

2 TRACK AND FIELD 25

Derek Drouin, 2012, 2016	27
David Neville, 2008	35
DeDee Nathan, 2000	39
Bob Kennedy, 1992, 1996	45
Jim Spivey, 1984, 1992, 1996	57
Dave Volz, 1992	65
Sunder Nix, 1984	69
Willie May, 1960	74
Milt Campbell, 1952, 1956	77
Greg Bell, 1956	83
Fred Wilt, 1948, 1952	90
Roy Cochran, 1948	93
Charles Hornbostel, 1932, 1936	96
Don Lash, 1936	99
Ivan Fuqua, 1932	103
LeRoy Samse, 1904	107

3 SWIMMING 111

Lilly King, 2016	113
Cody Miller, 2016	121
Blake Pieroni, 2016	128
Gary Hall, 1968, 1972, 1976	133
Jim Montgomery, 1976	138
Mark Spitz, 1968, 1972	145
Mike Stamm, 1972	160
John Kinsella, 1968, 1972	163
Charlie Hickcox, 1968	168
Don McKenzie, 1968	174
Chet Jastremski, 1964, 1968	179
Kathy Ellis, 1964	184
Fred Schmidt, 1964	188
Frank McKinney Jr., 1956, 1960	190
Mike Troy, 1960	194
Bill Woolsey, 1952, 1956	198

4 DIVING 205

Michael Hixon, 2016	205
Mark Lenzi, 1992, 1996	209
Cynthia Potter, 1972, 1976	214
Lesley Bush, 1964, 1968	219
Ken Sitzberger, 1964	223

5 SOCCER 229

Brian Maisonneuve, 1996	229
Steve Snow, 1992	233
John Stollmeyer, 1988	237
Angelo DiBernardo, 1984	241
Gregg Thompson, 1984	245

6 OTHER SPORTS 249

Michelle Venturella, Softball, 2000   251
Mickey Morandini, Baseball, 1988   255
Dick Voliva, Wrestling, 1936   258

Sources   261

Indiana University Olympians   265

PREFACE

INDIANA UNIVERSITY HAS LONG BEEN KNOWN FOR BASKETBALL, AS IT should be. Only UCLA (eleven), Kentucky (eight), and North Carolina (six) have won more NCAA championships than the Hoosiers' five.

But Indiana's legacy at the Olympic Games is no less impressive. The Hoosiers have collected fifty-five gold medals for the United States since the modern Olympics debuted in 1896, a figure exceeded by just seven schools: Stanford, UCLA, the University of Southern California, Texas, Michigan, and Florida. Indiana's ninety-five total medals rank eleventh.

This book has profiles of forty-nine IU Olympians. In the following pages, you will read that:

- The greatest athlete in IU history was not actually recruited by IU.
- A long jump gold medalist had such humble beginnings that he grew up in a chicken house.
- The Hoosiers produced the first African American gold medalist in the decathlon.
- A diver who had never before competed on the 10-meter platform won a gold medal a few months after she first tried it.
- The soccer player who helped build the Hoosiers' dynasty was discovered on Chicago playgrounds.
- A swimmer later became head valet for a Saudi Arabian prince and then a master chef.
- A swimmer was part of rescue missions for astronauts who walked on the moon.
- A double gold medalist won a Silver Star for heroism in the Vietnam War.
- Two distance runners became FBI agents.

Those athletes, in order, are Mark Spitz, Greg Bell, Milt Campbell, Lesley Bush, Angelo DiBernardo, Mike Stamm, Fred Schmidt, Mike Troy, Don Lash, and Fred Wilt.

The event in which the Hoosiers have the most gold medals (ten) is swimming's 4×100-meter medley relay: Frank McKinney, 1960; Kathy Ellis and Fred Schmidt, 1964; Charlie Hickcox and Don McKenzie, 1968; Mark Spitz and Mark Stamm, 1972; Mark Kerry (Australia), 1980; Lilly King and Cody Miller, 2016. Through 2016, the US men had never lost the 4×100 medley relay at an Olympics.

The Hoosiers also have four gold medalists in track and field's 4×400-meter relay: Ivan Fuqua, 1936; Roy Cochran, 1948; Sunder Nix, 1984; and David Neville, 2008.

The Hoosiers have earned a medal in every Olympics in which they competed, except 2004. In 1968, Indiana came away with seventeen medals, a total exceeded by only eight countries.

Indiana features 223 total Olympic berths, including athletes, coaches, and judges. Those are led by one hundred in men's swimming and diving, thirty-nine in men's track and field, and thirty in women's swimming and diving.

The twenty-four nations or territories besides the United States that a Hoosier has represented include Australia, Austria, Brazil, Canada, Colombia, Denmark, Dominican Republic, Egypt, France, Germany, Greece, Honduras, Hong Kong, Hungary, Ireland, Jamaica, Mexico, Nigeria, Puerto Rico, Saudi Arabia, Slovenia, Spain, Ukraine, and Venezuela.

This book is devoted to athletes, but Indiana has had multiple coaches on US staffs. Those include Bob Knight and Tara VanDerveer in basketball; Billy Hayes and Sam Bell in track and field; Doc Counsilman and Ray Looze in swimming; Hobie Billingsley, Jeff Huber, and Drew Johansen in diving; and Billy Thom and Jim Humphrey in wrestling.

The Hoosiers inevitably will send more athletes to Tokyo for the next Olympic Games, which were postponed from 2020 to 2021 by a pandemic. They will bring more medals back to Bloomington and build on a tradition that few universities can emulate.

INDIANA UNIVERSITY OLYMPIANS

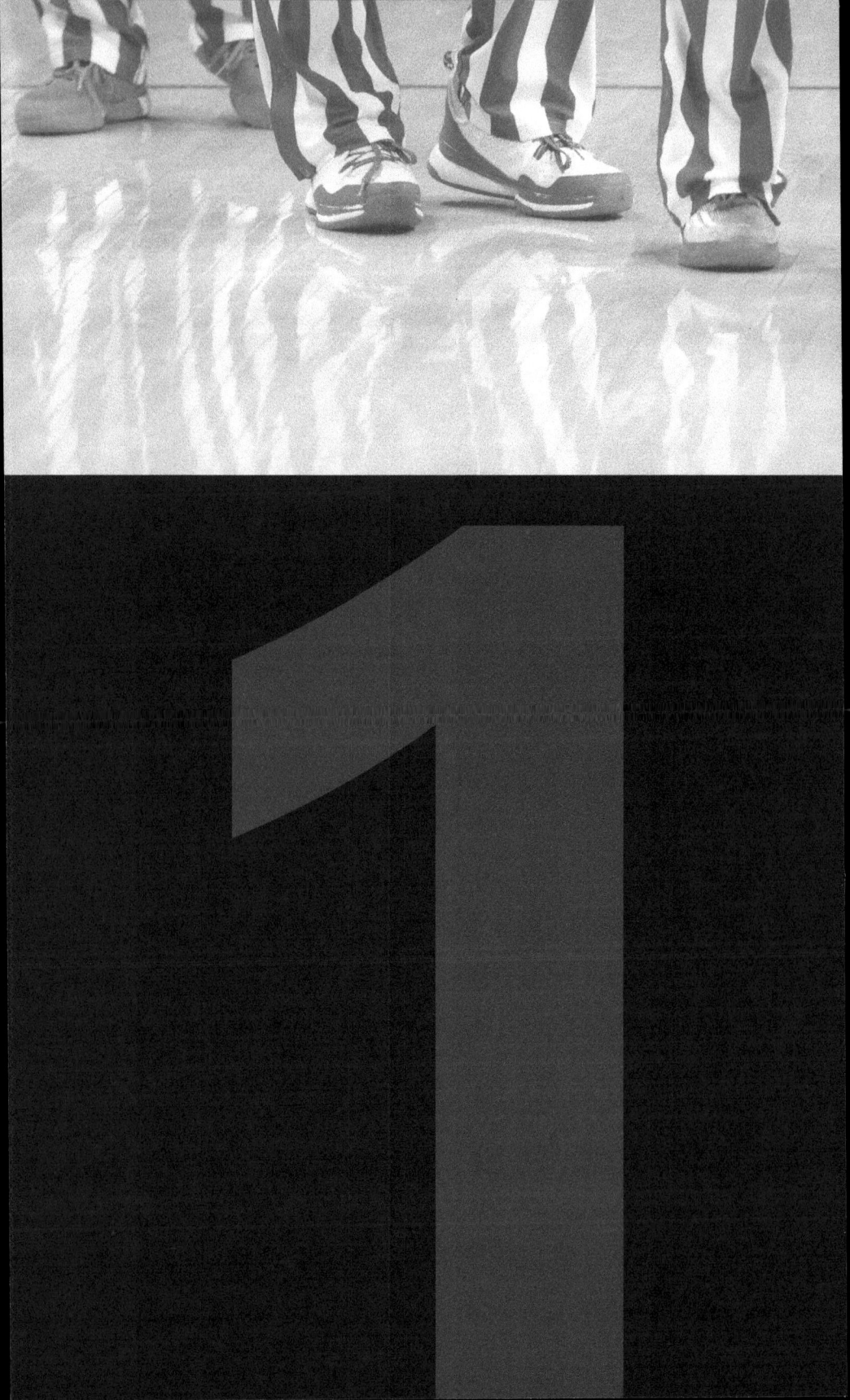

Steve Alford, 1985.
IU Archives P0030877.

Steve Alford
1984

America's Last Amateur Gold

STEVE ALFORD WAS COMING OFF A MOMENTOUS FRESHMAN BASKETBALL season. He averaged 15.5 points a game, scoring 27 in the Indiana Hoosiers' 72–68 upset of top-ranked North Carolina and Michael Jordan in the NCAA tournament's Sweet 16.

Although the Hoosiers didn't make it to the 1984 Final Four, coach Bob Knight did. He appeared on TV at halftime of one of the games on CBS. Alford was watching at home in New Castle, Indiana, with friends.

Knight looked into the camera and said, "I know Steve's watching back home. The thing I want him working on all summer is his defense and moving without the ball."

Alford shook his head. Here was Coach, two thousand miles away, chiding him about his defense. The next week, back in Bloomington, Alford was playing pickup. Those games were strictly for fun because no coaches were watching.

"I've got the whole summer to get better," Alford told Todd Meier, another freshman for the Hoosiers. "And no Coach Knight on my butt!"

Or so everyone thought.

Days later, Alford went to the mailbox at his dormitory, which usually had nothing other than letters from his mother. This time, there was an invitation to be among seventy-three players trying out for the US Olympic team, coached by Knight. That started the Hoosier on a summer in which he would see plenty of his coach... and Jordan.

Alford not only made the team, he was fourth in scoring (10.3 points a game) and second in assists for the 8–0 gold medalists. The Los Angeles Olympics were the last played before NBA pros were allowed. Alford is the fourth-youngest gold medalist in Olympic basketball history, at nineteen years, 260 days.

"To be the last amateur team to win gold is pretty special," he said.

Alford had not expected an invitation to the trials. The only younger players were Delray Brooks, eighteen, the Indiana Mr. Basketball who had committed to IU, and high schooler Danny Manning, seventeen, of Greensboro, North Carolina. Of the twelve players chosen, eleven were selected in the first round of the 1984 or 1985 NBA draft. The twelfth was Alford.

Six invitees went into the Naismith Basketball Hall of Fame: Jordan, Patrick Ewing, Chris Mullin, Charles Barkley, Karl Malone, and John Stockton. And Barkley, Malone, and Stockton did not make the Olympic team.

"Back then, when it was strictly amateur, no pros, you really had to hit it right," Alford said. "You almost had to hit the Olympics when you were a junior or senior in college. I was very fortunate I got invited."

He was a gym rat with a chance to play against some of the best players in the sport. That was going to be enough. Making the team was out of the question.

Trials began April 17. They were held at the IU Fieldhouse, across the street from Assembly Hall. Players were assigned to teams on each of eight courts with a simple instruction: play. Knight watched from a scaffold as a football coach would do.

Knight assembled a staff of nineteen college coaches to conduct three-a-day workouts and coach the games. There was a seven-player selection committee, although it was widely assumed Knight would have the final say.

In addition to the fact Alford played without burden of expectation, he found he had two other advantages: he knew Knight's motion offense and thus did not move tentatively, and he was in the best shape of his life. The workouts, drills, and scrimmages were as much a test of stamina as skill. He grew more confident after shooting seven of seven in his first scrimmage, and three of five in the second.

Alford was trying to study for final exams but found himself writing down names of players he would have to beat out to make the team. Also trying to guess those making the first cut were hundreds of pro scouts and journalists.

Alford recalled the sentimental favorite being Barkley, then a 280-pound forward out of Auburn nicknamed the "Round Mound of Rebound." Barkley's thunderous dunks and demonstrative fist pumps delighted onlookers but did not impress Knight. Coincidentally, Barkley was Alford's roommate during the trials on the top floor of the Memorial Union.

In a 1989 autobiography (written with John Garrity), Alford speculated that pairing him with Barkley was "one of Coach's little jokes, putting me with a guy who looked as if he could eat the furniture."

Alford hid food from his roomie. "If I had any Cokes or candy bars, I stuffed them away in my gym bag," Alford wrote.

Otherwise, Barkley was delightful, playing H-O-R-S-E with ball boys after practice or wrestling Auburn teammate Chuck Person on Alford's bed.

Alford was mesmerized by Jordan, whose maneuvers were so unconventional that those at the trials could barely describe them. There were dunks with 360-degree spins, jump hooks, alley-oops—you name it. The one thing that Jordan did that Alford also could was wipe the soles of his shoes on a wet towel on the floor. Knight spotted the mimicry and yelled, "See that, Jordan? You think Alford can leap from the foul line and dunk now?"

Alford could not. He could shoot.

So when the cut to thirty-two players was made, and the list was announced, Alford was on it.

Public scrimmages moved to Assembly Hall, which featured the atmosphere of college games, complete with cheerleaders and the IU pep band. Behind the scenes, Barkley was wavering on whether he wanted to play in the Olympics at all. He had already planned to leave college early, and if he went pro before Jordan, Barkley speculated he could make more money from endorsements.

Following weekend play, another cut was made, this time to twenty. Among those not making it was Antoine Carr of Wichita State. Carr was good enough— he already had a $225,000-a-year contract with an Italian team and had played for the silver medalists at the 1982 World Basketball Championship. Carr played for sixteen years in the NBA. Yet Knight's message had been clear: he would not be picking the twelve best players but the twelve making the best team.

There were no leaks about who was going to make it and no politicking by players or their advocates.

"I played in an era when there was no social media," Alford said. "Not every person was able to voice their opinion publicly like they do now."

Players returned for a minicamp in May and full practices June 15. The NBA draft, held June 19, was not the spectacle that it is now. Instead of traveling to New York for the draft at Madison Square Garden, those still in contention for the Olympics watched from Bloomington. Once drafted, players were led to a WTTV studio for a live feed to the USA Network.

Eight of the first eighteen selections were would-be Olympians: Jordan (drafted third); Sam Perkins (fourth); Alvin Robertson (seventh); Lancaster Gordon (eighth); Leon Wood (tenth); Tim McCormick (twelfth); Jeff Turner (seventeenth), and Vern Fleming (eighteenth). That did not include two players—Barkley (fifth) and Stockton (sixteenth)—who did not survive the cut to sixteen.

In 1985, five of the top seven picks in the NBA draft were from the Olympic team: Ewing (first), Wayman Tisdale (second), Jon Koncak (fifth), Joe Kleine (sixth), and Mullin (seventh).

The Olympians had multimillion-dollar contracts waiting, but there was a gold medal out there waiting too. Knight "didn't deny" the draft happened, according to Tim Garl, the IU basketball trainer who served in that same role for Team USA. "But he said, 'Hey, you need to do the Olympic thing first. We have a job to do.'"

When it came down to the final cut, Alford did not have to sit in a chair and wait for names to be called. Knight told him, and told him he earned it. Predictably, there was an outcry that an Indiana player had been picked by the Indiana coach. Knight responded just as predictably.

"We had twenty coaches who voted unanimously to keep him on the team," Knight said. "What am I supposed to do, keep him off because he played at Indiana?"

Alford felt no resentment from teammates. Knight yelled at him too often for that to happen. Alford and Tisdale were the most frequent targets of Knight's invectives.

Before heading to Los Angeles, the Olympic team went 7–0 on an exhibition tour against NBA players. The Olympians averaged 103.6 points a game and weren't challenged against out-of-shape, out-of-season pros.

One exhibition, on June 20, was played against a team of former Indiana greats: Ted Kitchel, Isiah Thomas, Kent Benson, Tom and Dick Van Arsdale, Randy Wittman, Mike Woodson, and 1976 gold medalists Quinn Buckner and Scott May. Team USA won 124–89.

Patriotic and Indiana fervor were underscored in a July 9 game against NBA stars, which drew 67,596 fans—then the most ever to witness a basketball game—to the Hoosier Dome in Indianapolis. The NBA team included Thomas, Magic Johnson, Larry Bird, and Kevin McHale. Team USA won that one 97–82.

The Olympic team practiced in San Diego for two weeks before heading to Los Angeles. There were team-building activities such as trips to the San Diego Zoo and a Padres baseball game, and Alford said some players slipped away for some "cheap thrills" in Tijuana, Mexico. Players took a bus trip to a JCPenney warehouse, where they were issued credentials, outfitted for uniforms, and allowed to stuff as much Olympics swag into a shopping cart as they could: T-shirts, jackets, caps, bags, sweats, shoes, pins, mugs, posters, and so forth.

It would be no exaggeration to assert the Americans won the gold medal not by what they did in Los Angeles but by what they did in Bloomington, San Diego, and elsewhere. Alford said they had the best player on the planet, Michael Jordan, and the best coach on the planet, Bob Knight. Give Knight time to prepare for an opponent, Alford said, and "he was almost unbeatable." And Knight had all summer.

"We had a phenomenal leader in Jordan," Alford said. "He's as good as it got.... It was a phenomenal team that couldn't help but get better. Those guys really did get better and better during that time."

In Los Angeles, players stayed in the Olympic Village on the University of Southern California campus. The team rode on the same bus with athletes such as gymnast Mary Lou Retton and boxer Pernell Whitaker. Alford met sprinter Carl Lewis and diver Greg Louganis. Alford said the experience gave him a lifelong appreciation of athletes from other sports.

"We were a part of the Olympics," he said. "We weren't the Olympics."

Team USA swept through group play with a 5–0 record, beating China 97–49, Canada 89–68, Uruguay 104–68, France 120–62, and Spain 101–68. Alford came off the bench to score thirteen points against Canada on six-of-eight shooting. Against Uruguay, the Americans once made fifteen consecutive shots.

Alford was taking antibiotics for a staph infection before the game against France, but it was not evident. In twenty-three minutes, he shot eight of eight from the field and two of two on free throws for eighteen points. For years, he has teased his basketball-playing children about it.

"Anytime France comes up, whether it is in french fries or anything to do with France, I tell them, 'That country can't get over me. I shot that country out. I was eight for eight.'"

His shooting in the quarterfinal was more consequential, considering he led the Americans with seventeen points in a 78–67 victory over West Germany. It was their closest game of the Olympics.

Knight was so vexed that he did not allow players to address the media afterward. He surprisingly pulled Alford aside to ask what was wrong with the team. Alford said he "took a deep breath" and responded that players were not paying attention to their notebooks during pregame. At Indiana, Alford said, players studied information Knight asked them to write down.

"You know, Steve, if you're not with us tonight, we probably don't win," Knight said, according to Alford's autobiography.

Alford could not respond. His coach had never paid him such a compliment.

At practice the next day, Knight said players would study those notebooks or would not play. No exceptions.

Mullin scored twenty points in a 78–59 victory over Canada, setting up what Knight and the twelve American players had focused on since mid-April: the gold-medal game. They would face Spain, a team they had already beaten by thirty-three points, at the Forum in Inglewood.

The Americans needed no more preparation, explanation, or motivation. After Knight stepped out into the hall for final consultation with assistant coaches, Jordan went to the whiteboard, picked up a marker, wrote a message, and signed it "The Players." He wrote: *COACH: DON'T WORRY. WE'VE PUT UP WITH TOO MUCH SHIT TO LOSE NOW.*

Knight returned, started to speak, and saw Jordan's message. He smiled, looked at each player individually, and said, "Let's go play."

Knight told the other coaches the game against Spain would be over in ten minutes. It was. Alford started for Team USA.

By halftime, amid chants of "U-S-A! U-S-A!" the score was 52–29. In a 96–65 victory, Jordan scored twenty points, Tisdale fourteen, and Perkins twelve. Alford added ten points and seven assists.

Spectators stormed the court. Alford was hoisted up and handed a pair of scissors to cut the net; he then handed them to a teammate. Players were going to lift Knight on their shoulders, but he pointed to eighty-year-old Henry Iba, who had been a consultant. Knight wanted to honor Iba, who was coach for the US team that controversially lost the gold-medal game to the Soviet Union at the 1972 Munich Olympics. Witnesses said Knight might have shed a tear for the coach he respected above all others. After players put Iba down, they carried Knight off the floor to chants of "Bobby! Bobby! Bobby!"

Of all the days, weeks, and months of his journey, the Olympic moment Alford remembers best is of standing on top of the podium and hearing the national anthem. He said he gained a better appreciation of the entire experience as the years passed.

"The thing I watch the most in each Olympics since is the playing of the national anthem when you're on the gold-medal stand," he said.

He did not see any other sports while at the Olympics, and that wasn't really the point anyway. That was reiterated regularly by Knight.

"He was there to win the gold medal," Alford said.

Alford did not stick around for the closing ceremony. He and his parents and brother, Sean, rode home in a van at a leisurely rate. They stopped for two hours in Las Vegas and walked around Caesars Palace. Steve had been "put through the ringer," as his father, Sam, put it, and he slept a lot. As they crossed the Illinois-Indiana border, he saw the first sign: *"WELCOME HOME, STEVE. CONGRATULATIONS."*

There were more signs and banners on Interstate 70 overpasses. East of Indianapolis, he saw a police car in which a girl was waving from the backseat. It was Tanya Frost, his girlfriend at the time and his wife since 1987. Past the Greenfield exit, the Alford van pulled over, and Steve and Tanya loaded into a convertible for a caravan home.

For six miles along I-70, all the way to the State Highway 3 exit, cars lined both sides. Helicopters hovered overhead for TV cameras. After arrival in New Castle, townspeople reached out to shake Alford's hand, and hundreds of people were lined up on both sides of the family home on Hickory Lane.

"The reception in New Castle is something I'll never, ever forget," Alford said.

Two nights later, on Steve Alford Day in New Castle, the world's largest high school gym filled with spectators. The ceremony was capped by Alford's speech, in which he lamented never winning a state championship for Sam, his father and high school coach. Steve took the gold medal off his neck and put it around his father's.

As his father had told him on the phone while the Olympic team was in San Diego, "There's a lot of players in Indiana who can say they've won a state championship. Very few can say they've won an Olympic gold medal."

Steve Alford was seemingly fated to be basketball royalty in Indiana.

He was born November 23, 1964, in Franklin, Indiana, the son of a coach. Soon after his second birthday, his parents, Sam and Sharan, sent Christmas cards forecasting that their son would be a Mr. Basketball in Indiana. Mom and Dad were right.

By age three, Steve was sitting on the bench at Monroe City High School, where his father was the coach. He learned to add by watching numbers on the scoreboard and to read and spell by looking at game programs and last names on the backs of uniforms. At five, he was playing in a YMCA league in Vincennes while his father coached at South Knox.

He would shovel snow from the driveway to shoot baskets if he couldn't get in a gym, practiced broadcasting games in a closet, and kept journals of his progress. Until he left for IU, he missed just two of his father's games—one when he had the chicken pox, another when he finished fourth in a regional Elks Hoop Shoot free throw contest at age ten in Warren, Ohio.

Sam Alford coached for four years at Martinsville, where local hero Jerry Sichting was idolized by his young son. (Sichting went on to be an All–Big Ten guard at Purdue and played and coached in the NBA.) Then his father moved onto New Castle and its 9,325-seat gymnasium.

If there is anywhere in the world for a basketball junkie to grow up, it is New Castle. Alford was no physical specimen—he was all of five foot ten and 125 pounds when he got his driver's license—but he tirelessly worked on his body as well as his game. He would shoot one hundred to three hundred free throws a day, charting them all and punishing himself with fingertip pushups or sprints when he missed.

He played in nineteen varsity games as a freshman, totaling 30 points, and averaged 18.1 for the 13–9 Trojans as a sophomore. He averaged 27.3 as a junior and 37.2 as a senior for teams that went 12–10 and 23–6. He was indeed Mr. Basketball in 1983, finishing with 1,078 points, one off the single-season state record set by Carmel's Dave Shepherd in 1969–70. Alford was 286 of 304 on free throws for .944, which would have led the NBA or NCAA that year.

In the next-to-last game of his high school career, he scored fifty-seven points—one off a state postseason record that has stood since 1915—at the Hinkle Fieldhouse semistate in Indianapolis. New Castle beat Broad Ripple 79–64 but lost to eventual state champion Connersville 70–57 that night, despite Alford's thirty-eight points. So he scored ninety-five points in one day. He was eighty-two of eighty-three on free throws in seven sectional, regional, and semistate games.

He and Tanya missed prom so he could play in the Dapper Dan Roundball Classic at Pittsburgh. Alford scored just four points, but he said, "The basketball game still was better."

At IU, Alford averaged 15.5, 18.1, 22.5, and 22.0 during four seasons in which the Hoosiers were a collective 92–35. As a senior, he was a consensus All-American for the 30–4 Hoosiers. He scored 23 points, featuring seven-of-ten shooting from the three-point line, as Indiana beat Syracuse 74–73 for the 1987 NCAA championship. Alford shot .530 on threes in the first season it was used by the NCAA.

He left Indiana as the Hoosiers' all-time scoring leader with 2,438 points (a record broken by Calbert Cheaney) and a record .898 percentage on free throws.

Alford was the first pick of the second round by the Dallas Mavericks in the NBA draft. He lasted four seasons as a pro, three with Dallas and one with Golden State, before retiring at age twenty-six. He totaled 744 points in 169 NBA games, more than 300 points less than he scored as a high school senior.

He became a college head coach at twenty-seven, returning to his home state at Manchester University. After a 4–16 first season, he was 78–29 in four years, including a 31–1 final season in which Manchester lost in the NCAA Division III championship game.

He subsequently coached four seasons at Southwest Missouri State (78–48), eight at Iowa (152–106), seven at New Mexico (155–52), and more than five at UCLA (124–63). He was fired at UCLA after a 7–6 start to the 2018–19 season. He returned to the Mountain West Conference when he was hired by Nevada in April 2019.

He took teams to the NCAA Sweet 16 four times, including three with UCLA and once (in 1999) with Southwest Missouri. His best records are 31–5 with UCLA in 2016–17 and 30–5 with New Mexico in 2009–10.

His sons, Bryce and Kory, both played college basketball for their father. Kory set a New Mexico high school record with 1,050 points in his senior season, averaging 37.7 per game. Kory left UCLA with the school's career record for threes made.

Quinn Buckner, 1973.
IU Archives P0020733.

Scott May, 1976.
IU Archives P0039895.

Quinn Buckner and Scott May
1976

Winning Back the Gold "Stolen" at Munich 1972

NO AMATEUR BASKETBALL PLAYER HAS EVER HAD, OR EVER WILL HAVE, A year like Quinn Buckner and Scott May did. It is no longer possible in a one-and-done era that features pros in the Olympic Games.

It was momentous enough that the 1975–76 Indiana Hoosiers, at 32–0, are the last NCAA champions to go undefeated. Buckner and May? They were 40–0.

They were key pieces on the US team that exacted revenge in the Montreal Olympics for what happened at Munich in 1972. Officials had awarded a do-over to the Soviet Union, which beat Team USA 51–50 for the gold medal.

"That was all part and parcel to the additional drive that many of us had, to right that wrong," Buckner said. "They stole it. It's that simple."

Buckner and May were 32–0 in college and 7–0 in the Olympics. They were 1–0 versus the Soviet Union. They helped the Hoosiers to a 94–78 victory over the reigning world champions in an exhibition before a sellout of 17,377 at Indianapolis's Market Square Arena on November 5, 1975. May scored thirty-four points on thirteen-of-fifteen shooting.

That was not Buckner's first experience against the Soviets, nor was it his first in international basketball. He was on a team that toured China in 1973 as part of US diplomacy.

After his sophomore year, nineteen-year-old Buckner was on the youngest and least internationally experienced team the United States had ever assembled. The Americans played in the world championship held in July 1974 at San Juan, Puerto Rico. The Soviets had five veterans from their 1972 Olympic gold medalists.

After the round-robin medal round, the United States, Soviet Union, and Yugoslavia were all tied at 6–1. The Americans defeated Yugoslavia 91–88 but lost to the Soviets 105–94. On a tiebreaker, the Soviets were awarded gold, Yugoslavia silver, and the USA bronze. Buckner averaged 6.6 points a game, eighth on the team, and learned what international basketball was about.

"First of all, they're men," Buckner said of the foreign opponents. "We found that out along the way. I even say this now to some people. The want to take kids from the Baltic... guys, they live in some war-torn place. They're tougher than you think they are."

No one ever questioned the toughness of Buckner and May, who were all-state players in football and basketball. Buckner played two years of football for the Hoosiers. Both players belong to the National Collegiate Basketball Hall of Fame. Also, Buckner is one of three men to have won a high school state title plus NCAA, Olympic, and NBA championships. The two others: Jerry Lucas and Magic Johnson.

Buckner was born August 20, 1954, in Phoenix, Illinois. His father, Bill, played football for the Hoosiers' unbeaten Big Ten champions in 1945. Quinn played football and basketball at Thornridge High School in Dolton, a suburb south of Chicago, and was on hoop teams that went 32–1 and 33–0 in his junior and senior years. In 1971–72, the Falcons won every game by fourteen or more points and won the state championship 104–69 over Quincy. That Thornridge team is still considered the best in Illinois history.

Scott May was born March 19, 1954, in Sandusky, Ohio, the son of a steelworker. He was a high school All-American and averaged twenty-five points as a senior. He was academically ineligible as a freshman at IU but soon found his footing in the classroom and on the court. Without May, Indiana reached the 1973 Final Four and lost to number one UCLA 70–59 in a national semifinal in St. Louis.

Buckner once thought about transferring from Indiana but eventually developed a close relationship with coach Bob Knight. Buckner said his father told him to get used to the way Knight communicates.

"That was the switch," Buckner said. "That's just the way Coach Knight communicates. He was right 99.9 percent of the time, so I fully appreciated what Coach Knight was saying."

In 1974–75, the Hoosiers became the first team to sweep an eighteen-game Big Ten schedule, winning by an average of 22.8 points. But in their twenty-sixth game—an 83–82 victory at Purdue, clinching the Big Ten championship—May broke his left arm. He returned to play limited minutes in a few games, but the goal of an unbeaten season and national championship ended in a 92–90 loss to Kentucky in the Mideast Regional final.

There was no stopping the Hoosiers that next season. Not only did they beat the Soviet Union, they opened with an 84–64 victory over UCLA's defending national champions in St. Louis. May scored thirty-three. Then he scored twenty-four in an 83–59 rout of Florida State, which trailed by twenty-seven at the half. The Hoosiers' route to the championship was so difficult—number one Indiana met number two Marquette in a regional semifinal—that the NCAA subsequently began seeding the tournament.

In order, Indiana defeated St. John's 90–70, number seven Alabama 74–69, number two Marquette 65–56, number five UCLA 65–51, and number nine Michigan 86–68. In Philadelphia, the Hoosiers beat the Wolverines for a third time. May scored 26 points, Kent Benson 25, and Buckner 16. Benson was most outstanding player of the Final Four, and May swept the college player of the year awards. May averaged 23.5 points and 7.7 rebounds a game, and he shot 53 percent.

"Scotty," Knight once said, "can do it all."

In three seasons together, Buckner and May were 86–6 and won the Big Ten championship each year. Soon after they cut down the nets in Philly, there was another mission ahead: recapture Olympic gold.

The two Hoosiers went to the Olympic Trials in North Carolina—Dean Smith was the US coach—and then awaited the NBA draft. May was the second pick, by the Chicago Bulls, and Buckner the seventh, by the Milwaukee Bucks. It was all a "whirlwind," Buckner recalled. "There was really no time to reflect that we had such a great college season," Buckner said.

Perhaps Buckner's greatest contribution to Team USA was to persuade May to come along. May was understandably conflicted. If he played poorly or was injured, he could be jeopardizing his NBA dollars. Others, notably UCLA centers Lew Alcindor (not yet Kareem Abdul-Jabbar) and Bill Walton, had passed on the Olympics.

May ended up sharing the cover of *Sports Illustrated* magazine's Olympics preview edition with marathoner Frank Shorter and swimmer Shirley Babashoff. As the Olympic tournament evolved, May became as invested as he had in the NCAA tournament. "I had the same sensation," he said. "The same feeling."

Smith endured criticism for choosing four North Carolina players—Phil Ford, Walter Davis, Mitch Kupchak, and Tom LaGarde—and two others from the Atlantic Coast Conference, Kenny Carr of North Carolina State and Steven Sheppard of Maryland. Buckner said the coaching staff wanted "continuity," which was one shortcoming of the 1972 Olympic team. Even so, Buckner said Smith's offense "was perfect" for a smart player like May.

"It really couldn't have worked out better," Buckner said. "I played for, easily in that era, maybe the two greatest coaches of all time. They went about the game very differently. Coach Smith was Coach Smith. He never swore; he never raised his voice. Coach Knight, he raised his voice all the time. One was very demonstrative, and the other really wasn't."

In Montreal, the Americans opened with a 106–86 victory over Italy. In their second game, Marquette's Butch Lee, a New Yorker born in Puerto Rico, nearly led his team to a historic upset. Lee scored thirty-five points on fifteen-of-eighteen shooting but was called for charging with eight seconds left and Puerto Rico trailing 93–92. Ford made two free throws to cap a twenty-point game, and the United States won 95–94.

"They had us in a tough spot. I will not kid you," Buckner said.

The Americans rallied for a 112–93 victory over Yugoslavia behind Adrian Dantley's twenty-seven points and May's twenty-four. Egypt withdrew from the tournament for political reasons, so the United States won by forfeit. After beating Czechoslovakia 81–76, the Americans faced host Canada in a semifinal before a crowd of nineteen thousand. May and Buckner led the Americans to an early 22–8 lead, and then rolled into the gold-medal game with a 95–77 victory. May finished with twenty-two points and Buckner with twelve.

There was no rematch with the Soviet Union, which lost to Yugoslavia 89–84 in the other semifinal. In a rematch with Yugoslavia, Dantley scored eighteen of his thirty points in the first half, and redemption was complete with a 95–74 victory. The United States won an eighth gold medal in nine Olympics.

Dantley, of Notre Dame, was Team USA's top scorer with a 19.3 average. May was second in scoring at 16.7 and led in rebounding at 6.2. Buckner was the fifth-leading scorer (7.3) and totaled eighteen assists, second to Ford's fifty-four.

Buckner said he was indifferent to missing out on avenging the 1972 loss to the Soviet Union. That's not what the Hoosiers, and Americans, were thinking atop the podium with gold medals around their necks and "The Star-Spangled Banner" ringing in their ears.

"It is by far the best feeling," Buckner said. "Winning a national championship is tremendous. But there's nothing better than representing your country and have that success. That's the world stage, and you just showed you stand above all."

The magnitude of it was underscored to Buckner in Barcelona, where he was an NBC reporter at the 1992 Olympics. Within the first few minutes after the Dream Team went into the locker room, somebody spoke the words "got you" to Buckner.

"I didn't pay any attention. It was Magic," Buckner said. "I had not even thought about it. That's how important it was to him."

The Los Angeles Lakers superstar had joined Lucas and Buckner in that state/NCAA/Olympics/NBA championship club.

Buckner went on to a ten-year career in the NBA with the Bucks, Boston Celtics, and Indiana Pacers. As in college, he was a defender and playmaker rather than a scorer. He made the NBA all-defensive second team four times with the Bucks. In 1980–81, he had career highs in scoring (13.3 points per game [ppg]) and steals (197, third in the NBA), and the Bucks were 60–22 in the regular season.

In 1982, the Bucks traded him to the Celtics for center Dave Cowens. In 1984, with Buckner coming off the bench, the Celtics went 62–20 and beat the Lakers 4–3 in the best-of-seven NBA Finals. The Celtics also made the 1985 finals but lost to the Lakers 4–2.

After that season, Buckner was traded to the Pacers but waived after thirty-two games. So he retired in 1986 at age thirty-one. For his career, he averaged 8.2 points, 4.3 assists, and 1.9 steals. He ranks just outside the NBA's all-time top fifty for steals.

Despite lack of experience, he was hired to coach the Dallas Mavericks in 1993. The Mavs, coming off an 11–71 season, started 1–23. They finished 13–69, and Buckner was fired two days after the season ended.

After being a network sportscaster, he was hired as vice president of communications for Pacers Sports & Entertainment in 2004. He became color analyst on TV broadcasts for Fox Sports Indiana.

May's NBA career was even shorter. He made the all-rookie team in 1977, averaging 14.6 ppg for the Bulls, but was impaired by injuries thereafter. He averaged 10.4 ppg in a seven-year career with the Bulls, Bucks, and Detroit Pistons. He played seven more years in the Italian League.

May made his home in Bloomington and became an owner of apartment complexes. Two sons, Scott Jr. and Sean, both played for Bloomington North High School. Sean, a high school and college All-American, helped North Carolina win the 2005 NCAA championship and was most outstanding player of the Final Four. Sean was chosen thirteenth in the first round of the draft by the Charlotte Bobcats and played four NBA seasons before leaving for Europe. Scott and Sean are one of four father-son duos to win NCAA championships.

In May's hometown of Sandusky, the Scott May Courts are named in his honor at Jaycee Park.

Walt Bellamy
1960

Hoops Hall-of-Famer (Twice)

BEFORE BASKETBALL'S DREAM TEAM WAS ASSEMBLED FOR THE 1992 OLYMPIC Games, there was an original version.

"This was the authentic Dream Team," Walt Bellamy once said of his 1960 Olympians. "I'd like to think that we were the best team that has ever played basketball."

Before pros were allowed in the Olympics, the six-foot-eleven Indiana center was a starter on a team of college and amateur players that crushed all opposition in

Rome. The Americans won the gold medal, outscoring eight teams by an average of 102–59.5. Indeed, the United States won by a cumulative 339 points, nearly as big as the 1992 margin (350).

The 1960 team, coached by Pete Newell, featured four members of the Naismith Hall of Fame—Oscar Robertson, Jerry West, Jerry Lucas, Bellamy—plus future NBA stars such as Terry Dischinger, Darrall Imhoff, and Bob Boozer. Robertson and West each averaged 17 points a game, and Bellamy averaged 8.1.

The Americans beat Italy 88–54, Japan 125–66, Hungary 107–63, Yugoslavia 104–42, Uruguay 108–50, Soviet Union 81–57, Italy 112–81, and Brazil 90–63.

In the gold-medal game, Bellamy was ejected by a Mexican referee for landing an elbow to the mouth of a Brazilian player, although it did not appear deliberate. As Bellamy pleaded his case with the referee, he had tears in his eyes. The Brazilians played timidly thereafter, however.

"That was the end of the game for them," Robertson said. "They were out of it at that point. They were not going to win anyway, but they didn't put up a big battle at all then."

Bellamy protested that it was ordinary rebounding.

"That was just coming off the board with the ball," he said.

Few rebounded better than "Bells." He played in the NBA during the era of Wilt Chamberlain and Bill Russell, so it is unsurprising that he never made an all-NBA first team. When Bellamy retired in 1974, he was third in league history in rebounds (14,241)—behind those two other centers—and sixth in points (20,941). As of 2019, Bellamy was still eleventh all-time in rebounds.

Walter Jones Bellamy was born July 24, 1939, in New Bern, North Carolina. He was six foot one by age fourteen, and his best sport was football. As a senior end, he led Barber High School to a state championship and was an all-state selection. In basketball, he acquired the nickname "goaltending kid" for blocking shots. He scored forty-seven points in a 1956 game against Durham.

A trip to Bloomington in summer 1956 was influential in his decision to enroll at IU. His high school coach, Simon Coates, was doing undergraduate study there, and he invited Bellamy to visit. During that time, the teenager played pickup ball with Hoosiers such as Wally Choice, Hallie Bryant, and Gene Flowers.

"Indiana at the time was the closest school to the South that would accept African Americans," Bellamy said. "It was an easy transition for me to make. Not that I was naive to what was going on in Bloomington in terms of the times, but it didn't translate to the athletic department or the classroom. Every relationship was good."

A case could be made for Bellamy as the top player in IU history. In three college seasons from 1958 to 1961—freshmen were ineligible—Bellamy set school records

Walt Bellamy, 1958.
IU Archives.

for rebounds in a season (649), rebounds in one game (33) and double-doubles in a career (59). He averaged 20.6 points and 15.5 rebounds for his career.

He rounded out the best decade of center play by any school in Big Ten history: from Bill Garrett to Don Schlundt to Archie Dees to Bellamy. All four Hoosiers made a major All-America team.

Bellamy averaged 17.4 points and 15.2 rebounds as a sophomore, then 22.4 and 13.5 on coach Branch McCracken's 20–4 team. As a senior, coming back from the Olympics, Bellamy averaged 21.8 and 17.8 (still the IU record) for a team that once ranked number four but ultimately fell to 15–9. In his final college game, he set a Big Ten record of 33 rebounds that still stands, and he scored 28 points in an 82–67 victory over Michigan.

Talents like Bellamy don't remain in college for four years anymore. Yet his Indiana years are among his most treasured.

"I would go so far as to say that they should at least experience the college atmosphere," he said. "There is no better atmosphere."

Bellamy became the first Hoosier chosen number one overall in the NBA draft by the Chicago Packers. He lived up to it, becoming 1962 Rookie of the Year by averaging 31.6 points and 19.0 rebounds a game. In NBA history, only Chamberlain—with 37.6 and 27.0 in 1960—averaged more as a rookie. For instance, Michael Jordan averaged 28.2 points a game in winning Rookie of the Year in 1985.

Bellamy's rookie season is nearly lost to history because Chamberlain averaged 50.4 points and 25.7 rebounds that year. Yet Bellamy was instant offense. He scored 35 in the home opener in Chicago, and 35, 37, and 45 over the next three games. In a loss to the Philadelphia Warriors, he scored 45 to Chamberlain's 55. In the NBA All-Star game—when those games were more competitively played—Bellamy had 23 points and 17 rebounds.

"To play against guys you watched on television . . . little did I know my talent would mesh with theirs," he said.

Bellamy merits a couple of footnotes. Only a decade after the color barrier in the NBA was broken, and with racial quotas commonplace, he played on the first all-black lineup during a Packers game. (The franchise later moved to Baltimore and then Washington, DC.)

He also owns an NBA record that might never be broken: eighty-eight games in one season. In December 1968, he was traded from the New York Knicks to the Detroit Pistons. The Knicks had played thirty-five games, but the Pistons only twenty-nine, so he played an additional fifty-three games for the Pistons.

Bellamy was omitted from the NBA's fiftieth anniversary team in 1996, despite statistics exceeding many of the big men who made it. One of them, Wes Unseld, asked, "Do you know what Bellamy did?"

What did he do?

He was an All-Star four times, and he averaged 20.1 points and 13.7 rebounds over fourteen seasons and 1,043 games. He was twice inducted into the Hall of Fame—belatedly as a player in 1993 and as part of the 1960 Olympic team in 2010.

The only other enshrined Olympic team is that of 1992. He was inducted into IU's Hall of Fame in 1982.

"I just like to think I made a contribution to basketball," Bellamy said in a 2007 interview.

He wore seven NBA uniforms: Chicago Packers and Zephyrs, Baltimore Bullets, New York Knicks, Detroit Pistons, Atlanta Hawks, and New Orleans Jazz. He was traded three times: from the Bullets to Knicks in November 1965, from Knicks to Pistons, and from Pistons to Hawks in February 1970.

Russell once told *Sports Illustrated* that Bellamy, at his finest, was one of his toughest rivals. Bellamy, sometimes critiqued for not always being at his best, was often stuck on rebuilding or expansion teams.

Before he coached the ABA's Indiana Pacers, Hoosier great Bobby "Slick" Leonard coached the Bullets. The Bullets were 31–49 in 1963–64, and Leonard largely blamed Bellamy. The coach frequently chided the center for not hustling, and twice Bellamy was fined ... despite a season in which he averaged 27.0 points and 17.0 rebounds.

Under a new coach, Buddy Jeannette, Bellamy was made captain the next year. Beyond his production—24.8 and 14.6—he led the 37–43 Bullets to the 1965 Western Division finals, where they lost to the Los Angeles Lakers in six games.

After Baltimore traded him, Bellamy helped the Knicks climb out of the cellar and into the playoffs in 1967 and 1968. His presence displaced Willis Reed, a natural center, so the Knicks in turn traded Bellamy and Howard Komives to Detroit for forward Dave DeBusschere.

After the third trade, Bellamy teamed with Walt Hazzard and Lou Hudson to push the Hawks to the 1970 Western Division finals. They were swept by the Lakers 4–0. Bellamy, with "Pistol" Pete Maravich in the backcourt, also made the playoffs in 1971, 1972, and 1973. Bellamy played one game for the Jazz in 1974 and retired at age thirty-five.

His home remained in Atlanta, where his wife, Helen, was a middle school science teacher. He was especially active in the NAACP.

He was a public affairs consultant, four-time delegate to the Democratic National Convention, commissioner of Atlanta's Police Athletic League, a special events director for a scholarship fund for minority students, a mentor at a local YMCA, a board member for a nursery school, and a member of two African Episcopal Methodist Church boards.

In 1977, he was a sergeant-at-arms at the door of the Georgia Senate. Bellamy escorted Prince Charles and introduced him to the legislature.

He died November 2, 2013. He was seventy-four.

Derek Drouin
Courtesy of Indiana University Athletics.

Derek Drouin
2012, 2016

Canada's Humble Superstar

DEREK DROUIN IS AN ANONYMOUS, AND RELUCTANT, SUPERSTAR. YET CONsidering what he achieved and what he overcame, the Indiana University high jumper had one of most epic double comebacks in Olympic history.

In March 2011, he tore two ligaments in his right foot, an injury known as a Lisfranc fracture. Doctors conceded it was potentially career ending. A little more than sixteen months later, he won a bronze medal at the London Olympics.

In May 2016, an MRI scan revealed he had a double stress fracture in his back. The Olympic Games were set for three months later in Rio de Janeiro.

"I was optimistic that if I did everything people told me to do, it was going to be fine," Drouin said. "I was confident I could deal with the pain. I only needed to get to Rio, where I knew the adrenaline and the competition would mask any pain."

In Rio, he applied pressure on his competition when he was first over the bar at 7 feet, 9¾ inches. No one else could clear it.

Qatar's Mutaz Essa Barshim won silver at 7–8¾ and Ukraine's Bohdan Bondarenko bronze at 7–7¾. When Bondarenko missed his only attempt at 7–9¾, the gold medal was Drouin's. He missed once at what would have been an Olympic record of 7–10½, then ended proceedings. He draped himself in the Maple Leaf and posed for photographers.

"It feels pretty sweet," Drouin said. "There have been some sacrifices, but I've always prided myself on my mental toughness."

He became the Hoosiers' first individual gold medalist in track and field since long jumper Greg Bell and decathlete Milt Campbell, both in 1956. Drouin and decathlete Milt Campbell are the only athletes out of IU to win track and field medals in two Olympics.

"The last couple of days I had a realization that I wasn't nervous at all," he said in Rio. "I was so excited to be out there because I was confident in my preparation, and also I just love the Olympics and was really just taking the whole moment in. I thrive in a situation where there is a lot going on. I don't sense a whole lot of distractions."

Drouin had been numbingly consistent in an event in which a miss can separate gold from no medal at all. After he won bronzes at the 2012 Olympics and 2013 World Championships, he won four successive major championships: the 2014 Commonwealth Games, the 2015 Pan American Games, the 2015 World Championships, and the 2016 Olympics.

Obviously, Drouin had a long résumé before he became an Olympic champion. Not that it made him a celebrity.

When he was surrounded by Canadian reporters in London, it was apparent they knew almost nothing about him. Life did not change after that. Nor did it after he won a historic three-way jump-off to win gold at the 2015 World Championships.

"The only time I think about it is when a reporter asks," Drouin said. "I'll basically go back to my regular routine as soon as I could after World Championships."

Students at IU knew less than Canadian media. Drouin took a lifeguarding class in fall 2011 with Chad Canal, who remembered how hard it was to simulate saving someone as tall as six foot five who had "zero body fat." Later that semester, Canal received a campus email and realized he had been partnered with an NCAA high jump champion.

"We had no idea he was a track superstar," Canal said. "And he acted like a normal student. Nobody understood this guy being a big deal. Yes, he was tall and very lean, but that's it."

Canal, a dentist, later sent Drouin a message apologizing for not recognizing him. Drouin's response: "Haha. I'm quite content with not a lot of attention."

He once sat at a table at York University in Toronto next to a sign asking, "Who am I?" Only one in ten could identify him, and he was already an Olympic medalist. That might have been welcomed by Drouin, but it sometimes rankled Jeff Huntoon, his coach since 2009.

"There's not the level of respect that he deserves to have. It disappoints me greatly, actually," Huntoon said.

Drouin's technique was so good that colleagues told Huntoon that once the high jumper checks in for his event, the coach's job is over. TV analyst Dwight Stones, a two-time Olympic bronze medalist in the high jump, called Drouin "maybe one of the best technicians in the event today."

Drouin was born March 6, 1990, in Sarnia, Ontario, the largest city on Lake Huron (population 72,000). He grew up in nearby Corunna. He played hockey—don't all Canadian boys?—and soccer, basketball, volleyball, and tennis. Because the landing area was viewed as dangerous, the high jump was not allowed in elementary school, and he did not begin that event until high school.

Nor did he confine himself to one event, training for the decathlon. His spurt in the high jump mirrored that of his height. He was five foot seven when he began high school and six inches taller a year later. In about eighteen months, his best jump increased from six foot one to six foot eleven.

His introduction to international competition was the 2007 World Youth Championships at Ostrava, Czech Republic, where he finished tenth, and 2008 Commonwealth Youth Games at Pune, India, where he won a bronze medal. His club coach, Joel Skinner, said the different sports were complementary. Once Drouin specialized in the high jump, improvement accelerated.

"Obviously, his basic athleticism helps him out a lot," Skinner said.

Indiana would not have recruited Drouin if he did nothing but high jump. Huntoon said the fact Drouin wanted to do other events, and the Hoosiers wanted him to do so, influenced both sides. He eventually scored points at Big Ten meets in the hurdles and javelin.

As a freshman, he finished second in the 2009 Big Ten indoor meet but won every conference high jump title thereafter. He made a breakthrough that summer when he jumped a school record 7–5¼ in the Pan American Junior Championships at Port of Spain, Trinidad. When he swept NCAA indoor and outdoor titles in 2010 and repeated indoors in 2011 with a 7–7¾ jump, the 2012 Olympics seemed inevitable.

But in an outdoor meet at Starkville, Mississippi, he tore ligaments off his right (takeoff) foot. He looked up what the injury was on a website, and he despaired. His distress was eased by a call to his sister Jillian, who once finished third in the NCAA heptathlon for Syracuse University.

"She calmed me down. I knew that it was serious," he said. "I knew that it would be a lot of hard work. But I never really had a dark moment after that."

The surgery required two metal screws to be inserted, then removed three months later. The procedure made Drouin's foot feel arthritic. His rate of recovery astonished everyone. In one practice session, his approach to the bar was so swift and effortless than Indiana coach Ron Helmer, standing across the track, thought Drouin was bounding off a ramp used as training tool. Not so. He was jumping off level ground. Soon thereafter, Drouin won the 2012 Big Ten title, setting a meet record of 7–7.

"Big Ten's where it turned around," he said. "I think I really needed that emotionally."

He jumped 7–7 at the NCAA Championships to finish second to Kansas State's Erik Kynard, and 7–7 again at the Canadian trials. His build-up to the Olympics included a 7–5 jump for victory in a July 13 meet at London, then 7–6½ for third July 20 at Monaco.

Still, Drouin was neither ranked in the world's top ten nor projected to be a medalist. He trained with the Canadian team in Kamen, Germany, and didn't arrive at the Olympic Village until nearly a week after the opening ceremony.

In Olympic qualifying, the customarily precise jumper missed twice at 7–3, a low bar for him. All he could think about was what he would say to his parents, who made the 5,350-mile trip from Corunna.

"'I'm so sorry I put you through this.' I'm sure they were more nervous than I was," Drouin said.

He cleared the bar on his third and final attempt, and kept climbing. He eventually finished sixth, leaping 7–6 to join thirteen other finalists. Drouin was already eleventh in the standings and might not have needed to clear 7–6 but said he wasn't sure, so he took his third attempt anyway. He missed once at 7–5 and twice at 7–6.

"I don't think I've ever had that many misses in my life," he said.

The final had a different kind of drama. Drouin made 7–2½, 7–4½ and 7–6, all on first attempts. Eight jumpers cleared 7–6, but only Drouin and three others did so without a miss. Kynard and Russia's Ivan Ukhov cleared the next bar, 7–7¾. After Drouin missed three times, he said it was "the worst feeling ever" to watch others attempt the same bar. Anyone else's clearance would have knocked him off the podium.

No one did. Ukhov won gold at 7–9¾ and Kynard silver. Drouin tied for third with Barshim and Great Britain's Robbie Grabarz, so all three earned bronze medals.

Drouin said he was "hanging on" at the Olympics because he was weary from a long season and inability to train as he had previously. He acknowledged he was lucky because 7–6 was the lowest height to win an Olympic medal since 1976. He actually forecast difficulties because the four-centimeter increase to the next bar—2.29 to 2.33 meters—was so great. A clean sheet—no misses—was going to matter.

Drouin's parents, Gatetan and Sheila, came prepared. The jumper ran to where they were seated a few rows up, hugged them, and took the Maple Leaf they brought on a lap of honor. He also had with him a Canadian flag signed by those in his hometown. His longtime club coach, Skinner, "almost broke a couple of ribs" from hugging him so hard, he said.

"I didn't notice how big the stadium actually was until I was doing my victory lap," Drouin said. "I do a pretty good job of zoning everything out."

The Canadian prime minister, Stephen Harper, tweeted congratulations. Drouin's medal was the first for Canada in men's track and field since 1996 and first in a field event since high jumper Greg Joy took silver at Montreal in 1976.

Drouin could have become a pro after that but returned to campus in 2013 for a final season of eligibility. He won national titles indoors and outdoors, making him the first five-time NCAA high jump champion. He won the Bowerman Award, college track and field's version of the Heisman Trophy. He and two other Hoosiers—Jim Spivey (1982) and Sunder Nix (1984)—are the only track and field athletes ever to win the Jesse Owens Award as the Big Ten's male all-sports athletes of the year.

Although he didn't break the collegiate record of 7–9¾ held by Southwestern Louisiana's Hollis Conway, Drouin had one of the most prolific seasons ever by a collegiate high jumper. Conway had fourteen meets of 7–7 or higher in 1989, seven coming after the college season. Drouin had eleven such meets, four after the college season. During an indoor heptathlon, he jumped 7–6½, a world record for multievents.

"I love being a part of a team. That's why I chose to go to Indiana—because I love the team," Drouin said. "I had one more season of my life that I could be on a team like that. I wasn't going to give up being a part of something like that. That was my main reason for going back, and I loved it. And I'm so happy that I did."

If he left IU with one regret, it might be failure to score in the 110-meter hurdles at the 2013 Big Ten meet. He was going so fast while leading a semifinal that he smacked barriers late and didn't advance.

He completed a four-year Big Ten outdoor sweep, then finished third in the Prefontaine Classic at Eugene, Oregon, setting a Canadian record of 7–8¾. Six days later, he beat Kynard at Eugene to win the NCAA title at 7–8.

If London was an occasion in which a low jump realized a medal, the 2013 World Championships in Moscow were the antithesis of that. To stay in contention, Drouin had to make 7–2½, 7–4½, 7–6, 7–7¼ and 7–8½, all on his first attempts. Then he broke his own seventy-five-day-old Canadian record by jumping 7–9¾ for a bronze medal. It was the highest third-place jump in history. Drouin said he never thought 7–9¾ would be worth only third.

"I had no choice but to be composed in such a final," Drouin said. "I am proud of myself. It feels really good."

Drouin became the first IU male athlete to win a world medal since Jim Spivey's bronze in the 1,500 meters in 1987.

Ukraine's Bohdan Bondarenko won gold with a World Championships record of 7–10¾. Barshim took silver, also at 7–9¾, because he cleared that height on the first attempt and Drouin on the second. Olympic champion Ukhov finished fourth at 7–8½ and Kynard fifth at 7–7¼.

In 2014, a year without a global championship, Drouin was ranked fourth in the world. On April 24, in the Drake Relays at Des Moines, Iowa, he raised his Canadian record to 7–10½ (2.40 meters). Through 2019, only six men in history had gone higher. He jumped 7–7 to win a gold medal in the Commonwealth Games at Glasgow, Scotland, and 7–7 again to finish fourth in the Continental Cup at Marrakesh, Morocco.

After the college season, Huntoon was fired as an assistant coach for the Hoosiers. He continued to coach Drouin, though, and took a job with Athletics Canada.

In 2015, Drouin won golds in his two major competitions: Pan American Games at Toronto (7–9¼) and World Championships at Beijing (7–8). He won the world title in a dramatic jump-off against Bondarenko, the defending champion, and China's Guowei Zhang. Drouin became Canada's first high jump world champion, and first world champion in any event out of IU.

"I was telling myself that if there was ever an opportunity (to win gold), this was it," Drouin said. "I really felt like I was the one to beat, that this was my championship to lose. I told myself so many times that 'you can win this, you can win this,' that when it finally happened, it was just a relief."

Rain stopped shortly before competition began, erasing his takeoff mark. He adjusted, and was one of three jumpers tied for first at 7–7¾. They missed three times each at 7–8¾, and then a fourth time. The bar was lowered to 7–8, and Drouin cleared on his first attempt. When the two others missed, Drouin was gold medalist. Bondarenko and Zhang tied for silver. Oddly, Drouin said he had been so frustrated with a new approach that he just wanted the season to be over.

"Luckily, I was patient, and things finally worked out and things clicked, and when they clicked, they really clicked," he said.

Leading up to the Rio Olympics, he relocated from Bloomington to Toronto so he could work more closely with Huntoon on a daily basis. Drouin amended his technique, speeding up and taking longer strides toward the bar. But he began feeling back pain in January, so he cut short his indoor season. After jumping 7–6 at Qatar in early May, he learned the diagnosis of the two fractures but did not reveal the condition publicly.

There were days he wondered if he would jump in Rio de Janeiro. Over time, his condition improved. He met with a sports psychologist for the first time. Then, less than a month before the Olympic final, he jumped 7–9¾, beating top rival Barshim. It was Drouin's highest jump in twenty-seven months, since his Canadian record in Des Moines. He did not raise the bar, so he ended that meet without missing once. That is called a clean sheet, and few keep it as clean as Drouin.

He said pressure in Rio could be viewed in two ways: that because he had an Olympic medal, he had none; or because he was world champion, he had much.

"Dealing with pressure is something I've been pretty good at," he said.

In the Olympic Village, several days before he was to compete, he dreamed he won the gold medal. He said he felt relieved, then reminded himself that he spent his entire life dreaming about going to the Olympic Games.

"Yet here I am wishing it away," he said. "I had to stop wishing this was over and enjoy the moment."

He breezed through qualifying, jumping 7–6, the same height he had cleared to win bronze four years before. In the final, he was as precise as a Swiss timing device. He cleared six bars on first attempts: 7–2½, 7–4½, 7–6, 7–7¾, 7–8¾, 7–9¾.

No one else could match that. He missed once at what would have been an Olympic record of 7–10½, then stopped. Winning gold was "probably one of the most powerful emotions I've ever felt," Drouin said.

"He focuses on what he's going to do, and he goes through the process," Huntoon said. "That's why he looks like he does. Some may call it boring, but it was awfully damn exciting tonight."

Prime Minister Justin Trudeau congratulated him on Twitter. Radio stations in Canada were "buzzing with his performance," according to Matheiu Gentes of

Athletics Canada. His countrymen gathered around TVs to watch. Drouin subsequently held a news conference at Rio's Main Press Center.

Only two other men had ever won high jump gold with zero misses en route: Russia's Andrey Silnov in 2008 and West Germany's Dietmar Mogenburg in 1984.

Drouin became the second Canadian to win gold in the high jump, after Duncan McNaughton at Los Angeles in 1932, and first in a field event since then. Drouin was Canada's first gold medalist in individual track or field since 100-meter winner Donovan Bailey in 1996.

Considering his injured back, Drouin's comeback was reminiscent of several others in Olympic lore:

- In 1964, Al Oerter endured a chronic cervical disc injury, then tore cartilage in his lower ribs while practicing in Tokyo less than a week before discus qualifying. In the final, he set an Olympic record of 200–1 to win the third of his four gold medals.
- In 1968, Tommie Smith pulled an adductor in his groin in the 200-meter semifinals. Two hours later, he won the gold medal and set a world record of 19.83 seconds. That prefaced the demonstration by himself and John Carlos during the medal ceremony.
- In 1984, Joan Benoit underwent arthroscopic surgery on her knee seventeen days before the US marathon trials. She won, then became the first women's marathon gold medalist.

Drouin always trained as if he were competing in the decathlon. Contrary to the if-it's-not-broke-don't-fix-it maxim, he broke down his technique to fix it. His approach to the bar became faster, creating high risk for high jumps.

In April 2017, he jumped 7–5¾—a world record for a decathlon—en route to a score of 7,150 points. He also owns the high jump record, 7–6½, for an indoor heptathlon. An Achilles injury knocked him out of the 2017 World Championships, and he missed the 2018 and 2019 seasons because of a spinal injury causing pain in his neck.

If he could return to form, he would have a chance to be the second three-time high jump medalist ever. The only one is Sweden's Patrik Sjoberg, who won silvers in 1984 and 1992 and bronze in 1988.

David Neville
Courtesy of Indiana University Athletics.

David Neville
2008

He Kept the Faith and Dived to Glory

DAVID NEVILLE FOUND HIS RHYTHM BEFORE FINDING HIS STRIDE.
He was once better at music than he was at track and field, playing percussion instruments from fourth grade. His mother has a master's degree in piano performance. He played in the marching band at Indiana University and graduated in 2007 with a music education degree.

But he was a runner. As was his father. As was his grandfather.

Neville himself didn't necessarily see it that way. He quit track after breaking his foot as a high school sophomore in Merrillville, Indiana. He discovered that he missed it and returned to the team the next year, just a few weeks before the sectional. He qualified for the state meet and finished seventh in the 100 meters.

Then, six years before the 2008 Beijing Olympics, he imagined himself being there. He was wearing a Team USA singlet. He was winning medals. The vision was so vivid that he told a reporter about it.

"I stuck with it, stuck with it. And I kept my faith," said Neville, a devout Christian. "And my faith is the only reason why I can say with assurance that I would be in Beijing."

He was not only there. He won a bronze medal in the 400 meters, diving to the finish line to complete a 1–2-3 American sweep, and a gold in the 4×400 relay.

Neville's epiphany came as he began specializing in the 400, a long sprint that has been characterized as the most painful race in the sport. His father, David Neville II, was convinced it would be the best race for his six-foot-three son. The father ran 800 meters in 1:48.54 for Virginia Military Institute in 1982, setting a school record that lasted twenty-six years.

The son was not as convinced, especially after his first 400. He ran that distance in a relay after a few days of training.

"It was horrible," Neville recalled.

It was fate.

As a Merrillville senior, he set what was then an Indiana high school record of 46.99 seconds in winning the 400-meter state championship. He was fourth in the 200 in what was surely the best Indiana field ever assembled. Gary West Side's Mark Jelks set a state record of 20.88, and South Bend La Salle's Leroy Dixon was second. Jelks later became a national indoor champion at 60 meters and first native Hoosier to run 100 meters in less than ten seconds (9.99). Dixon won a gold medal in the 4×100 relay at the 2007 World Championships.

Neville's gold medal was years in the making. On enrolling at Indiana, he was ineligible for college competition in his first year. He had adequate grades and test scores, but the NCAA did not count an eleventh-grade English course as part of core curriculum. So he trained alone after the Hoosiers' practices ended, doing workouts timed by a friend. He took classes in hapkido, a Korean martial art.

So his father continued to coach him and travel with his son to meets. At the 2003 Pan American Junior Championships in Bridgetown, Barbados, Neville won a silver medal in the 200 in 20.63. The gold medalist was a sixteen-year-old Jamaican who also made it to Beijing: Usain Bolt.

By 2004, Neville appeared to be accelerating the timetable toward an Olympics. He won the 200 and 400 at the Big Ten meet—the times of 20.39 and 45.05 were both the fastest ever by a graduate of an Indiana high school—and was seventh in the 400 at the NCAA Championships. His 45.05 was among the top ten times in the world, and six would be chosen for the 4×400 relay pool from the Olympic Trials. Yet it was perhaps a case of too much too soon, because Neville was eliminated in his first-round heat at the trials. He would not be going to Athens.

By 2006, he was back on track. He had his best NCAA finish in the 400 meters, third, and ran the USA Championships at what amounted to a home stadium in Indianapolis. He was assigned the unfavorable lane 8 in the final, much like being adrift on an island. Nothing but open space ahead of you, nothing to signal who might be behind you. Nonetheless, he again finished third, lowering his time to 44.75. It was a race of inestimable value. Not only was it his last as a collegian—setting himself up for a pro contract with Nike—but it supplied experience in that outside lane.

He completed his degree in 2007 but had an undistinguished season, culminating with seventh place at the USA Championships. Afterward, he and his wife, Arial, moved to Valencia, California, so he could be coached by John Smith. Smith, who once set a 440-yard world record, had previously coached Olympic gold medalists such as Maurice Greene, Quincy Watts, Kevin Young, and Steve Lewis.

"I saw a level in him, a spirit it him, that only lives in certain people who are really and truly champions," Smith said.

Neville's 2008 season began auspiciously when he won the national indoor championship at Boston in the 400 meters, his first major title. Yet that race did not include Jeremy Wariner, the defending gold medalist, or LaShawn Merritt, the favorites to take two of the three US team spots. Neville was one of many given a chance for third in the Olympic Trials at Eugene, Oregon.

Again, Neville drew lane 8 for the final. He ran scared. He ran into the lead through 300 meters, conceding he was "kind of shocked." He was passed by Merritt and Wariner but comfortably claimed the third Olympic berth, clocking a personal best of 44.61, or four-tenths of a second ahead of fourth place. He did not take the traditional Hayward Field victory lap, explaining, "I didn't feel too good afterward."

Lead-up to the Olympic Games wasn't too good, either. He raced poorly in Europe, then developed a sore Achilles tendon while training in China. He underwent near-constant medical treatment in Beijing.

In Olympic semifinals, two per heat qualified for the final, plus the next two fastest times. Neville was second in his semifinal in 44.91. Just as in Eugene, two medals seemed secure in the hands of Wariner and Merritt, followed by a mad dash for bronze.

Coincidentally, Neville drew lane 9, again putting him on the outside, unable to see those he was racing. At least, he was unable to see them until it mattered. As he approached the finish, out of the corner of his eye, he saw others nearby. He made a hasty decision. He dove. He slid across the wet track as a baseball player would sliding head first into second base.

"I did it because it was the only thing I could think to do in the last second," Neville said. "God might have pushed me over."

Merritt won gold in 43.75 over Wariner's 44.74, representing the biggest margin at an Olympics since 1896. Neville was a close third in 44.80, and .04 ahead of fourth. It was the Americans' fifth sweep of 400-meter medals, following 1904, 1968, 1988, and 2004. Neville became the Hoosiers' first medalist in an individual track and field since hurdler Willie May won a silver in 1960.

Neville's was the slowest medal-winning time since 1980. That was irrelevant. So were the bruised chest and scrapes from his dive onto the track.

"Sometimes we have to sacrifice our body and our mind and our spirit for what we really want," he said.

This time he did take a victory lap, albeit a slow one. He repeatedly stopped and crouched, wrapped in an American flag, while making his way around the Bird's Nest. He hugged his wife and parents, who came to the rail to share in the celebration.

The reluctant quarter-miler had thus run the three fastest 400s of his life in the most unconventional way—all out of the outside lane.

"I didn't look behind, I didn't look back, and I just kept my eye focused on the prize that was ahead," Neville said. "That's why I have medal around my neck right now."

Although acknowledging he felt "pretty beat up," he was chosen to run a semifinal of the 4×400 relay for Team USA. He ended his leadoff leg in first place with a time of 44.92, and the Americans won to qualify for the final a day later. Team USA coach Bubba Thornton said Neville deserved to run the final after diving for bronze in the 400 meters. It had not been a particularly successful Olympics for Team USA, so Thornton exhorted the relay team to "kick butt." Which is what they did.

Merritt (44.35), Angelo Taylor (43.70), Neville (44.16), and Wariner (43.18) combined for a time of 3:55.39, breaking the Olympic record and beating silver medalist Bahamas by almost three seconds. The previous Olympic record was 2:55.74 by the United States in 1992.

"I was just soaking it in, and I was saying, 'Do what you've got to do. Bring it home,'" Neville said. "To have a gold is great, but it's even sweeter to have an Olympic record."

He became the fourth gold medalist out of IU in the 4×400 relay. Others were Ivan Fuqua in 1932, Roy Cochran in 1948, and Sunder Nix in 1984.

Neville, at twenty-four, was young enough to have tried for one and perhaps two more Olympics. He never again ran as fast as he did in 2008, and only in 2009 did he reach another national final (he finished fifth). Because of recurring Achilles injuries, he retired soon after finishing last in a first-round heat at the 2012 Olympic Trials. Track was never his primary mission anyway.

He was once a minster at the Merrillville Unity AME Zion Church, which had been founded by his father. In California, he led youth ministry at Santa Clarita Christian Fellowship Church. In May 2014, he returned to his home state as head track and field coach for Taylor University, a small Christian college in Upland, Indiana. He left Taylor in 2017 to become an assistant coach at Tennessee.

Neville returned to a big stage in 2016 as one of sixteen cast members on Fox's nationally televised reality show *American Grit*, supplying a glimpse of life in the military. Filming took place in the wilderness of Pack Forest outside Eatonville, Washington. One of his team's early challenges was carrying a 125-pound log for 3.6 miles through forest and up hills. Taylor track athletes held a weekly watch party to see how their coach fared.

Neville's team did not win. But his college athletes could see for themselves that their coach had grit.

DeDee Nathan, 1997.
Photo by Nick Judy.
IU Archives P0021549.

DeDee Nathan
2000

Serving a Mission Beyond Sports

SHE SHARES A BIRTHPLACE WITH CARL LEWIS, GREATEST MALE ATHLETE OF the twentieth century. She shares an event with Jackie Joyner-Kersee, greatest female athlete of the twentieth century.

Yet DeDee Nathan's life has largely been an unshared experience. She lived alone. She trained alone. She competed alone. Success and failure were hers alone.

"I'm an island," she once said.

Except, she said, when she opened herself up to the Lord. Nathan became a Christian when she was twenty-one.

"You know, it has shaped my life, as it should," she said. "That's the way it's supposed to be. I wouldn't take anything for my journey now."

Nathan's journey is unique in Indiana sports history. She has been a state champion, Big Ten champion, national champion, and world champion; she has been on a state championship team and coached a state championship team. She made it to her only Olympic Games at age thirty-two, but she came ever so close to being a four-time Olympian. Doing so would have tied her with JJK. She came within twenty-four points of beating JJK at the 1998 Goodwill Games.

With three women in the heptathlon going to the Olympics, Nathan finished fourth at the US trials in 1992 and 1996, and fifth in 2004. She won the 2000 trials and finished ninth at Sydney in what was an uncharacteristic performance. Afterward, she said, "I was out there long jumping, and God said, 'You are already a champion. You've accomplished your goal.' You do so much and you get to the pinnacle, what else is there to do? Yeah, you can win, but at the same time I could have missed this whole thing.... So this is really a blessing, it really is."

Family heartache preceded Nathan's Olympic blessing.

Her mother, Beverly, was eighteen when she gave birth to LaShundra Denise on April 20, 1968, in Birmingham, Alabama, also the birthplace of Lewis. Beverly's sister began calling her niece DeDee, and the name stuck.

Beverly left Nathan's father, moved to Fort Wayne, Indiana, in 1970, and married a police officer. The daughter never saw her father again until she was twenty-one. He was in and out of prison, Nathan said.

Beverly and Robert Nathan had a son, Keith. DeDee took her stepfather's name. The couple divorced while DeDee was in high school. She said her stepfather was overbearing and that his relationship with her mother was volatile. Theirs was not a spiritual home.

However, Nathan and her half-brother were picked up by a Baptist church bus for Sunday services. Beverly said her daughter was strong-willed and energetic. DeDee liked to run and climb trees and fences.

"Everything had to be DeDee's way," the mother said. "I'd tell her life doesn't work that way. You have to bend down sometimes."

For years, Nathan, five foot eleven and 170 pounds, was judged as an athlete of talent but had no discipline. She has stated her progression was gradual because she stayed clean and did not use performance-enhancing drugs, as she claimed other heptathletes did.

As a high school freshman for Fort Wayne South Side, she ran on a 4×400-meter relay team that won a 1983 state title in 3:48.18, a record that stood for twenty-eight years. She won five state titles in the 100- and 300-meter hurdles.

At Indiana University, she was a six-time Big Ten champion in four different events: indoor 55-meter hurdles, pentathlon, long jump, and 400-meter hurdles.

As a junior in 1989, she was fourth in the long jump and sixth in the 400 hurdles at the NCAA Championships. She culminated her college career in 1990 by finishing second in the NCAA heptathlon with a school record of 5,855 points. That started a fifteen-year streak of ranking in the top ten in the United States in the hep.

Nathan was gold medalist at what proved to be a contentious Pan American Games at Havana in 1991. There were charges of Cuban corruption. Nathan said distances in the heptathlon were consistently shortened for the Americans, but she won nevertheless with 5,778 points. She affirmed she was a contender to make the Olympic team a year later.

In the Olympic Trials at New Orleans, Nathan was in the top three until the closing 800 meters. She finished thirty-eight points behind Kym Carter (6,200–6,162) for the final spot on the team going to Barcelona. She returned to the Pan Am Games in 1995, at Mar del Plata, Argentina, and won a bronze medal before finishing eighth at the World Championships in Rome.

She conceded she was angry sometimes because she had so little financial support. She worked twenty hours a week in an Indianapolis loan office. Eventually, she lived rent-free in a Bloomington apartment and collected financial support, including proceeds from her high school's ten-year reunion.

"I feel like I owe a lot of people who invested a lot of time and energy in me to see it through," she said then.

In the 1996 Olympic Trials at Atlanta, Nathan was first through two events (13.10 in the 100-meter hurdles and 6 feet in the high jump) and sixty-nine points behind JJK after day one. A poor javelin distance cost her in the next-to-last event—a throw ruled a foul would have meant 100 more points—and she again fell from third to fourth in the closing 800. Sharon Hanson edged Nathan, 6,352–6,327.

Nathan's score would have placed seventh and made her top American at the Atlanta Olympics. The thirty-four-year-old JJK dropped out, and perhaps should have dropped out before the Olympics, allowing Nathan on the team. Nathan said it was her own "epic fail," that she was in the best shape of her life and had no excuses.

"Nobody really knows this because I never talk about it. But it all had to do with spirituality and being obedient to God," she said. "Every single time that I failed—and I failed big, and I always failed big because I succeeded big—it was a spiritual thing. God just had to get me in a certain spot. He let me know in '96 when I didn't make that team, He let me know, 'If you're not going to be obedient and do what I want you to do, I will never let you go to the Olympics. You don't go.' And that's the only thing I hadn't done yet."

In 1999, Nathan had her best year. At thirty, she became a world champion, winning the pentathlon in the World Indoor Championships at Maebashi, Japan. She set an American record of 4,753 points, smashing Carter's record of 4,632 from 1995. Through 2019, Nathan's record had been raised only fifty-two points.

Nathan said she came in expecting to win, did so emphatically, and earned $50,000 in prize money. World record holder Irina Belova of Russia won the silver medal with 4,691 points. Nathan was first in the 60-meter hurdles (8.26), high jump

(6–1¼) and shot put (49–6½), third in the long jump (20–5¾) and second in the 800 meters (2:18.98), setting indoor personal bests in all five events.

Less than three months later, she won the heptathlon at Götzis, Austria, with 6,577 points, a career best and the world's highest score in twenty-one months. It was a total that would have earned a bronze medal at the 1999 World Championships in Seville, Spain, but she inexplicably failed to clear a bar in the high jump at the nationals and did not qualify. It was reminiscent of the pole vault failure that kept Dan O'Brien out of the 1992 Olympic decathlon.

Finally and inevitably, in 2000, Nathan achieved her long-sought goal of making it to an Olympics. In the Olympic Trials at Sacramento, California, she won—by four points, 6,343–6,339, over Sheila Burrell—despite winning just two of seven events and turning in no personal bests. Nathan said it was as if God decided it was her time.

"I'm a lot older, a lot wiser, a lot stronger, mentally and physically," she said. "I'm glad He had me stick it out these last four years."

In Sydney, Nathan and decathlon bronze medalist Chris Huffins rented a house at a three-week cost of $15,000, sharing lodging with Nathan's pastor and his wife, plus family and friends. Even in a stadium with 104,228 in attendance, she could see her pastor and hear the voice of her brother.

If only she could have felt her legs and body. A slow 100-meter hurdles time of 13.74 put her sixteenth after one event, and her medal chances were effectively over. She blamed anti-inflammatory medication she took to treat sore Achilles tendons.

"I just numbed my nervous system," she said. "I got out with everybody; I just didn't move."

She finished ninth with 6,150 points, far off the bronze-winning score of 6,527. Gold medalist Denise Lewis of Great Britain scored 6,584, or just seven points more than Nathan had at Götzis in 1999. Nathan, standing next to Lewis, was the first to congratulate her when standings were announced.

It was the lowest-scoring heptathlon since the inaugural one at Los Angeles in 1984, when the top heptathletes were absent because of the Soviet-led boycott. Nathan was the top non-European finisher.

"Two days and eleven hours each day, we have nothing. There's nothing in the tank," Nathan said. "Our bodies are a mess. We're a mess. We're sore. We're just so fatigued, it's not even funny. When your body gives out on you, then your mind and heart kick in."

Nathan had begun the year in a quest to make it to the Winter Olympics, training with bobsledders in Park City, Utah. She had the requisite size, strength, and speed, and initial results were astounding. Her push times were coming within fifteen hundredths of a second of those by the men.

She teamed with driver Bonny Warner and finished second in the national championships behind Jill Bakken, who went on to win a gold medal at the 2002 Salt Lake City Olympics. Nathan said the sensation of sledding was like that of riding a roller coaster with eyes closed.

"I never would have thought in a billion years about bobsled," she said.

She did not pursue bobsled because she was not done with track and field, although it must have seemed like she was still on a roller coaster. She won her second national heptathlon title in 2001 despite arriving in Eugene, Oregon, at 4:30 a.m. on the day she was to open competition. Her flight was delayed in Denver by a hailstorm. After five hours of sleep, she competed in borrowed clothes, her college running shoes, and spikes a half inch too small. She nonetheless scored 6,174 points. At the World Championships in Edmonton, Alberta, she was seventh.

She tried once more to make it to an Olympics, and she said it was her "farewell to the sport." She was fifth in the 2004 trials at Sacramento. Coincidentally, she was again third heading into the 800 and scored 6,020 points, her best since 2001. She was 106 points behind third place.

"I'm an Olympian because I gutted my way through that," Nathan said. "It wasn't because I was the most talented. I lost all the time. I gutted my way to the Olympics. Period."

She became an educator in Indianapolis, first taking a position at Warren Central High School and later becoming an assistant principal at Pike High School. At Pike, she coached teams to girls' state titles in 2012 and 2015 and runner-up finishes in 2014 and 2016. She became the first woman in Indiana to both compete for and coach a state championship team.

Nathan left coaching after 2017, staying until Lynna Irby left Pike. When Irby was a freshman, Nathan said it was her job to put the sprinter in position to make history, and the teenager did so. Irby achieved the unprecedented feat of becoming a four-time Indiana champion in the 100, 200, and 400 meters (2014–17).

Nathan might have achieved more in her own track and field career but expressed no disappointment. Her legacy is secure. She attributed temporary setbacks to stubbornness in wrestling with God.

"Finally pulled it all together in 1999 and 2000. Now I see it for the way it was," she said. "He was trying to save my life. It's my story. It's my testimony. And I'm saved by it."

Bob Kennedy, 1995.
Photo by Guy Zimmer.
IU Archives P0041933.

Bob Kennedy
1992, 1996

He Made the Atlanta Crowd "Erupt"

WHEN BOB KENNEDY ARRIVED IN DURHAM, NORTH CAROLINA, FOR THE 1990 NCAA Championships, he was not even twenty years old. He had unexpectedly won at the NCAAs in cross-country as an Indiana freshman, and he would be in the mix for a 1,500-meter title in this sophomore season. Yet there were older runners in the 1,500—many of them non-US citizens who were "wicked fast," as Kennedy put it—and the young Hoosier might have been overmatched.

Hoosiers coach Sam Bell didn't think so. Bell knew Kennedy could win, citing this example:

In a 1971 mile at Philadelphia, in one of the most anticipated races ever on American soil, Marty Liquori upset Jim Ryun with a long, sustained kick. Liquori ran the closing 880 yards in 1:51.3 to beat Ryun, 3:54.6 to 3:54.8. The story resonated with Kennedy because his father, Bob Jr., had once beaten Liquori in a New Jersey high school race.

That's how you win, Bell told his nineteen-year-old runner.

"There are certain events, races, that you learn so much about yourself," Kennedy said. "And that was one. Especially when you're young enough and inexperienced enough to blindly trust... Sam Bell, in my case."

In that NCAA 1,500 final, the pace was neither fast nor pedestrian. Kennedy's strategy was to start a Liquori-like drive from 500 meters out. It "wasn't a violent acceleration," he said, but a fourteen-second 100 meters thrust him into the lead. Then he ran the next 200 meters in twenty-seven seconds. Still, he was closely pursued as he rounded the final turn.

"You don't get rid of anyone of that caliber by doing that," he said. "And everybody fanned out to go... and then they've just got nothing. They just kind of stay. So that's how we won that race."

Kennedy finished first in 3:40.42. Next came Providence's Bill Mullaney (Ireland), 3:40.59; Arkansas's Johan Boakes (Great Britain), 3:40.76, and Providence's John Evans (Great Britain), 3:40.76. Future Olympian Steve Holman of Georgetown, also a sophomore, was eighth.

Sophomores to win the NCAAs in the 1,500 meters or mile are among the biggest names in track and field: Joaquim Cruz, Liquori, Ryun, Dyrol Burleson, Ron Delany, Bill Dellinger, Louie Zamperini, and Glenn Cunningham. Cruz and Delany were Olympic gold medalists. Ryun, Dellinger, and Cunningham also were Olympic medalists. Zamperini, of Southern California, was the subject of *Unbroken*, a book and movie about surviving as a Japanese prisoner during World War II.

The most memorable moment in Kennedy's career came when he took the lead with less than two laps to go in the 5,000 meters at the 1996 Olympics Games. The Atlanta crowd of 83,313 "absolutely erupts," a British broadcaster said. Kennedy attempted to string out the field, reminiscent of the race in Durham six years before.

Kennedy went into the Olympic final with the fastest time in the field after others dropped out, chose other events, or didn't make national teams. If the pace had been slower, he said, he would have seized the lead with four laps left. In a fast race, with two left. More than twenty years later, he conceded he should have gone with three left.

"I just didn't. I ran 1:57-something for the last 800. And got sixth," he said.

"My philosophy always has been—put yourself in the best position for you to win, and then see what happens. But if you walk off the track or cross-country course and, 'Ah, I didn't put myself in the right spot,' then it's your fault."

Kennedy's time was 13:12.35, and his sixth place was best by an American in an Olympic 5,000 since Steve Prefontaine was fourth at Munich in 1972. No US-born runner has finished as high since 1996. In other words, in a span of nearly a half century, Kennedy is the best America produced.

He aimed at what was once the world record of 12:58. When he got there, Haile Gebrsellassie had lowered it by fourteen more seconds.

Kennedy never won an Olympic medal or became an iconic figure like Pre. Truth be told, if not for widespread doping, he might have been a medalist. That cannot be proved. Nor can it detract from what he did achieve.

"People that know the sport, they're amazed at what he did," said Todd Williams, a contemporary of Kennedy and two-time Olympian. "What he did was bring American distance running to a level they never even thought about."

At Indiana, Kennedy was a four-time NCAA champion and won twenty—*twenty*—Big Ten titles at distances from 1,500 to 10,000 meters. Added together, that required nearly fifty miles.

He won four US titles at 5,000 meters (1995, 1996, 1997, 2001) and set six American records (four at 3,000, two at 5,000). He won US cross-country titles in 1992 and 2004, setting a record for most years between first and last such victories in a championship dating to 1890. *Track & Field News* ranked Kennedy top American nine times in the 5,000, including every year from 1993 to 1999.

In 1988, he became the first American to win the NCAA cross-country race as a freshman. In 1992, on his home course in Bloomington, he won by 40.8 seconds, still the largest margin in history. That also made him the first to win NCAA and national titles in the same year since Al Lawrence in 1960.

Kennedy's lone international medal came in 2001, when he was twelfth in world cross-country and led the United States to a team bronze. He said the medal is stored somewhere in a box. Between 1987 and 2012, it was the Americans' only team medal. Through 2018, he had clocked sub-13:06 in the 5,000 nine times, most ever by an American. (Kenyan-born Bernard Lagat had eight and Galen Rupp six.)

Kennedy's best times:

- 1,500 meters, 3:38.32
- Mile, 3:56.21
- 3,000 meters, 7:30.84 (American record from 1998 to 2010)
- Two miles, 8:11.59
- 5,000 meters, 12:58.21 (American record from 1996 to 2009)
- 10,000 meters, 27:37.45

He had a long-standing contract with Nike, which created two racing spikes in his honor: the Nike Kennedy XC and Nike Zoom Kennedy. As a pro, he was coached by his British agent, Kim McDonald, who died in 2001 at age forty-five. Kennedy said he would be "shocked" if athletes coached by McDonald were using performance-enhancing drugs. Kennedy trained with Kenyan greats such as Moses Kiptanui and Daniel Komen in London and Australia.

Kennedy said he and McDonald once spoke about doping suspicions. The coach said he could go out that day and locate PEDs.

"And you probably will win Olympic gold medals and set records and make millions. But you'd have to sit on your couch and wonder where it came from," McDonald told him.

It is a conversation Kennedy has long remembered.

"Because it's twenty years later. And I sit it on my couch. And I'm proud of what I did," he said. "That came from my talent, my work, and I'm proud of that. I know there are some former athletes, 'Well, that guy was cheating.' It's gone. It's done. It's about what I feel good about. Not about, 'Well, I should have won the bronze medal in Atlanta.' It's gone. It's done. I don't stress about that stuff. Knowing my personality—I think everyone is a little different—if I had doped, I would be struggling right now."

Kennedy was born in Bloomington on August 18, 1970, the only child of Bob and Barbara Kennedy. Grit must have been hereditary. His mother's pregnancy was a balance between protecting her unborn son and fighting kidney cancer with radiation.

Bob Sr. once held the New Jersey high school two-mile record and ran for the Hoosiers' 1967 Big Ten cross-country champions. Barbara did not start running until later in life and was winning local races and finishing high in age-group competitions well into her thirties.

"So the joke in my family is, where did I really get my talent from?" Kennedy said.

The family relocated to suburban Columbus, Ohio, when he was a child. He was a soccer midfielder through middle school and ran a 5:16 mile as an eighth-grader. (That is not much faster than his daughter, Sophia, who ran a 5:19 mile in eighth grade.)

Running "was always fun," he said, even when he was "destroyed" in a cross-country regional as a freshman at Westerville North High School. The six-foot Kennedy grew four to five inches before his sophomore year, improving so much that he was second in Ohio in cross-country. In track, he was second in the state meet in the 3,200 meters behind Mark Croghan, who went on to become a three-time Olympian in the steeplechase.

As a junior and senior, Kennedy swept state titles in cross-country, 1,600, and 3,200 meters. His state meet record of 4:05.13 in the 1,600 from 1988 still stands. He also won in the Kinney (now Foot Locker) cross-country nationals. He was training fewer than thirty miles a week, so he left high school with unrealized potential. His college choices included Illinois, Wisconsin, Georgetown, and Texas. But it was hard to reject Indiana. Bell sent weekly newsletters to track alumni and parents of athletes, including comments, and young Kennedy had been reading those for years.

"I'm surprised that I thought this when I was seventeen. If you really looked at the history of what the various coaches produced, coach Bell by far produced more Olympians than any of those other coaches," Kennedy said.

Kennedy became misty-eyed when speaking about his Indiana coach, who died in 2016 at age eighty-eight. Bell could be crusty and blunt-spoken, and yet he was beloved by athletes. He considered himself their coach for life.

"He was very direct. Really passionate. Loved his athletes," Kennedy said. "If you messed up, he would get in your face. He had an expectation for you as an athlete, as a student, as a human being. And that's why I get emotional thinking about it. That's why you have hundreds of former athletes show up at this funeral or show up at reunions."

Kennedy conceded he "wasn't an angel" in college but never endured a Bell rebuke. "I'm just lucky I didn't get caught."

Kennedy did not often get caught by another runner, either.

As a freshman, he won the first of four Big Ten titles in cross-country. He was fourth on a cold, wet day in the Midwest Regional at Mahomet, Illinois, so his expectations diminished for the NCAAs. Asked by Bell where he thought he could finish, he replied in the top fifteen.

"You should be top five," Bell told him.

"We always connected brilliantly that way," Kennedy said.

On a 10,000-meter course at Granger, Iowa, he unexpectedly won with a time of 29:21, one second ahead of the runner-up. Kennedy reset his goals almost immediately, as he explained to his coach on the way back to the hotel.

"And Bob looked at the golf course from his window seat and said, 'Well, I've got to forget this and start looking ahead,'" Bell recalled.

By its nature, running is a selfish enterprise in which there is no ball to pass or playing time to share.

But Bell built a balanced program, and the Hoosiers were sometimes asked to sacrifice for team points. The coach kept Kennedy out of the 5,000 at NCAA Championships—even though both knew it would be his distance after college—so he could hone his speed in the 1,500. An exception was made at Big Ten Championships, when the coach asked Kennedy to commit to the team.

That's how Kennedy found himself tripling—mile, 3,000, 5,000—in indoor conference championships. He did so in 1990, 1991, and 1992, and won eight of nine races. Bell almost pulled him out of the 5,000 in 1991, but team standings were close enough against Illinois that he told Kennedy: "I need you to run the 5,000." During the race, Kennedy heard the words "We've got this," so he relented for perhaps the only time. He did not chase eventual winner Brad Barquist of Michigan—who made the 1996 Olympic team at 10,000.

"I just didn't want to put in that effort," Kennedy said.

This did not ruffle Bell in the least. If the Hoosiers needed those points, the coach told him, he would have won. Indeed, Indiana was Big Ten champion indoors in 1990, 1991, and 1992, and outdoors in 1990 and 1991.

In Kennedy's sophomore year, he was fifth in the NCAA in cross-country and third in the indoor 3,000 before winning that historic 1,500. After the college season, still a nineteen-year-old, he finished second in the USA Championships in the 5,000.

His junior year, 1991, was to last so long Kennedy red-shirted in cross-country the following fall. He was third in the NCAA in cross-country and won the indoor mile in 3:58.11, breaking four minutes for the first time at the RCA Dome in Indianapolis. Shockingly, he failed to make the outdoor final in the 1,500.

His resilience was underscored when, soon afterward, he finished third in the 5,000 at the USA Championships to make his first world team. He lowered his 5,000 time to 13:22.17 on July 6, at Oslo, Norway, but the favorable conditions there were nothing like the humidity he endured at the World Championships in Tokyo. In fact, because he barely made the final there, his response was: "Oh crap. Because you're not going to be in it." He was not. He finished twelfth.

On the other hand, Tokyo was an introduction to what became a fourteen-year career on the world stage: 1991–2004.

"Running rounds and running qualifying heats at the highest level, trying to figure out how to get through," Kennedy said. "They matter, and it's part of championship racing."

After training through autumn 1991, he nearly added another NCAA title indoors but was edged in the 3,000 by Washington State's Josephat Kapkory, 7:59.04 to 7:59.24. In the outdoor 1,500, Kennedy was again second, beaten by Holman, 3:38.39 to 3:39.10. That was Kennedy's last race wearing an IU singlet.

The 1992 Olympic Trials, held at New Orleans, were as muggy as Tokyo was the year before. The tactical 5,000-meter final left six runners clustered together at the bell lap. Kennedy seized the lead with 300 meters left but was overtaken by John Trautman, who sped past him 80 meters before the finish. Trautman, with a closing lap of 54.7, finished first in 13:40.30. But in the trials, second is as good as first, and Kennedy's runner-up 13:41.22 qualified him for his first Olympics.

He had kept a poster in his condominium that read, "Think Barcelona," and the goal he had envisioned as long ago as his teen years was met. At the Barcelona Olympics, he was second in his heat in 13:35.76. He was overmatched in the final, as he had been in Tokyo, and finished twelfth in 13:39.72. Coincidentally, gold medalist Dieter Baumann of West Germany was to become a friend of Kennedy on the European circuit. Baumann, a harsh critic of doping, twice tested positive for the steroid nandrolone in 1999 and served a two-year suspension.

Kennedy returned to IU for his final season of college cross-country, and it was on the IU course where he ran away from the field as no one has before or since. As Phil Richards of the *Indianapolis Star* wrote, "It was a command performance, one that exhibited Bob Kennedy's impressive level of fitness, strength, savvy and steel will."

His plan was to change tempo early and often to separate himself. He and Kapkory shared the lead through 3,000 meters, but Kennedy seized control on an uphill grade in the next kilometer. Kapkory could not respond, fading to twelfth. Kennedy kept extending his lead, delighting a large crowd, and crossed the finish with fists upraised. He covered the rain-soaked 10,000 meters in 30:15.3. He called it one of his most satisfying achievements, given how many supporters he had in Bloomington. This title, he said, was sweeter than that of his freshman year.

"The first one, I just played off everybody else," Kennedy said. "This one, I controlled it. I made the move, and that's more satisfying."

And he wasn't even done for the week. Five days later, Kennedy came from behind to win the US cross-country title at Kenosha, Wisconsin, beating defending champion Williams and eight-time winner Pat Porter. By four miles, Porter had a seven-second lead. Kennedy and Williams caught up by five miles, crossing together in 24:05. Porter went ahead again but was passed by Williams, who built a ten-meter lead over Porter with three hundred meters left.

Kennedy passed Porter and caught Williams, and the two sprinted up the final hill. Kennedy finally surged in front and raised his arms as he entered the finish chute, as he had done in Bloomington. He and Williams both clocked 29:41, followed by Porter in 29:45.

"I thought the race was over at six miles," Kennedy said. "But I saw I was close and dug down with what extra I had. I caught a gear that I haven't had to use this year."

For the rest of his career, many important races would be run not in the United States but in Europe.

In his first season out of college, he came as close as he ever would to an individual global medal, finishing fourth in the 3,000 meters in the 1993 World Indoor Championships at Toronto. Kennedy's time of 7:51.27 was .17 behind bronze. He was second in the 5,000 at the USA Championships but did not advance past the heats in the outdoor worlds at Stuttgart, Germany. He lowered his 5,000 time to 13:14.91, again at Oslo.

Kennedy's breakout year was 1994. A stress fracture in his shin kept him out of the World Championships in cross-country. But not since Prefontaine and Liquori in the 1970s, or Craig Virgin in the 1980s, had an American distance runner been such a force on the track. Bell conceded Kennedy "jumped the gate" in his development.

On July 8 at Lille, France, Kennedy lowered his 5,000 time by nearly ten seconds to 13:05.93 and finished second to Morocco's Khalid Skah, the Olympic champion at 10,000. On July 18, he set an American record of 7:35.33 in finishing fourth in a 3,000 at Nice, France. Four days later, he was second to Skah in a 5,000 at Oslo in 13:02.93, then making him the ninth-fastest in history. He finished sixth August 17 at Zurich in 13:12.98 and seventh September 3 in the Grand Prix final at Paris in 13:16.93.

Kennedy would leave for Europe after nationals and not return until after the Grand Prix final. He was based out of London, sharing a row house with Irish great Marcus O'Sullivan and Holman. They lived near a track and did long runs on grass and dirt trails in Bushy Park, the former hunting grounds of King Henry VIII.

"I just loved Europe," Kennedy said. "I loved being there, I loved racing there. I'm super comfortable. And a lot of my fellow athletes weren't."

His 1995 was less spectacular but foundational to the upcoming Olympic year. He finished fourteenth in world cross-country and won his only US indoor 3,000 and first US 5,000 title. He was seventh in the 5,000, behind six Africans, at the World Championships in Goteborg, Sweden. His fastest 5,000 time, 13:03.37, came in finishing fourth August 18 at Brussels, Belgium.

He showed early fitness in 1996 by running a 5,000 in in 13:12.14 in the Pre Classic at Eugene, Oregon, on May 26, finishing third behind Kenyans Paul Bitok (13:08.29) and Komen (13:12.14). Kennedy won by ten seconds at the 1996 Olympic Trials in a slowish 13:46.17 in hot, humid weather at Atlanta.

But the race that changed the pre-Olympics outlook was his American record of 12:58.75 at Stockholm, Sweden, on July 8 in finishing second to the twenty-year-old Komen (12:51.60). Kennedy became the first non-African ever to break thirteen minutes. Komen did not make Kenya's Olympic team, so Kennedy would not have to beat him at Atlanta.

It was to the Hoosier's advantage that the Olympic final of the 5,000 was the third round in four days. Kennedy knew he lacked his peers' finishing speed, but his attempt at a long kick came up short. Venuste Niyangabo, a bronze medalist in the

1,500 at the previous year's World Championships, blazed the last 400 in 54.93 to become Burundi's first-ever gold medalist. His time was 13:07.96, with Bitok taking silver in 13:08.16, and Morocco's Khalid Boulami bronze in 13:08.37. Bauman, the defending champion, was fourth in 13:08.81.

In sixth, Kennedy said at least he was "in the thick of it." At Barcelona, he said, he might as well have been a tourist.

"I'd love to have a medal," he told the media afterward. "But this is a positive thing for me. I'm not disappointed. An Olympic medal is an extremely hard thing to come by."

Kennedy, at twenty-five, would never run in another Olympics.

He ended 1996 ranked sixth in the world, and no runner born outside Africa finished that high again until Rupp ranked fourth in 2014. On August 14, Kennedy lowered his American record in the 5,000 to 12:58.21. He twice broke his own American record in the 3,000, clocking 7:33.96 and 7:31.69. He was fifth in the 5,000 at the Grand Prix final in 13:04.4 at Milan, Italy, on September 7. It was the year of his career.

It was far from his last year in the sport. He was competitive for eight more seasons. Indeed, he won that cross-country team medal at age thirty.

In 1997, he ran a USA Championships at home. Before 9,197 spectators at Indianapolis, he found himself in another duel against Williams, this time at 5,000 meters. It was a tumultuous occasion despite Kennedy's runaway victory. With temperatures near 80, Williams went down with three laps to go and required medical attention. Kennedy waved to the crowd as he crossed the finish to win in 13:30.86, then went to the other side of the track. He was greeted by about one hundred youths, many bare-chested, who were part of his runners' camp. The rail collapsed from the weight, leaving four teens with minor injuries.

"They were rushing to get the stadium done. I guess they forgot a few bolts in there," Kennedy said. "I scooted out of there in the nick of time."

Who said Bob Kennedy was not quick?

The season culminated in the World Championships at Athens, where he was sixth (again) at 5,000 meters. He was eight seconds behind the bronze medalist, so he was not in the mix as much as he was at the Atlanta Olympics.

Kennedy stayed on course for the 2000 Sydney Olympics. In 1998, he lowered his American record in the 3,000 to 7:30.84 at Monaco on August 8 and ran a 5,000 in 13:03.57 at Berlin on September 1. In 1999, he was a distant ninth in the worlds at Seville, Spain, but showed he contemplated moving up in distance by winning his first 10,000-meter race on the track in 27:38.37 at Stanford.

What happened to him in 2000 is why the Olympics are so glorious and yet so cruel. The Olympics are a moment in time, and sometimes it is not your time.

Kennedy's car was rear-ended on Fall Creek Parkway, near his Indianapolis home, on May 8. He felt unhurt, but while training in California a week later, his back was painful after a long run. A physician discovered a small fracture in his vertebrae. So in ten of the fourteen weeks leading up to the Olympic Trials at

Sacramento, California, he could not run at all. He cross-trained in a pool and on a bike, but he lacked his usual fitness.

At the trials, he barely got out of the 5,000-meter heats. After building a 40-meter lead through five laps of the final, he drifted back to the pack. Adam Goucher finished first in 13:27.06, and Kennedy was sixth in 13:42.15. He would not be going to Sydney. Not in any distance.

That is why 2001 turned out to be such a gratifying season. He led the Americans to that cross-country bronze at Oostende, Belgium. Then, on the track, he was an underdog thirty-year-old as he prepared for the USA Championships at Eugene.

"That's one of those things, 'OK, I'm not at the top of my game. I'm coming off injury. How am I going to do this?'" Kennedy said.

He won the last of his four US titles in the 5,000 by doing what the Kenyans often did—speeding up and slowing down, hoping to wear down or befuddle the other runners. He alternated laps of sixty-two and sixty-eight seconds, and the favored Goucher stuck with him. In the end, Kennedy held on to win in 13:28.72 and, uncharacteristically, raised his arms in celebration. Alan Culpepper was second in 13:29.66 and Goucher third in 13:30.36. Afterward, Goucher told his older rival: "I had no idea what was going on out there."

Kennedy: "To me, I love that stuff. I love that part of racing."

He had to pull out of that year's World Championships because of an underactive thyroid. That, plus iron deficiencies and nagging injuries, knocked him out of the 2002 season. He was not vintage Bob Kennedy in 2003, either.

By 2004, ahead of the Athens Olympics, he looked more like the man who dominated American running in the 1990s. For the first time since 1997, he raced at home in the February 8 cross-country nationals at Indianapolis. He broke from the pack near the end of the fourth of six laps on a snow-covered, two-kilometer loop at Fall Creek and Sixteenth Park. Before then, Kennedy said, it was "barely an effort." He finished the twelve-kilometer race in 35:03, four seconds ahead of Robert Gary.

"I've made a lot of friends since college who know what I do but have never seen me run," Kennedy said.

To secure his qualifying time for Athens, he ran 10,000 meters in a lifetime best of 27:37.45 at Stanford on April 30. He was thirty-three, but distance runners older than him had won Olympic medals. He could do it.

About ten days from the Olympic Trials, he was preparing a workout in which he would run four separate miles, each in about 4:12 to 4:15. His first mile was 4:07, and the second 4:08. He was "holding back," he said, because it was so effortless. "There's very few workouts when I feel that way. "You're on," he recalled. The third mile was run in 4:10. The fourth mile began, and his Achilles tendon tightened.

"And that was it. That's a thirty-three- or thirty-four-year-old body," Kennedy said.

He tried various treatments but knew he was vulnerable heading into the 10,000 at Sacramento. After two laps, he dropped out, and another Olympics would go on without him.

He had committed to running November's New York Marathon. So after his Achilles healed, he endured a nine-week training program in Boulder, Colorado, designed by Dieter Hogen, a German coach. Kennedy called it "one of my favorite running experiences." Hogen assured him he could run a marathon in two hours, ten minutes. However, a prerace evaluation showed Kennedy had an elevated white blood cell count, and that manifested itself in the race. He dropped out at New York after eighteen miles.

He intended to keep going but finally announced his retirement from elite running on January 20, 2006. He and then-wife, Melina, became parents of twins, Marcus and Sophia, on January 11, 2005. It was time to chase children, not records.

After the New York Marathon, he did not run a step for five years. He concentrated on fatherhood and ownership of stores selling running gear. Ten years after his first marathon, he was persuaded to enter another. He was in a contest against other former runners to see who could lose the most weight, and gradually he became fit enough to try New York again. He ran the 26.2 miles in 3:26:17 and said, "I'm happy that I did it." Publicity about his quest caused him to hear from people he had not spoken to in years. Some spectators and runners recognized him, including two men who ran with him for many miles.

Kennedy's career in retrospect shines more brightly than in his own era. If not for injuries, he would have been a four-time Olympian.

"I think the mentality of an athlete like myself is, I think you always feel you could have been better," he said. "Otherwise, you probably wouldn't have driven yourself so hard. There are those thoughts like, 'If I would have done this differently in Atlanta, I would have won a medal. If I had done this differently, I could have run a great marathon maybe.'"

No maybes: Bob Kennedy belongs in the pantheon of American runners.

Jim Spivey
Courtesy of Indiana University Athletics.

Jim Spivey
1984, 1992, 1996

One of America's Greatest Milers

AHEAD OF THE 1992 OLYMPIC TRIALS, JIM SPIVEY'S RUNNING LEGACY WAS secure. He was a world medalist, Olympian, NCAA champion, national champion, and American record holder. What more was there?

Redemption. He wanted that. In 1988, in what was otherwise one of his best years, he failed to make the Olympic team, passed near the finish by Mark Deady for the third and final spot in the 1,500 meters. How odd was that? Deady was not only another Indiana University runner, he was a tenant in an apartment owned by Spivey.

By 1992, Spivey was coached by Mike Durkin, an attorney who ran for Illinois and made two Olympic teams. The night before the final, Durkin called with specific instructions: "Go out with the leaders, then run the third lap in fifty-six seconds."

"The last straightaway," Durkin told Spivey, "don't go to your guns unless somebody comes alongside you."

And one more thing:

"These guys are trying to break into your home."

In New Orleans, in what was his fourth Olympic Trials, Spivey did as instructed. He stayed with the leaders, passing 400 meters in 57.5 seconds and 800 in 1:58.6. Then, when most runners are holding back for a finishing kick, he ran the third 400 in 57.1 to stretch the field. He seized the lead and held it.

"With two hundred to go, I started to think of people breaking into my home. I got to that level of energy on the turn," Spivey said. "Forty meters to go, I see Steve Holman. He's tight as a rock. Four steps later, the finish line came."

Spivey ran the last 400 in 54.4, last 300 in 40.4. He finished first in 3:36.24, followed by Holman, 3:36.48, and Terrance Herrington, 3:37.14. Those three were going to the Olympics, and everyone else stayed home—as Spivey did four years before.

Soon after crossing the line, Spivey bent over, held his head in his hands, and went to his knees as someone draped a towel over his shoulders. He sobbed and repeatedly cried out, "Thank you, Lord." He recalled telling Durkin afterward that it was the hardest race, mentally, he had ever run.

"All the dragons from 1988 were there," Spivey said.

Including road miles, he ran sixty-eight sub-four-minute miles between 1980 and 1996, plus the 1,500-meter equivalent of sub-4:00 in many other races. Track and field can be guilty of valuing clock over competition, but Spivey's times stand the test of time:

- In 1980, he set a Big Ten meet record of 3:38.56 for 1,500 meters. Through 2019, it was still the record.
- In 1982, he set an IU record of 1:46.5 for 800 meters. The record lasted thirty-six years.
- In 1984, he was fifth in the 1,500 meters at the Los Angeles Olympics in 3:36.07. It was the fastest time by an American at an Olympics until 2012.
- In 1986, he became the second American to run a sub-3:50 mile. Through 2019, only two more US-born runners had done so.
- In 1987, at Lausanne, Switzerland, he set an American record of 4:52.44 in the infrequently run 2,000 meters. He became sixth of all time, and four of the five then ahead of him were Olympic medalists. The time remains the American record.
- In 1988, he ran 1,500 meters in 3:31.01 at Koblenz, Germany, to become second in US history. Thirty years later, only three other US-born runners had run faster.

"For college, it was more about getting ready to run postcollegiately and staying in that mind-set that I want to continue on," Spivey said.

And to think it all started because he got a B in a high school phys-ed class.

He was born March 7, 1960, in Schiller Park, Illinois, a son of a Motorola TV technician. Spivey was a freshman basketball player at Fenton High School in the Chicago suburb of Bensenville when he was asked to race a mile for gym class. His time was 6:48. The gym teacher, John Kurtz, also the track coach, told Spivey he should go out for cross-country and track.

Spivey's response: "I'm a basketball player." The coach's response: He gave Spivey a B in class.

"He won't admit he gave me a B because I didn't go out," Spivey said.

His memories of high school are perhaps more vivid than those of his college and postcollege careers. Those were the days that laid the foundation for all that was to follow.

In sophomore gym class, without any training, Spivey ran a 5:48 mile. Once he began running, his times kept dropping: 19:08, then 17:17, then 16:48. By the end of his sophomore year, he had run a 9:21 two-mile.

The nearby powerhouse York High of Elmhurst awarded T-shirts to those on the team who ran one thousand miles over the summer. So Spivey and two teammates did so, too, wearing "Fenton 1,000-Mile Club" T-shirts that fall. He faithfully recorded his mileage inside the square of each calendar date. He would make a list of tasks, then check off each one.

"I think the biggest thing for me was that there was order," Spivey said. "It sounds so simple. You trained on your own. And you could see progress. Coach Kurtz would say, 'I want you to run this.' And you would do it. And you could see progress. And that carried over to my schoolwork."

He said he was once a B-student and ended up graduating thirtieth in a class of five hundred.

As a junior, he finished second in the state in cross-country and the two-mile, dropping his time to 9:00.3 in the latter. He was recruited by schools such as Wisconsin, Illinois, Kentucky, and SMU. Oregon coach Bill Dellinger visited his home but could not offer any scholarship money. He was second in cross-country again as a senior and signed with Indiana on his eighteenth birthday, which coincided with the fiftieth birthday of Hoosiers coach Sam Bell.

During Spivey's 1978 spring, he was entered in the 440-yard dash in a midweek meet, with the mile run scheduled seven minutes later. He ran the 440 in 49.7 (or 49.4 for 400 meters), followed by a 4:13 mile. Kurtz excitedly called Bell the next day to inform the Indiana coach. It was then, Spivey said, that he thought he could run a sub-four-minute mile someday. Sub-3:50 is not a goal when you're just eighteen.

Going into the state meet, he targeted the 880-yard run, preparing to run the third 220 especially hard. He was confident, then took it as a challenge when only half of the high school writers polled picked him to win.

"Really? I hadn't lost a race all outdoor season," he recalled.

He surged on the backstretch, as he had trained to do, and distanced himself from all other runners. Fans in Charleston, Illinois, gasped.

"To this day, I can remember the noise of the crowd," he said.

In the final, the first lap was faster than the day before (fifty-five seconds), and he said there was a "moment of doubt" whether he should surge as had done in trials. He decided to do so. "And the announcer said, 'He did the same thing yesterday.' I remember hearing that," Spivey said.

He finished in 1:50.3, the 800-meter equivalent of 1:49.7. It was the fastest time of 1978 by a high schooler. He went on to run 1,600 meters in 4:06.2 in the International Prep Invitational at Naperville, Illinois—a 4:08 mile that made him second nationally at that distance. Coincidentally, first at 4:05.4 was John Gregorek, who went on to become a longtime rival, fellow Asics sales employee, roommate, and one of Spivey's closest friends.

"I would consider him a brother," Spivey said.

At Indiana, Spivey thrived under Bell's methods, totaling thirteen individual Big Ten championships: six indoors, five outdoors, and two cross-country. Spivey's

1980 victory in cross-country helped the Hoosiers tie Michigan for the team title, and Indiana didn't win another until 2013. He said Bell became a mentor and a friend for life.

"Sam was good for me in getting me to do things I didn't think I could do in training and racing," Spivey said.

As a sophomore, he became the first IU undergraduate to run a sub-four-minute mile, clocking 3:58.9 indoors at Louisville, Kentucky when he was still nineteen. Spivey won the first of three Big Ten mile/two-mile indoor sweeps. He underscored his range by finishing sixth in the indoor NCAAs at 880 yards, then third in the two-mile, on the same day. In that two-mile, Spivey finished less than one second behind winner Suleiman Nyambui of Texas-El Paso. The twenty-seven-year-old Nyambui, of Tanzania, went on to win a silver medal in the 5,000 meters at the Moscow Olympics.

That May, Spivey ran for the first time at Eugene, Oregon, where Dellinger had tried to lure him. Spivey could not understand why the Hoosiers would travel across the country for a dual meet... until he saw the large crowd at Hayward Field. He recalled winning a 1,500/5,000 double in 3:43.12 and 13:38.97, although Indiana lost the closing 4×400 relay and thus the meet 80–74. An Oregon fan waited afterward so he could speak to Spivey, telling him it was the fastest such double ever in a dual meet there. "Surely," Spivey replied, "Steve Prefontaine won a faster double."

"No. Not that fast," the fan told him.

Also that year, at Champaign, Illinois, he set a Big Ten meet record for 1,500 meters. In the same stadium where Red Grange and Dick Butkus once roamed, and where Herb McKenley and Renaldo Nehemiah made track history, Spivey was headed toward one of the fastest college times ever. Spivey hit 2:38 with a lap to go but "the wheels came off about one hundred meters to go," he said, and he finished in 3:38.56. Nevertheless, because championship races are typically slow and tactical, no one has bettered that at a Big Ten meet.

In his first Olympic Trials, Spivey finished seventh in the 1,500 at Eugene, a valuable experience for a twenty-year-old. Those making the team—Steve Scott, Steve Lacy, and Durkin—did not make it to Moscow anyway because of the US boycott. Spivey missed the 1981 indoor season but came back in June to finish third in the NCAA 1,500.

In 1982, he was the Big Ten's first all-sports athlete of the year, outpolling Michigan halfback/sprinter Butch Woolfolk. Spivey actually won his first national title, in the mile, before his first NCAA title. He set a Big Ten record of 3:57.04 in the USA Indoor Championships at New York's Madison Square Garden. He set another Big Ten record, in the outdoor mile, with a time of 3:55.56 at UCLA. Besides winning a Big Ten double-double, that year he became the first Indiana miler to be an NCAA champion by taking the 1,500 in 3:45.42 at the 4,550-foot altitude of Provo, Utah.

As a redshirt senior, he won his second Big Ten cross-country title. In the indoor NCAAs, he clocked a 3:59.95 mile at Pontiac, Michigan, becoming the first US winner since North Carolina's Tony Waldrop in 1974. With collegiate eligibility expired in 1983, Spivey moved up to 5,000 meters for the USA Championships, finished second, and qualified for the inaugural World Championships at Helsinki, Finland. Yet the year's highlight was the July 9 mile at Oslo, Norway, where he dropped his time all the way to 3:50.59 and finished second to Scott's 3:49.49.

Heading into the 1984 Los Angeles Olympics, he decided to leave Bell and change coaches, getting workouts from Durkin and Ken Popejoy, another Chicagoan who was an NCAA champion for Michigan State. Spivey reasoned that Bell was busy coaching his college team. What Durkin brought, Spivey said, was proper peaking. On the climactic day, "He got it right," Spivey said. As he was to do at an Olympic Trials eight years later, Spivey heeded Durkin's prerace strategy of staying closer to the front.

"You know," Durkin told him, "if you're fourth instead of ninth, you have a much better chance of making an Olympic team and winning."

Trials favorites were Scott, the American record holder and 1983 world silver medalist, and South African-born Sydney Maree. Spivey was fourth with a lap left, trailing front-runner Maree. Expectedly, Scott went to the lead around the final turn. But he was passed by Spivey, who won by three yards in 3:36.43. Scott was second in 3:36.76, Maree third in 3:37.02.

Spivey went on to qualify for the Olympic final, in which Scott tested the field by passing 800 meters in 1:56.81. Spain's Jose Abascal moved ahead with about 500 meters left, chased by Great Britain's Sebastian Coe and Steve Cram. Spivey passed a fading Scott and moved to fifth with a lap to go. Britain's Steve Ovett dropped out with 350 meters left, suffering from a respiratory problem, and a gap was created between Spivey and the eventual medalists.

"That was it. I was done," Spivey said.

Coe repeated as Olympic champion with an Olympic record of 3:32.53, followed by Cram and Abascal. Spivey was fifth. He had not won a medal, but he put himself in position to medal.

"I ran back to the Olympic Village," Spivey said. "I'm going to look in the mirror and ask myself, 'Did you do everything you could do?' I remember saying, 'Yes, I did.'"

He broke through the 3:50 mile barrier, also at Oslo, on July 7, 1986. He finished third in 3:49.80, behind Cram, 3:48.31, and Scott, 3:48.73. On his website, Spivey wrote that he was losing oxygen so rapidly at the end of the race that he was becoming disoriented and struggling to sign autographs for children afterward. Surely he broke 3:50, he told himself, because this is what it should feel like.

"I found my sweats and jogged off to warm down by himself," he wrote. "After about a half mile, I stopped. I went down to one knee, with tears streaming down my face. I looked at my watch. It was 12:30 a.m. The practice track was almost deserted. I asked, 'Lord, what did I do to receive such wonderful talents?' The tears fell heavier now. I thanked Him many times, but the question resurfaced—what was my time? I picked myself up, smiling, and continued on my warmdown."

"Back at the hotel, the results were posted. The mile was the last event on the program, so they did not have the results after we finished. I quickly scanned down to third place. I saw 3:4x, and I did not need to know the next number. I had run under 3:50!"

The next year, 1987, featured three major championships: indoor worlds at Indianapolis, Pan American Games at Indianapolis, and outdoor worlds at Rome. Spivey missed a medal by .12 at indoor worlds, finishing fourth in 3:39.63 at the Hoosier Dome.

The Pan Am Games lack the appeal they once had, but most top Americans competed then because the event was at home and the Olympic Trials were to be in Indy the next year. Spivey led the 1,500 heading into the home stretch but was overtaken by Brazil's Joaquim Cruz, the 800-meter gold medalist from the LA Olympics. Cruz won the slow race in 3:47.34, with Spivey taking silver in 3:47.46 and Scott bronze in 3:47.76.

The worlds 1,500 at Rome was arguably Spivey's greatest achievement. He was fifth with 300 meters left but fell farther behind when Cram sped to the front in a prolonged kick, ahead of Spain's Jose Luiz Gonzales and Somalia's Abdi Bile. Spivey passed Kenya's Joseph Chesire for fourth, then overtook the fading Cram, who ultimately was eighth. Bile, the NCAA champion for George Mason University, was gold medalist in 3:36.80. Gonzalez took silver in 3:38:03 and Spivey bronze in 3:38.82.

"I remember thinking, 'All Mike said was for me to be with the leaders with three hundred to go, and I couldn't even do that,'" Spivey said.

However, Bile had run the closing 800 in an unprecedented 1:46.6, so Spivey's time was 1:47.9. The Hoosier "didn't feel so bad" after that. Also, no US-born runner subsequently won a world medal in the 1,500 until Matthew Centrowitz—the 2016 Olympic champion—in 2011.

If 1987 was Spivey's year, 1988 should have been. At twenty-eight, he was in his prime. He was coming off that world bronze and American 2,000-meter record. Indoors, he won his only national title in the 3,000 meters.

But a late-April stress fracture in his left tibia cost him a month of training. Worse, it cost him confidence heading into the Olympic Trials, even though he had run a 3:50.57 mile to finish sixth July 2 at Oslo.

"Physically, I was ready," Spivey said. "But mentally, I was not ready."

In the Olympic Trials at Indianapolis, he remembers being nudged by another runner with a lap to go, nearly tripping him. He accelerated from three hundred meters to go until the closing one hundred . . . "but then I used so much energy, that was it," he said.

Jeff Atkinson surprisingly won in 3:40.94, followed by the thirty-two-year-old Scott in 3:41.12. Just before the finish, Deady overtook Spivey for the third Olympic spot, 3:41.31 to 3:41.52.

"I think in the long term, it was probably the best thing for me," Spivey said. "I was putting too much emphasis on my running."

He lost out on Seoul but said the outcome was good for his soul. He changed priorities after that, dedicating himself to his Christian faith; his wife, Cindy; and two sons. Later in 1988, he ran the second-fastest 1,500 in the world for that year (3:31.01), but then had to end his season because of back pain. Nike offered him so little money to renew his contract, he switched to ASICS for free.

"Then you realize, 'How bad do you really want it?'" he said. "How far do you want to go?"

Although he was fourth in the 1,500 at the 1991 nationals, he ran a series of fast times thereafter and was poised for a breakthrough summer. He ran another sub-3:50 mile, finishing third at Oslo in 3:49.83. But after a solo 3:52.74 in 100-degree heat in New York, he developed a small tear in his hip and was out of the 1991 worlds in Tokyo.

Early end to that season prefaced an early beginning to the next, which Spivey said contributed to the redemptive 1992. After his front-running victory at the Olympic Trials, he made the final in what evolved as a wide-open 1,500 at Barcelona. Reigning world champion Noureddine Morceli of Algeria would have been favored, but he lost six weeks of training and had his twenty-one-race winning streak end.

Kenya's thirty-four-year-old Joseph Cheshire led the finalists through a slow 800 meters in 2:06.83. Heading into the back straightaway of the final lap, Spivey and Spain's Fermin Cacho were fighting for third when they briefly jostled each other. Cheshire drifted to the outside of lane 1, and Cacho, on the rail, sped by him and Germany's Jens-Peter Herold. With the Spanish crowd roaring, Cacho sprinted to victory off a closing 400 of 50.5. His winning time, 3:40.12, was the slowest since 1956. Spivey, caught up in traffic like so many others, closed in 52.2 but finished eighth in 3:41.74, or .04 behind Morceli. The Algerian broke the world record four weeks later and won the next three global titles.

"Today, I would have rather pushed the pace and got twelfth than sit back and get eighth," Spivey said.

At thirty-two, he was racing as well as ever. Eleven days after the Barcelona final, he was fourth in a 1,500 at Zurich in 3:32.94, behind Morceli and Cacho. It was the second-fastest time of Spivey's career.

A year later, in the 1993 worlds at Stuttgart, Germany, he was fifth behind medalists all familiar to him: Morceli (gold), Cacho (silver) and Bile (bronze). Spivey also ran what was then the fourth-fastest 3,000 ever by an American, 7:37.04, in Cologne, Germany.

He could have retired after 1993 but unexpectedly broke an eleven-year-old personal best with a 5,000-meter time of 13:15.86 in 1994. He was fourth in the 5,000 at the 1996 Olympic Trials in Atlanta, and that ordinarily would mean he was off the team. Third-place Ronnie Harris did not meet the Olympic qualifying standard. Spivey did. He ran 13:24.23 on July 8 at Stockholm, Sweden, in a race in which Bob Kennedy set an American record of 12:58.75.

For the Olympics, Spivey took a flight from Chicago for the opening ceremony, in which he had never walked. Then he flew back from Chicago and drove to Atlanta from Glen Ellyn, Illinois, with his family. As he awaited his first-round heat, he could not help but think about another race. He jogged over to the 1,500 start, as he had done in 1984 and 1992.

"I hit my spikes on the line," he said, "and it sent chills up my spine."

He advanced out of the first round. After leading for part of his semifinal, he finished thirteenth and was eliminated. He walked off an Olympic track for the last time.

"How can you be disappointed at thirty-six years of age?" Spivey said afterward.

During his European summers, he rented a room in the London suburb of Southgate, passing the time by reading Charles Dickens novels. During early postcollege years, he worked for the NBA's Indiana Pacers as an account executive. Beginning in 2006, Spivey was employed by ASICS in college team sales and sports marketing. Before that, he was track coach at University of Chicago from 1997 to 2001 and women's cross-country coach at Vanderbilt from 2001 to 2005.

He started the Jim Spivey Running Club in 1990 in Wheaton, Illinois, and designed workouts for runners of all ages. He has been an assistant coach at Wheaton Academy, Wheaton North High School, and Latin High School in Chicago. His signature as a coach is to hand out half-sticks of gum after workouts.

Dave Volz, 1981.
IU Archives P0021975.

Dave Volz
1992

Monroe County's Best Ever

HUNDREDS OF OLYMPIANS, ALL-AMERICANS, AND FUTURE PROS HAVE PASSED through the Indiana University campus. When it comes to homegrown athletes out of Monroe County, there has been no one like Dave Volz.

His is another what-might-have-been story. Yet what the pole vaulter did achieve was something for the record books.

As a twenty-year-old sophomore in 1982, Volz twice raised the American record, to 18 feet, 9¼ inches and then 18 feet, 10½ inches—two inches from the world record. Days after the latter, he severely injured his left ankle practicing in Zurich. He never recovered completely.

He limped through the 1984 Olympic Trials. However, by 1986, he became the fourth American to clear 19 feet, doing so at the indoor Millrose Games in New York. Then he broke his leg in 1987, and his athletic career was over. Or so he thought.

Volz was born May 2, 1962, in Long Beach, California. He was two when his family moved to Bloomington.

Vaulting was appropriate for his risk-taking personality. He used to dive into water-filled limestone quarries from as high as one hundred feet. As an IU freshman, Dave kept looking at the catwalk atop the fieldhouse, then looking back at the vault pit. Wonder what it would be like to jump?

He determined that he could make the sixty-five-foot leap. So he pulled a high jump pit on top of the vault landing pad for extra cushion, climbed to the catwalk and went flying, making sure he was out the necessary twenty feet. The padding wasn't directly underneath ... and he nearly missed the pit, pushing off too hard.

He later told former Indiana coach Marshall Goss, who coached him at Bloomington South High School, that no one should assert you can't change direction in midair.

"If you look down and don't see any place to land," Volz told him, "you can change directions."

He said he did a forward roll on landing—"it basically just folded me in half" and came away with bruised vertebrae, a sore back, and an injured hamstring. That wasn't as calamitous as subsequent misadventures.

Volz could have been a decathlete. He ran the hurdles in 14.2 seconds, long jumped over twenty-three feet and high jumped 6-8¾. He could dunk a basketball as a five-foot-eight freshman, and he once picked up a javelin and threw it 168 feet.

In high school, he and thrower Kevin King competed in a home meet on a Friday night, then immediately left for Ohio. There was no lodging available, so the two boys slept overnight in a pickup truck ... then went out and finished second in the Mansfield Relays by themselves.

Volz won state titles in the pole vault in 1979 and 1980. He won the AAU Junior Olympics in 1980, becoming the first Indiana high school vaulter over seventeen feet. The next year he set an American junior (under-twenty) record of 18-3¼ and won the NCAA title.

He was fast and explosive with extraordinary upper-body strength. One of his vaulting contemporaries, Billy Olson, who set eleven world records and was the first American over nineteen feet, once said, "He's an animal. He goes down that runway so hard he's almost out of control."

The name Volz always will be part of vaulting lore because he popularized the technique known as "volzing," or placing a dislodged bar back on its pegs while in midair. He said he began doing it because he did not want to be smacked in the face by the bar on his descent.

"It didn't take me long to figure out that if I could control the middle of the bar, I could control the ends of it," he said. "The less violently it moved, the less violently the ends moved, and the more likely it would stay up. You had to get your body over the bar to get on top of it anyway."

"Volzing" was eventually banned.

That 1982 injury was debilitating. It could be argued that the history of the event changed because of it.

"If the guy wouldn't have been hurt, he could have been the best in the world for the next five years," said Earl Bell, a former world-record holder.

As a junior, in March 1983, Volz limped to an 18–0½ vault to finish sixth in the NCAA Indoor Championships. It was, Hoosiers coach Sam Bell said, the gutsiest effort he had ever seen. Volz had reconstructive surgery on his ankle a month later.

Volz limped through the 1984 Olympic Trials. He didn't make it to the 1988 trials, breaking his right leg in three places in a 1987 incident in which he was demonstrating the long jump for a college track class. He had never made it to an Olympic Games.

His comeback started after Bell asked the late Bill Cook, a Bloomington billionaire, to find the vaulter a job that would allow him to resume training. So Volz worked in an Ellettsville warehouse early in the day and worked himself back into shape. In 1992, at age thirty, he vaulted 19–0¼ at the trials, finished second, and made his first Olympic team.

At the Barcelona Olympics, swirling winds were so vexing that Ukrainian vaulter Sergey Bubka, the defending gold medalist and world record holder, missed all three attempts at his opening bar of 18–8¼. Bubka was history's first world champion (1983) and first twenty-foot vaulter (1991), two goals that Volz might have reached. Volz finished fifth in his only Olympics at 18–6½, one clearance from a medal.

Afterward, he said he could not have written a much better ending.

"A lot of people were involved getting me back to here, and I'm thankful," he said. "It took everybody working together to make things possible, just to give me a shot. It means a lot. I couldn't have made it on my own."

The Vaulting Volzes start with Dave but don't end there. Three sons—Drake, Drew, and Deakin—were also pole vaulters. Their collective personal bests add up to more than seventy feet, or about seven stories high. Dave, Drew, and Deakin each won two state titles. Deakin set what was then a national high school indoor record of 17–11¼ in 2015. As a Virginia Tech freshman, he won a gold medal in the World Junior Championships with a vault of 18–6½ at Bydgoszcz, Poland, in 2016.

Dave added a higher ceiling to the pole barn on his twenty-three-acre property in south Monroe County so his sons could vault there. He has coached all three and once served as a volunteer assistant coach for Hoosier vaulters. He stayed with Cook Inc., which manufactures medical devices, and became vice president of manufacturing operations.

Sunder Nix
Courtesy of Indiana University Archives.

Sunder Nix
1984

Track and Field Changed His Life Path

IF NOT FOR TRACK AND FIELD, SUNDER NIX NEVER WOULD HAVE MADE IT TO Indiana University, much less the top of an Olympic podium. He might not have graduated from high school. As a freshman, he considered dropping out.

"My grades were so bad, so horrible, I had to go to summer school just to catch up with my class," Nix said.

He was motivated to stay enrolled because the track coach at Phillips High School, in Chicago, saw him in gym class. The coach, Ken Musial, told Nix he should be a sprinter.

"I said, 'What's that?' I had no idea what sprints was," Nix said.

He was a fast learner. And he was fast.

Nix stayed in school, raised his grades. He became the nation's fastest high school quarter-miler, national champion, world record holder, and Olympic gold medalist. If you ask him the highlight of his college career, however, he will tell you it was the day he earned his degree.

"When people show an interest in you," he said, "you don't want to let them down."

Nix was born December 2, 1961, in Birmingham, Alabama. He was raised in Sylacauga (population 12,000), a town in Talladega County. Sylacauga is known as "The Marble City" for its white marble bedrock. Coincidentally, Nix made his way to Bloomington, known for its nearby limestone quarries.

Nix was the third of four children raised by a single mother, Johnnie Mae Nix. Three earned college degrees. When Nix was eight, the family moved to Chicago. His mother worked for RCA and became a secretary for Jane Byrne, the Chicago mayor from 1979 to 1983. Nix earned extra money as a part-time housekeeper for

Byrne. The sprinter was guided by Musial, a father figure who peeked into athletes' classrooms to make sure they were in school.

Training was effective, albeit confined, in the inner city. With no indoor track, athletes ran in the hallways in winter. When Nix was a freshman, someone slid a trombone case in front of him as a prank. He was not seriously hurt.

"We almost lost him right there," Musial said. "It wasn't anything done intentionally, but he could have gotten killed."

Oddly, Nix was a never an individual state champion in Illinois. As a junior, he was third in the state in the 100-yard dash and ran on Phillips's winning 440 relay team. He was timed in a wind-aided 9.3 for 100 yards. As a senior, he tripled in the sprints: fourth in the 100 and 220, second in the 440. But weeks later, in the International Prep Invitational at Naperville, Illinois, he was fourth in the 220 in 21.3 after winning the 400 in 46.6—fastest by a high schooler in 1980.

During the recruiting process, he considered Arizona, Texas, Kansas, and Tennessee. Yet he did not want to stray far from Chicago. All he knew about Indiana was basketball. Then he researched the successes the Hoosiers had in track, and learned Bell produced Olympians. Nix said he was impressed by the facilities—there was a real indoor track—as well as the campus and academic support.

"This is it, right here," he told himself.

He said a tone was set for his college career when he won the Big Ten 440-yard dash title as a freshman, the first of a four-year indoor sweep. He won the outdoor 400 meters in 1981 and again as a senior in 1984.

He said his biggest victory came in the 1982 National Sports Festival at Indianapolis. The twenty-year-old finished first in 44.68, the fastest time in the world that year, in nipping Darrell Robinson of Tacoma, Washington. The eighteen-year-old Robinson's time of 44.69 set a world under-twenty record. Nix's time—originally recorded as 44.67—remains the school record nearly four decades later. It is so important that he includes it in his email address: SunderNix4467.

"I was at home, it was a new track, and the stadium had [13,000] people," Nix recalled. "Coach Bell said, 'Just run.'"

Bell, who died in 2012 at age eighty-eight, had a profound influence. The coach was "direct," Nix said, and another father figure. Athletes, parents, and track alumni would receive a weekly newsletter with comments. If someone performed poorly, Nix said, "They would know." He said the Hoosiers did not want to disappoint their coach, comparing him to E. F. Hutton. When Bell spoke, you listened.

"Whatever they asked me to do, I done it," Nix said. "Because he knew what he was doing. He had all those Olympians. I never questioned Coach Bell's style."

A foot injury during the 1983 indoor season impaired Nix briefly, but he went on to have a momentous year. He won his only NCAA and US titles, plus bronze medals at the World University Games in Edmonton, Alberta, and World Championships in Helsinki, Finland. His 600-yard indoor best of 1:09.26—the race he won at NCAAs—prefaced what could have been a career as a half-miler. His indoor title also helped the Hoosiers place fourth in NCAA team standings, a finish they have bettered just once subsequently.

Helsinki featured the first World Championships and first worldwide track and field gathering since the 1972 Munich Olympics. Cold War tension was evident between the United States, which had boycotted the 1980 Olympics, and Soviet Union, which in turn would shun Los Angeles in 1984. The Finns, who were invaded by the Soviet Union in 1939 during World War II, rewarded Russian winners with polite applause. They cheered loudly for red-clad Americans such as Carl Lewis, a triple gold medalist, and Mary Decker, who memorably achieved the "Double Decker" by beating Russians in the 1,500 and 3,000 meters. The forty-thousand-seat stadium, built for the 1952 Olympics, was filled for what resembled eight straight days of college football championships.

There was speculation that none of the American collegians—Nix, Michael Franks (Southern Illinois), or Eliot Tabron (Michigan State)—could medal in the 400 meters. They were too young, and competition was too strong. That's what skeptics were saying anyway.

"It really irritated us," Nix said.

Four rounds were required, and on the third day, Franks won his semifinal in 45.44. Nix barely advanced out of his semifinal, edging Olympic champion Viktor Markin of the Soviet Union for fourth. Both clocked 45.73, and officials took times to a thousandth of a second. The outcome was debated for thirty minutes before Nix was declared the fourth qualifier.

There was a rest day before the final, something Nix said came "in the nick of time." In the final, he was in last place through 200 meters in 22.2. Yet even at the end of a January-to-August season, he had the strength to power through to a bronze medal in 45.24. He nearly caught Franks, the silver medalist in 45.22. Jamaica's Bert Cameron took gold in 45.05.

In 1984, Nix was the Big Ten all-sports athlete of the year. He set a 440-yard world record of 46.40 in the Big Ten indoor meet March 3 at Ann Arbor, Michigan. The time was intrinsically not as fast as a hand-timed 46.2 by Tommie Smith from 1967, nor the 400 meters of 45.79 by Antonio McKay from three weeks earlier. Nonetheless, Nix signaled he was on track for the Los Angeles Olympics.

His chances looked less certain after he finished fifth and fourth in NCAA indoor and outdoor meets, respectively. He was in top form by the Olympic Trials, though, held in the LA Coliseum, same as the Olympics. Nix won heat, quarterfinal, and semifinal races in 45.22, 45.07, and 44.93, respectively. In the final, Nix led through two hundred meters before being overtaken by Alonzo Babers and then McKay. McKay, of Georgia Tech, completed an NCAA indoor/outdoor/trials sweep, clocking 44.71. Babers, 44.86, and Nix, 45.15, took the two other spots.

Nix skipped the opening ceremony, preferring to rest. His most memorable moment inside the Olympic Village was being in an elevator with gymnastics gold medalist Mary Lou Retton—"I couldn't believe how small she was"—and Indiana's

Bob Knight, coach of the US basketball team. There were no track and field events in the first week, but athletes in the village could hear cheering from the nearby swimming venue.

As in Helsinki, Nix barely advanced to the final, finishing fourth in a semifinal in 45.41. He was the slowest of eight finalists. All but Darren Clark, eighteen, of Australia were college sprinters.

"The rounds take a lot out of you," Nix said. "People think it's easy. It's hard."

In the final, Clark went out strongly and led until the closing fifty meters. He was overtaken by Babers and Ivory Coast's Gabriel Tiacoh. Babers, a twenty-two-year-old second lieutenant in the Air Force, surprisingly won the gold medal in 44.27, fastest in the world since Alberto Juantorena's 44.26 at the 1976 Montreal Olympics. Tiacoh, who was just seventh in the NCAA for Washington State, took silver in 44.54. A three-way duel for bronze was won by McKay in 44.71, followed by Clark and Nix, both in 44.75.

It was the first 400-meter race ever in which six men ran under forty-five seconds. Nix said he was tiring and leaning back at the finish instead of forward.

"That's the difference between no medal and a bronze medal, right there," he said.

Nix's Olympics were not over. He led off the climactic 4×400 relay for the US team, which won gold in 2:57.91, fastest in the world since the 1968 Mexico City Olympics. Nix, starting in lane 8, handed off in second place behind Nigeria's Sunday Uti.

Great Britain won silver in 2:59.13 and Nigeria bronze in 2:59.32. Australia was fourth in 2:59.70 in the first 4×400 ever to have four teams under three minutes. Nigeria's foursome included twenty-eight-year-old Rotimi Peters, a former Hoosier sprinter.

Nix said he was tired from his Olympic races, and he wanted to go home. He said he regrets not attending opening or closing ceremonies in Los Angeles. On his return to Bloomington, students on campus congratulated him.

"The crazy thing, though, was that they would take roll call and when the teacher got to my name, people would look at me funny," he said. "I was kind of embarrassed with the situation."

He completed his degree in criminology. He did not end his track career but never ran as fast as did on that fateful day at Indianapolis in 1982.

In 1986, he won the Prefontaine Classic at Eugene (45.39), plus 400s at Stockholm (44.84) and Helsinki (45.18). He finished second (45.01) at Zurich, Switzerland, and ended that year seventh in the world.

In 1987, he contributed a 44.9 anchor leg to a second-place 4×400 in the Sports Festival at Durham, North Carolina. At the 1988 Olympic Trials in Indianapolis, site of his breakthrough race six years earlier, he won a heat in 45.88 before being eliminated in a quarterfinal.

Nix regretted that he delayed a move up to the 800 meters, which Bell had encouraged him to do. If Nix had done so, he believes he could have made it to the 1988 Olympics.

"I was stubborn and didn't listen to his good wisdom," Nix said.

As a collegian, he once ran 800 meters in 1:49.91. The question of what-might-have-been was raised when he finished second in the 1994 USA Indoor Championships at Atlanta in 1:48.37, behind Kenya's David Kiptoo, who went on to finish sixth at the 1996 Olympics. Among those the thirty-two-year-old Nix beat were Rich Kenah, a 1997 world bronze medalist, and Stanley Kersh, who was twice fourth at the US Olympic Trials.

Fitness remained a priority even after Nix's retirement. He won multiple masters national championships and, at age forty-two, ran 400 meters in 50.42.

Nix said youths he encounters need discipline more than anything. He has been employed as a probation officer, juvenile detention center supervisor, and counselor at a minimum-security prison in Plainfield, Indiana. He was also an assistant track coach at Ball State from 2007 to 2011 under Randy Heisler, an Olympic discus thrower and former IU women's head coach.

Willie May
1960

One Hundredth of a Second from Gold

A TIE HAS NEVER BEEN DECLARED IN OLYMPIC TRACK AND FIELD. THE 110-meter hurdles final at Rome in 1960 came as close to a tie as any.

The two semifinal winners, both in 13.7 seconds, were defending gold medalist Lee Calhoun of Gary, Indiana, and Indiana University hurdler Willie May. In the final, they were placed in adjacent lanes, May in 1 and Calhoun in 2. Calhoun led by half a meter by the first hurdle, but May's speed allowed him to draw even coming off the tenth and final one. Straining shoulder to shoulder, both finished in a pronounced lean.

After examination of a photo finish, Calhoun was determined to be the winner over May, both in 13.8. Electronic timing had been available at the Olympics since 1952, and those times were 13.98 for Calhoun, 13.99 for May. (There was a headwind of 1.9 meters per second, slowing the times.) Indeed, the head of the six-foot-three May crossed before that of the six-foot-one Calhoun. It is the torso that counts, and that was Calhoun, who became the first two-time gold medalist in the 110 hurdles. The only other hurdles final in Olympic history as close came at Moscow in 1980, when East Germany's Thomas Munkelt beat Cuba's Alejandro Casanas, 13.39 to 13.40.

Calhoun had won gold at Melbourne four years before with a similar lunge. His two Olympic victories were thus by a cumulative four-hundredths of a second. Calhoun had to sit out the 1958 season for receiving gifts on the television game show *Bride and Groom*. Hayes Jones won bronze over West Germany's Martin Lauer, who shared the world record with Calhoun at 13.2. It was the fourth consecutive 1–2–3 sweep by the United States.

William Lee May was born November 11, 1936, in Knoxville, Alabama. His family moved north to Robbins, Illinois, a suburb south of Chicago. He led Blue Island

Willie May, 1957.
IU Archives P0066633.

(now Eisenhower) High School to a state championship in 1955, winning both hurdles races and running a leg on a winning 880-yard relay team.

At Indiana, May won seven Big Ten titles in the hurdles from 1957 to 1959. His first, in 1957, came in the indoor 70-yard hurdles over Olympic gold medalist Glenn Davis of Ohio State and helped the Hoosiers to the team championship. His last, in 1959, came in the 220-yard low hurdles in 22.9—a time bettered in Big Ten meet history only by Ohio State's Jesse Owens, who set a world record of 22.6 in 1935.

May never won a national title in the high hurdles but was forever close: third in 1958 and second in 1959 in the NCAAs; sixth in 1958, fourth in 1959, third in 1960 in the AAU; second to Calhoun in the Olympic Trials and Olympics in 1960; second in the Pan American Games at Sao Paulo, Brazil, in 1963 at age twenty-six. His best time was 13.4.

May's greatest contribution to track and field might have been as a coach. He followed a former high school teammate, Ron Helberg, to Evanston (Illinois) Township High School. May had a commanding but gentle presence. In an email, Evanston athletic director Chris Livatino said: "In a word, he was nobility."

May was Helberg's assistant coach for Evanston teams that won four state championships in the early 1970s. May became head coach in 1975 and led the Wildkits to twenty-six conference titles—twenty-four straight from 1976 to 1999—and a state championship in 1979. He became athletic director in 1983, a position he held for sixteen years. He retired as head track coach in 2006 but continued to serve as an assistant coach until his death.

He died March 28, 2012, from amyloidosis, a rare blood disease. He was seventy-five.

"While all of the trophies and medals distinguish Coach May in the history books, what will always define Coach May for me was the grace, humility, and strength with which he carried himself and his teams at Evanston Township High School," Livatino wrote.

Milt Campbell, 1955.
IU Archives P0029640.

Milt Campbell
1952, 1956

First Black Decathlon Gold Medalist

THERE IS MELANCHOLY IN REFLECTING ON THE ACHIEVEMENTS OF MILT Campbell, as great as they were, and as he was. He does not require revisionist history. He does not require the record be set straight.
 Let the record be known.

The fact that he lamented lack of recognition during much of his life does not mean he was wrong. He was right. He could be characterized as the greatest athlete ever to come out of Indiana University, even over Mark Spitz.

During the 2012 Olympic track and field trials, all of America's living gold medalists were brought together for the one hundredth anniversary of the decathlon: Campbell, Rafer Johnson, Bill Toomey, Bruce Jenner, Dan O'Brien. The only one who recognized Campbell, or acknowledged him, was Elliott Denman, longtime journalist, fellow New Jersey native, and Olympic teammate.

"He was completely overlooked," Denman said, "which to me is the story of his life."

Part of the story anyway. Other parts of the story seem more like myth.

The abbreviated version:

In 1956, Milt Campbell became the first black gold medalist in the Olympic decathlon. He set world records and won an NCAA titles in the hurdles for Indiana University. He played pro football and excelled in swimming, wrestling, judo, tennis, and bowling.

"Campbell was, to me, the greatest athlete who ever lived," Olympic filmmaker Bud Greenspan once said.

So there is no valid reason, beyond lack of knowledge and research, as to why forty-eight years after he won a silver in the Olympic decathlon while in high school and forty-four years after he won gold, that Campbell did not make ESPN's Top 100 Athletes of the 20th Century or its Top 50 Black Athletes survey.

Mathias (twice), Johnson, Toomey, and Jenner all won Olympic decathlons between 1948 and 1976, and all received endorsement contracts and acting roles. Not Campbell. Part of that can be attributed to racism, although Johnson is also black. Part can be explained by the fact the 1956 Olympics were in Australia in November—during football season—and were the last Olympics without worldwide television coverage. Part was Campbell's outspokenness on civil rights and justice issues.

"I've probably been the greatest athlete this country has ever seen," he said in a 1980 interview with the *New York Times*. "I guess I sound angry about it. I think I have a right to be. I've paid my dues, but the advertising and commercial worlds don't call me."

Campbell was born December 9, 1933, in Plainfield, New Jersey. His father, Thomas, was a New York City cab driver and mother, Edith, a domestic houseworker. The couple split up when Milt was young, and he and his older brother, Tom, moved in with their grandmother.

Tom was a hurdler for Plainfield High School. Milt, determined to follow his brother, built hurdles out of wooden slats and set them up in the driveway. Milt kept tumbling over them until his brother pointed out that the hurdles were placed too close together.

Campbell did not confine himself to the high school track or football field. When he walked into the pool, he was told by a swimmer that a "colored boy" had never been on the team because crocodiles made them afraid to swim. That was preposterous, and Campbell took it as a challenge. Coach Vic Liske encouraged Campbell, who formed a lifetime bond with that coach. He swam the freestyle anchor for Plainfield's eastern states champion team in the medley relay.

"That first year I was second to him all year long," Campbell said of the swimmer who'd scoffed. "But the next year, I broke all his records and made All-America."

In wrestling, Campbell once subbed for a sick heavyweight and proceeded to pin the boy who went on to become state champion. He was proclaimed the world's greatest high school athlete—not that it could be proved. Yet how could that be disproved?

Before the 1952 Olympic decathlon trials at Tulare, California, Campbell had never competed in a decathlon. Nor had he long jumped, vaulted, thrown the discus or javelin, or run 1,500 meters in a competition. Defending Olympic champion Bob Mathias easily won the trials, setting a world record of 7,829 points (old scoring tables). Campbell was second with 7,055, and he was on his way to Helsinki.

In Finland, Mathias repeated as gold medalist and set another world record, 7,887 points (7,580 on 1985 scoring tables). Mathias won by the largest margin in Olympic history, but that should in no way diminish Campbell's silver score of 6,975 (6,948 on 1985 tables). After all, the eighteen-year-old Campbell was still in high school, as Mathias was in 1948.

Campbell returned to New Jersey and resumed high school football, scoring eighty points in his first four games for Plainfield. Arthur Daley of the *New York Times* referred to him as "fullbacking terror," a combination of Army's Blanchard and Davis, Mr. Inside and Mr. Outside. Like Bronco Nagurski, Campbell could be restrained "only by gang tackling," according to Daley.

Campbell, six foot three and 210 pounds, was told he would be unable to hurdle if he grew any bigger. He tuned out those voices. He said it was not important what someone else said but what he told himself.

"So I used to tell myself every day that the bigger I got, the stronger I would get, and the stronger I got, the faster I would get," he said.

Then it was off to Bloomington. He played two football seasons for the Hoosiers, 1954 and 1955, both ending with 3–6 records. He still shares the school record for interceptions in a game with three against Ohio University on October 29, 1955, helping Indiana to a 21–14 home victory. Earlier that year, he won the 120-yard high hurdles in 13.9 at the NCAA Championships and repeated that victory in the AAU nationals, also in 13.9.

Campbell left Indiana to join the navy in 1955. He was stationed in San Diego and competed on military track squads while training for the 1956 Melbourne Olympics.

He thought he would qualify for Melbourne in the 110-meter hurdles. At the US trials in Los Angeles, he finished fastest of all the finalists and nearly caught Joel Shankle for the third place on the team, both timed in 14.1. World record holder Jack Davis and NCAA champion Lee Calhoun took the top two spots and would reverse positions in the Olympic final.

The decathlon trials, held in Crawfordsville, Indiana, brought together three of the greatest athletes in history: Johnson, Campbell, and Bob Richards, who already had won Olympic gold in the pole vault. On day two, before a capacity crowd of forty-two hundred at Wabash College's Ingalls Field, Richards set a decathlon world record by vaulting fifteen feet to earn 1,122 points.

Yet it was Campbell who pushed Johnson, then the world record holder. Johnson's day-one total of 4,639 points was highest in history and 98 points ahead of record pace. But he reinjured his left knee in the high jump and aggravated it the next day in the discus. Moreover, the track and runways were slow from heavy rain, and Johnson fell short in a bid to break his own record. He finished with 7,775 points to Campbell's 7,559 and Richards's 7,054.

With the Olympics in the southern hemisphere, there were nearly five months until Melbourne, where it would be spring. On November 4, the day after the Olympic torch began its journey from Greece, army divisions from the Soviet Union invaded Hungary to suppress an uprising. International tensions were so great that there were worries over nuclear war and whether the Olympics should be canceled or the Soviet Union banned. In the Sinai Peninsula, Egyptian and Israeli forces clashed, and Britain and France bombed Egyptian military targets in an attempt to ensure control of the Suez Canal.

With that as backdrop, the US team headed to Hawaii on a chartered flight. Athletes stayed on Waikiki Beach for a day and half, resting and sightseeing. After a brief stop in Fiji, the Americans arrived in Melbourne. Switzerland, Spain, and the Netherlands boycotted the Games over the dispute in Hungary, and Iraq, Egypt, and Lebanon withdrew because of war in the Sinai. China pulled out because the International Olympic Committee continued to recognize Taiwan.

Johnson's knee pain persisted, and he withdrew from the Olympics in the long jump, for which he had also qualified. During the decathlon, he tore stomach muscles. Meanwhile, Campbell was confident and said so, even though he was projected for third behind Johnson and the Soviet Union's Vasily Kuznetsov.

In an Olympics documentary, Campbell said, "Rafer asked me how did he think it would all turn out. And I remarked to him that I thought this was a very bad time that he showed up because this Olympic Games was mine, and I was willing to do everything that I had to do to get it. I looked at the expression on his face and realized he also felt that I was ready."

Campbell opened by winning the 100 meters in 10.8, and he broke Johnson's day-one record with 4,654 points. The margin was 189 points, and it widened after Campbell started day two by clocking 14.0 in the hurdles, which would have earned bronze behind Calhoun and Davis. Campbell lost his grip on the world record—his vault of 11 feet, 1¾ inches was nearly twenty inches off his best—but not on the gold medal. In frustration, Campbell threw himself on the ground in the infield and banged his head on a blanket as Richards tried to console him. Campbell followed the vault with a javelin throw of 178–11, losing just 50 points off his lead.

Campbell needed only to stay within one minute of Johnson to claim gold, and he found an ally in Ian Bruce of Australia. The two began the final lap together. As Campbell recalled:

> All of a sudden I hear this voice off my shoulder, saying, 'Come on, big boy. It's time to run. I'm sure you can do better than this. Come on, let's run.' I turned around and looked at Ian Bruce, and he was running like he had just walked onto the track and started running. He wasn't breathing hard, and he wasn't sweating. He just seemed to keep yelling at me at this particular point. So we started picking up the pace. As we picked it up a little faster and a little faster, we began to close on the Russian tremendously.
>
> I can remember going into the last turn and thinking that I want to catch this guy. I've got to catch him and I've got to beat him. And Ian Bruce was saying at the same, 'Come on. Pick it up, pick it up, pick it up.' I thought this was fantastic because I could feel the speed picking up. And coming off the last turn, Ian Bruce and I got into a sprint, stride for stride. We came down, we passed the Russian, and we were driving for the tape. I can remember having an edge on him right down to the wire. When we got down to the wire, he nipped me out.

Nonetheless, Campbell's 1,500 time of 4:50.6 secured gold and give him an Olympic record of 7,937 points (7,565 on modern tables). After Johnson finished his heat to secure silver, Campbell threw a blanket over his countryman's shoulders. The two walked off the track with arms around each other. Kuznetsov was the bronze medalist. Without Campbell around, Johnson went on to win decathlon gold four years later, breaking Campbell's Olympic record with 8,392 points (7,901).

At twenty-two, Campbell was on top of the world. Or so he thought. He came home to little fanfare and no product endorsements. The snubs, real and imagined, continued for decades. It was not because of the calendar or lack of TV coverage, he said.

"No, I think it had to do with the fact that America was not ready for a black man to be the best athlete in the world. And now the press refuses to go back and do the research," he told *Sports Illustrated* in a 1996 interview.

Los Angeles Times columnist Jim Murray wrote that Campbell was "as magnificent an athlete as any Thorpe or anyone who come before or after him." Yet Campbell had the misfortune to be between Mathias, a future member of the House of Representatives, and Johnson, a future confidant of the Kennedy family. It was like "playing a scene with a baby and a dog," Murray wrote.

That doesn't explain how Mathias and Johnson were among twenty inaugural members of the US Olympic Committee's Hall of Fame and Campbell was not on the ballot. It was 1992 before the Hoosier was elected.

Melbourne was Campbell's fifth and last decathlon. His track and field career did not end there. In 1957, he set world hurdles records at 70 yards indoors (7.0 at New York on February 9) and 120 yards outdoors (13.4 at Compton, California, on May 31.) Campbell remains the only Olympic decathlon champion to set a world record in an individual event.

He was selected in the fifth round of the 1957 NFL draft by the Cleveland Browns, who chose Jim Brown out of Syracuse with their first pick. The two rookies roomed together. Campbell lasted one season, rushing seven times for twenty-three yards. He was cut, he said, because of his offseason marriage to Barbara Mount, a white woman. The New York Giants had expressed interest in signing Campbell, telling him to report to training camp, but then would not return his calls.

"And I was blackballed out of the league," Campbell said.

He went instead to the Canadian Football League, where he played for the Hamilton Tiger-Cats, Montreal Alouettes, and Toronto Argonauts until retiring at age thirty in 1964.

Campbell and his first wife were married for twenty-five years before divorcing in the early 1980s. They had three children together. He was married again and spent the last thirteen years of his life with companion Linda Rusch.

He was an advocate for self-help through education and was outspoken about civil rights causes. During the Newark riots of 1967, he returned to New Jersey from Canada and started a community center and alternative school that emphasizes black history and culture.

He later became a motivational speaker, with failure in his own meat-trucking business as his motivation. He fought prostate cancer for a decade until he died November 2, 2012, in Gainesville, Georgia. He was seventy-eight.

He is the sole member of both the National Track and Field and International Swimming Halls of Fame. He was voted New Jersey's athlete of the twentieth century. Toward the end of his life, Campbell said he got enough satisfaction from knowing he was the best at what he did. It was sadly paradoxical that more recognition came his way so late.

"He didn't get the recognition in the fifties," Rausch said in a 2012 interview. "He got it all this year, and he died."

Greg Bell, 1957.
IU Archives P0066629.

Greg Bell
1956

A Life of Serendipity

GREG BELL IS NEITHER A COWBOY IN ONE OF THE WESTERN NOVELS HE reads nor a creation of Horatio Alger. Yet there is a fictional element to Bell's story.

He spent his first twelve years living in a chicken house. He was the seventh of nine children whose father never made it past fifth grade. When Bell began high school, he did not know it had a track and field team. He worked odd jobs after graduation, was drafted into the US Army, and had to be persuaded by the family doctor to enroll in college at age twenty-four.

So Bell went to Indiana University. He never lost a collegiate competition in the long jump, won two NCAA titles, and twice leaped to within about an inch of Jesse Owens's world record. In 1956 at Melbourne, Bell became the twelfth American to win the long jump in thirteen editions of the modern Olympic Games. He is also a dentist, poet, writer, speaker, and woodworker.

"When I read about some of the things that I have done," he said, "I think I'm reading about somebody else. That does not sound like me."

Bell was born November 7, 1930, on a thirty-six-acre truck farm ten miles south of Terre Haute, Indiana. His mother, the former Essa Manual Bradshaw, had six children from a previous marriage. His father, Curtis Bell, had built a house on the property, but it was destroyed by fire. Without insurance to replace it, the father modified the twenty-by-thirty-foot chicken house into living quarters. Children slept three to a bed. Until Greg was seven, there was no electricity. One year, the family subsisted on almost nothing but potatoes.

Bell said he was a shy child, hiding behind his mother's apron. Speaking was a struggle into adulthood.

"I was insecure. Didn't know I was worth anything," he said.

The farm produced vegetables, strawberries, and melons. A horse-drawn plow tilled the soil, and there were cows to milk, hogs to butcher, and livestock to feed. Bell's father did own an old Model T Ford truck. If young Greg wanted a toy, he had to be imaginative enough to make one himself. That is, until a friend of his mother donated a scooter.

"A real scooter!" Bell recalled.

That was not his only entertainment. An uncle gave him the complete works of Paul Laurence Dunbar, a black poet who wrote in Negro dialect. Bell said he "just got hooked on Dunbar," leading to a lifetime love of poetry. Bell can recite twenty-one Dunbar poems from memory and in dialect.

An old Philco radio offered dramas such as *The Lone Ranger* and *Mr. District Attorney*. Nearly eighty years later, Bell can recite the lead-in for *Mr. District Attorney*. Bell's father listened to broadcasts of boxing matches featuring Joe Louis, who was an icon to black Americans in the 1930s. Young Bell was mesmerized by the delivery of sportscaster Don Dunphy from New York's Madison Square Garden. Oh, if he could only see the famous arena someday.

"Turns out, not only did I see it. I competed in it and won a national championship in it," said Bell, who won a national AAU title there in 1958.

For school, he took a nine-mile bus trip to the unincorporated town of Pimento. But in 1942, everything changed for the Bells. World War II had begun, and the government wanted four hundred thousand acres of Indiana farmland to build an ammunition depot. The Bell farm was on that land, and all they got for it was $1,500.

Greg was twelve, and he remembers the guards on horseback coming to the house daily to say they had to leave.

"We were the last ones out. Because we had nowhere to go," Bell said.

The family moved to what was known as the Underwood neighborhood, just north of the city limits of Terre Haute, in a house at 2913 N. Fourteenth Street. It could have been called a ghetto, Bell said, if there had been enough residents to make it a ghetto.

As a sophomore, he enrolled at Garfield High School. He conceded there was racism there but did not allow that to scar him.

"I accepted it for what it was," Bell said. "That was the way times were. But I detested it."

That was especially so in an English class in which the teacher said "colored children" could never be awarded higher than a C. In that class, Bell said, that was true. He said he always wanted to return to Garfield and show the teacher he earned As at IU in English composition and literature.

Bell had always been a fast runner, beating children two or three years older, but had never participated in anything resembling organized sports. He was drawn to the pole vault because *Tarzan* was his new favorite radio show, and that event seemed closest to swinging from a jungle vine. Using a bamboo pole and a sawdust or sand landing pit, he could vault as high as eleven feet.

"I had no idea what I was doing," he said.

He once wrenched his back in practice, knocking him out of the pole vault. The principal, James Conover, asked him if he had ever done broad jumping, as the event was then called. Again, Bell had never heard of it. "What is it?"

"You run and then jump," the principal replied. Bell tried it, and the jump was measured. It was longer than the school record.

Bell began running sprints and relays, too, but long jump was his signature event. As a senior, in 1948, he finished second at the state meet with a distance of 22 feet, 2 inches, or 4 inches from first. He figured that was it. End of track career. He knew about the Olympics—they were held in London that year after a twelve-year hiatus caused by World War II—but that is all.

He remained home, working odd jobs. He cleaned mortar from bricks, pulled nails from used lumber, cut weeds with a scythe, worked in a feed mill, cleaned a poultry house, shucked corn. He moved to Chicago and roomed with his brother, taking a job at meatpacking company. He shook salt from cowhides in what he said was the worst job he ever had, "maybe that anyone ever had."

He was an apprentice truck driver, hauling eggs, paper, and cotton. Then fate intervened again. He was drafted into the army in 1950. Not that he minded, really. He did not have a decent job, he said, and "at least they're going to pay me."

After basic training, he speculated he would be sent to war in Korea. Instead, he was among the occupying US forces in Western Europe. He awaited orders in Sonthofen, Germany, which was bombed twice during World War II because that is where Hitler organized training for boys in the Nazi Party. Bell was eventually deployed to Captieux, France, in wine country about sixty miles south of Bordeaux. Coincidentally, an ammunition depot changed his life again, because one was located in Captieux.

His track career was resurrected when he learned about a meet being held in Bordeaux. He secured a pair of spikes and had all of four days to train. He won the high jump and pole vault, placed second in the 100 meters, and ran on a winning relay.

That earned him a spot in the 1953 European championship of the US Armed Forces, held in Nuremberg, Germany. Not only did he win the long jump, he did so by jumping nearly eighteen inches farther than he did in high school.

"And I hadn't done anything," he said.

Again, he assumed he could put away the spikes for good. At least he had gone out with a championship.

Bell returned to the family home and took a job with Allis-Chalmers, a manufacturer of machinery. It was a good job, paying $1.69 an hour on the night shift. Bell had a future, even if that employment was not it.

He developed what seemed to be an annual case of tonsillitis, and his mother asked a physician she knew, William Bannon, to pay a house call. Dr. Bannon noticed Bell's Armed Forces trophy sitting on a piano given to his mother, and asked about it. Bell, expecting some sympathy from the doctor, instead was told to get out of bed and get his butt to college.

"I looked at him like he had lost his mind," Bell said.

Dr. Bannon persisted, badgering him about college for a year and a half. Finally, the twenty-three-year-old relented. He would enroll in fall of 1954 at IU, where Dr. Bannon was a trustee. Bell spoke to track coach Gordon Fisher, who didn't even have to recruit him. Before leaving for Bloomington, Bell was awarded ten dollars from Dr. Bannon with instructions to buy himself a steak dinner. That did not happen.

"I ate off that for about a week and a half," Bell recalled.

Classes were difficult. He had always been an indifferent student, and here he was taking algebra, chemistry, and trigonometry. For instance, he was asked to balance an equation. Bell's thought was, what's an equation? He said he might as well have been studying books written in Russian "because I had no understanding at all." By the end of his freshman year, Bell made the dean's list.

"This is my life on the line. I don't have an option," he told himself.

He was married by then, to the former Clara Stewart, a nurse, and had an infant daughter. They lived in a small trailer off campus, and Bell acknowledged he was despondent sometimes. His track scholarship did not pay all expenses, so he had a part-time job at a residence hall snack bar. He mopped floors, cleaned tables, grilled hamburgers and hot dogs, and did janitorial labor.

Freshmen then were ineligible for varsity meets, but that didn't mean he couldn't train or jump. Indeed, he had been largely self-coached anyway. Bell could not be in the Big Ten or NCAA Championships but went to the 1955 indoor AAUs, realizing a lifelong dream of seeing Madison Square Garden. He finished second to Rosslyn Range, who weeks later jumped 26–4¼ to win a gold medal in the Pan American Games at Mexico City.

That should have signaled Bell's arrival on a world stage, but he was just getting started at age twenty-four. Bell won his first national title in the outdoor AAUs that year at Boulder, Colorado, becoming the eighth in history to jump twenty-six feet. "No one had ever heard of me. I literally came from out of nowhere," he said.

The next year, there would be an Olympics, and Bell could not help but think about it. He did not know a lot about Olympics lore, other than that Jesse Owens won four gold medals in 1936 and, like Joe Louis, became a hero to black Americans. Bell once appeared on *The Ed Sullivan Show*, a televised variety show popular in the 1950s and '60s, with Owens. Dr. Bannon was thinking about the Olympics, too. He told the Hoosier jumper if he made it to Melbourne, he would be there.

In 1956, Bell first won the long jump in the Big Ten, then in the NCAAs. In the Olympic Trials at Los Angeles, he tied John Bennett for first at 25–8¼, followed by Rafer Johnson in third. Under international rules, Bell would have finished second on the basis of next-best jump, but that did not matter. He was on the team. In a tune-up meet October 20 at Ontario, California, Bell came within two inches of Owens's world record with a distance of 26–6½, then the second-longest jump ever.

There were several stops on the trip of nearly eight thousand miles to Australia, allowing Bell to spend his twenty-sixth birthday on Waikiki Beach. The Olympics were in the southern hemisphere, so they were held in November, or late spring.

After the November 22 opening ceremony at Melbourne Cricket Grounds, the actual competition two days later was almost anticlimactic. That is because the long jump was held in the "worst conditions I could imagine competing in," Bell said. The runway was short, surface soft, and headwinds strong. He opened with a jump of 22–10¾, far below his usual standards. Worse, he strained a leg muscle. He knew such a distance wouldn't get him on the podium. The other jumpers didn't care how good he was supposed to be.

"So I got myself together," Bell said.

In the second round, he jumped 25–8¼, which proved to be the winning distance. Only two men in Olympic history—Owens (26–5½) and Germany's Luz Long (25–10), both at Berlin in 1936—had gone farther. Bell aimed at the Olympic record, but conditions made that out of the question.

"It was one of the worst performances I could have imagined," he said.

He jumped 25–6 in the third round, which turned out to be the second-best jump of the final. After a foul, a pass, and another short jump, it was over. Bell was Olympic champion. Bennett took silver at 25–2½. Johnson had withdrawn from preliminaries because of injury. More than six decades later, Bell was philosophical about his achievement.

"I don't know that I'd have been heartbroken if I hadn't won," he said.

As promised, Dr. Bannon was in Melbourne. He took Bell out to dinner, where he was recognized and approached by a white Australian. The man introduced himself as Melvin Teasdale and invited Bell to spend the rest of his time in Melbourne, nearly three weeks, with his family. Bell accepted. He traveled to sites away from the usual tourist attractions, including the Dandenong Mountain Ranges and an Aboriginal village.

Forty-four years later, before the 2000 Sydney Olympics, Bell was surprised by a call from Eric Teasdale, who located his phone number via the Internet. Teasdale was a teenager when Bell spent those weeks with his family, and seeing video of Bell jumping evoked memories. The reconnection, to Bell, "testified in favor of the brotherhood of man."

After the Olympics, Terre Haute gave Bell a welcome home with ceremonies at city hall and a Rotary Club luncheon. Mayor Ralph Tucker designated him honorary mayor. Bell was also honored at Garfield High School.

He still had two more college seasons and was, if anything, better in 1957. He was most outstanding athlete of the Penn Relays, winning the long jump at 26–1½ and 100-yard dash in 9.7 seconds. His long jump stood as a meet record until it was broken by Carl Lewis in 1981.

Bell helped the Hoosiers win Big Ten team titles indoors and outdoors, placing second in both sprints outdoors in addition to winning the long jump. In the NCAAs at Austin, Texas, he set a collegiate record of 26–7—just 1¼ inches from Owens's world record—and had another jump of 26–5 in the series. The NCAA record lasted seven years. Bell also placed fifth in the 220-yard dash, behind winner Bobby Morrow, a US teammate who had won three golds in Melbourne.

In 1958, Bell won at the Penn Relays for a third successive year and a third indoor/outdoor sweep in the Big Ten. He also added that AAU indoor title. Injury prevented him from going for a third NCAA title. His studies paid off so much that he was awarded a Big Ten Medal of Honor, which goes to one male (and now one female) student per year for proficiency in academics and athletics at each Big Ten university.

His undergraduate days ended, but not his studies or long jumping. He moved from Bloomington to Indianapolis for dental school. In 1959, at twenty-eight, he had his last outstanding season—indeed, one of his best.

In June, he won his second AAU title (26–1¼) at Miami. In July, in the second dual meet held between the United States and Soviet Union at Philadelphia, Bell was the American captain. He beat Russian long jumper Igor Ter-Ovanesyan, again jumping 26–7—thus giving him three of the four longest jumps in history, all behind Owens's 1935 world record of 26–8¼. Bell capped the summer by winning a silver medal in the Pan American Games at Chicago.

He continued into 1960 and finished fourth in the Olympic Trials at Stanford. His distance of 25–4 was 1¼ inches behind third place, which would have put him on the team going to Rome and allowed him to defend his gold medal. He ended his career ranked first in the world three times (1956–58) and had thirteen jumps exceeding twenty-six feet, then the most in history.

While working his way through dental school, Bell worked on a farm outside Indianapolis, hoeing the ground, weeding garden areas, and picking beans and corn. He also worked for the parks department supervising children on outdoor playgrounds, and he raked the ground when construction began on a new medical science building. It could have been humbling for an Olympic champion, but Bell said it was honest labor and no different from what he had done growing up.

He began his dental career by teaching at Howard University in Washington, DC, and eventually became director of dentistry at Logansport State Hospital, which is Indiana's oldest psychiatric hospital. He began in 1970 and was still practicing dentistry there in 2019.

"The deeper I got into it, the better it seemed to suit me," he said in a 2018 interview on his four-acre estate. "I've been practicing for fifty-seven years. I'm going to get good at it pretty soon. I just can't imagine doing anything else with my life."

He has never attended an Olympic Games other than Melbourne and said he was disappointed that he has never been invited. When he asked the US Olympic Committee about attending the 1976 Montreal Olympics, he said he was told to put his name in the ticket lottery.

When he was inducted into the National Track and Field Hall of Fame in 1988, instead of donating his gold medal or an old pair of spikes, he gave three poems to be displayed in the museum. One of them is "I Believe in You," in Dr. Bannon's honor. Bell often recites poetry, either his own or that written by others, from memory. He remains in demand as a motivational speaker. He takes his gold medal with him to show others, as he did in a 2019 trip back to the Penn Relays.

"I am nothing special at all. I am Greg Bell," he said. "I do what I do because I enjoy doing it."

He was divorced in 1987. He remarried in 1990 to the former Mary Lawrie, who had four children from a previous marriage. Bell's three children are Valinda, a nurse; Gregory Kent, an engineering technician; and Shari, an attorney. He is a close friend of Hallie Bryant, the former Harlem Globetrotter.

Bell has been beset by vitiligo, a disease that causes loss of skin color in blotches. He joked that he is turning white, mindful of the indignities he endured for being black. Otherwise, he is content, explaining that he can separate who he is from what he has done. He is a charter member of the Indiana Track and IU Halls of Fame. In his will, he has left the gold medal to the Indiana Track Hall of Fame, located in Terre Haute.

"My whole life can be summed up in one word: *serendipity*," he said.

Fred Wilt
1948, 1952

Runner, Detective, Author, Coach

FRED WILT HAS AN UNUSUAL RÉSUMÉ FOR A MEMBER OF INDIANA UNIVERsity's Athletics Hall of Fame. His greatest contributions to track and field were as an author and coach, not a runner, and at Purdue rather than Indiana.

Yet it would be gross oversight to dismiss the credentials of someone who was an NCAA champion, two-time Olympian, and world record holder. Coincidentally, Wilt followed in the spikeprints of another IU Olympian, Don Lash, in that he became an FBI agent and Sullivan Award winner.

Wilt was born December 14, 1920, in Pendleton, Indiana. He started as a college basketball player at Indiana Central College (now University of Indianapolis), although there is no record of him earning a letter there. He eventually transferred to Indiana, wanting to run for coach Billy Hayes. Wilt was at IU for one year, 1941, but made the most of it.

He was 12–0 in races until beaten by teammate Wayne Tolliver in the Big Ten two-mile. Then Wilt won the NCAA two-mile in 9:14.4, and followed the next fall by winning another NCAA title, in cross-country. Wilt was the last great runner coached by Hayes, who died in 1943.

"With the exception of my mother, coach Hayes influenced my life more than any other individual," Wilt said. The coach inspired "unbelievable confidence," Wilt said.

After leaving IU, Wilt joined the navy. When World War II ended, he began a thirty-year career as an FBI agent while continuing his running career, representing the New York Athletic Club. He was AAU national champion eight times at distances from the indoor mile to cross-country, and top American in two other races he did not win.

When the Olympics resumed in 1948 at London, Wilt made the US team in the 10,000 meters and finished eleventh. He was twenty-first in the 10,000 at the 1952 Helsinki Olympics. He was twice in the top ten of *Track & Field News'* prestigious world rankings in the 5,000 meters—ninth in 1949 and tenth in 1950.

He won the Sullivan Award as the nation's top amateur athlete in 1950, the same year in which he lost an unusual vote to break a tie. Wilt and Wisconsin rival Don Gehrmann crossed the finish together in the Millrose Games indoor mile at New York, both in 4:09.3. It was so close that judges reversed their decision twice before settling on Gehrmann. The issue was put to a vote at the AAU convention, where delegates not at the race were asked to rule based on a head-on photo. Gehrmann won that, too. Wilt ran his fastest outdoor mile that year, 4:05.5, on April 30 on the boardwalk at Atlantic City, New Jersey. (The world record then was 4:01.4.)

In 1951, Wilt ran one of his most high-profile races, pitted against Gehrmann and Great Britain's Roger Bannister in the mile at the Penn Relays. Of course, Bannister in 1954 became the first to run a sub-four-minute mile. But there was so much prerace publicity in Philadelphia that Bannister called it "my first 'mile of the century'" in his autobiography. Bannister also read about an alleged "tiff" between the two Americans.

"Gehrmann's tactics were always the same. He followed Wilt's pace until the finishing straight," Bannister wrote. "Then, having a better 'kick,' he nipped past and won. These tactics were of course quite legitimate, but very aggravating to Wilt."

A crowd of forty thousand turned out. And Bannister had by far the best kick. The soon-to-be icon ran the closing 440 yards in 56.7 seconds for a time of 4:08.3, a Penn Relays record. He beat Wilt by 15 yards and Gehrmann by 30.

Fred Wilt, 1941.
IU Archives P0043872.

Although Wilt did not show it at the Olympics, he had his best season in 1952 at age thirty-one. He set a world indoor record of 8:50.7 in the two-mile February 23 at New York, breaking Greg Rice's mark of 8:51.0 from 1943. Then only Sweden's Gunder Hagg (whose mile world record was broken by Bannister) and Olympic champion Gaston Reiff of Belgium had better outdoor times. Wilt set an American record of 14:26.8 for 5,000 meters in 1952 but was fourth at the US trials and did not qualify for Helsinki at that distance.

After his running career ended, he set out to learn what the world's best runners knew that Americans didn't. His research became a *Track & Field News* book, *How They Train*, which reproduced scores of training programs and was long a best seller. That led to another book, *Run-Run-Run*. He was ultimately able to fill material for a quarterly journal, *Track Technique*. Wilt's contributions helped make American distance running in the 1950s and '60s an international force for the first time since early in the twentieth century.

"I do not recommend that any athlete copy the training procedure of another, but I do maintain that the material herein will suggest many ideas which may be adopted in formulating workout programs suited to an individual runner's needs," Wilt wrote in *How They Train*.

Wilt was not formally coaching in the 1960s but devised a training program for Buddy Edelen, an American living in England. Wilt submitted all the workouts from Indiana by mail. In 1963, Edelen became the first American in a half century to set a marathon world record, running a time of 2 hours, 14 minutes, 28 seconds in a race from Windsor to Chiswick, England.

"The pattern that enabled Edelen to break the world marathon record—weekend long run, medium-long midweek run, speed work and easy running sprinkled between—is the same pattern I have passed on to thousands in my books and online coaching," running author Hal Higdon wrote.

On retirement from the FBI, Wilt, at fifty-seven, became women's track and cross-country coach at Purdue in 1978. The Boilermakers finished second in the Big Ten in cross-country in 1983, second in outdoor track in 1986 and then won their first outdoor title in 1987.

Wilt kept writing, eventually publishing eight books. He belongs to both IU and Purdue Halls of Fame and to the National Track and Field Hall of Fame. He died September 5, 1994, at his home in Anderson, Indiana. He was seventy-three.

Roy Cochran, 1939.
IU Archives P0029377.

Roy Cochran
1948

Glory Delayed, Not Denied

ONE YEAR OUT FROM THE 1940 OLYMPIC GAMES, INDIANA UNIVERSITY SOPHomore Roy Cochran ran himself into medal contention. He won the 400-meter hurdles at the AAU national championships in 51.9 seconds, or three-tenths off the meet record. "I knew I could run fifty seconds flat, if necessary, to win," he said at the time.

Cochran's older brother, Commodore, had won a gold medal at the 1924 Paris Olympics in the 4×400 relay when Roy was five years old. Now it was going to be Roy's turn. But later in 1939, World War II broke out, and the 1940 and 1944 Olympics were canceled. He would have to wait.

Leroy Braxton Cochran was the ninth of ten children, born January 6, 1919, in tiny Richton, Mississippi. The family lived in a farm out in the country, and there wasn't much money or much to do.

"So they ran. They ran everywhere," said Cochran's daughter, Janice Cochran-Pendleton. "They ran to school. They raced each other. They ran for the fun of it. If they wanted to go somewhere, they went on foot. If they had to get there fast, they ran."

Commodore—whose nicknames were Com, Speed, and Racehorse—ran for Mississippi State, winning two NCAA 440-yard titles. Billy Hayes was Commodore's coach before taking the job at Indiana. Roy had an offer to play football for Tulane but was persuaded by his brother to run track for Hayes's Hoosiers.

As a sophomore in 1939, Cochran won the 440-yard hurdles at the Drake Relays, the 220-yard low hurdles in the Big Ten and the aforementioned AAU 400-meter hurdles. He won Big Ten 440-yard titles indoors in 1940 and 1941, and outdoors in 1941. While serving at the Great Lakes Naval Training Center, he won a national indoor title at 600 yards in 1942. That prefaced a world record of 52.2 in the 440-yard hurdles at the Drake Relays on April 25.

Then Cochran went to war, serving as navy lieutenant in the Pacific. He thought his athletic career was over. After the war, he enrolled at the University of Southern California to study for a physiology degree and resumed running for fitness. Surprisingly, his times were as fast as they were before a long layoff, and the twenty-nine-year-old began serious training. He was third in the AAU 400 meters (no hurdles) in a career-best 46.7 in 1946, and he finished second a year later in the 400 hurdles.

In 1948, Cochran won the 400-meter hurdles at the AAUs in 52.3, taking his second national title nine years after his first. Only Bershawn Jackson (twelve years, 2003–15) and Edwin Moses (ten years, 1977–87) have done so in that event so many years apart. Cochran proceeded to edge Dick Ault at the Olympic Trials, 51.7 to 51.8, and it was on to London.

At the Olympics, Sweden's Lune Larson won the first semifinal in an Olympic record of 51.9, and Cochran tied that in the second semifinal. Ceylon's Duncan White was off fastest in the final, but Cochran overtook him and decisively won the gold medal. He set an Olympic record of 51.1, or half of a second off the fourteen-year-old world record. Cochran's margin of seventh-tenths of a second was then the second-largest in Olympic history, and not until 1968 would anyone win by more. He became the Hoosiers' first individual gold medalist in any sport.

Yet Cochran was not finished. He ran third leg for the US team that won the 4×400 relay, the same event in which his brother won gold in 1924. Jamaica's Arthur

Wint tried to cut into Cochran's lead but pulled up injured and could not finish. The Americans' time of 3:10.4 was far ahead of silver-winning France, 3:14.8.

Inexplicably, Cochran was later singled out by King George VI during a cocktail party at Buckingham Palace. The *Indiana Alumni Magazine* of September 1948 reported the following, which originally appeared in the syndicated column of *Los Angeles Examiner* sportswriter Vincent X. Flaherty:

> For some reason, the King singled out Roy Cochran, America's 400-meter hurdles Olympic champion.... Roy, a real guy, who is extremely intelligent and versed, kept the conversation kicking 15 minutes with the King. The two sat off in one corner of the big room all by themselves. Other members of the party wondered why the King devoted so much time to one individual...
>
> "He's one of the swellest guys I ever met," said Cochran, thoroughly enthralled. "And do you know something else?" said Cochran. "It took a real King to make me taste my first drink of liquor. He didn't make me, of course. I just sort of felt it wouldn't be right if I didn't."

Cochran died in 1981 at age sixty-two. He accrued neither fame nor riches, and his daughter said he never boasted about his Olympic glory.

"That just wasn't his way," Pendleton said. "He used to tell me, 'These things won't get you anything but a cup of coffee, and that's if you've got a dime to go with them.'"

Cochran was inducted posthumously into the National Track and Field Hall of Fame in 2010. His gold medals are on display in the Mississippi Sports Hall of Fame.

Charles Hornbostel
1932, 1936

He Shot for Records, Not for Baskets

CHARLES HORNBOSTEL WAS A RELUCTANT RUNNER. HE WANTED TO BE A basketball player.

He became one of the greatest runners ever to come out of Indiana, despite his inauspicious teenage years. He ran in two Olympic finals, set two world records, ran on two relays setting world records, won three NCAA half-mile titles (still a record), and never lost a collegiate race in his specialty.

Charles "Chuck" Hornbostel was born September 26, 1911, in Evansville, Indiana, the son of a blacksmith. When he entered Evansville Central High School, he ran to develop fitness for basketball. He was not a standout in either sport, never breaking five minutes for a mile. On graduation, he worked as a bank teller for two years, earning twenty dollars a month. With less than three dollars to his name, he enrolled at Indiana University. He took a job at a sorority dining hall in return for free meals and small pay. His basketball dream had not died, and he went out for cross-country to get in shape for his favorite sport.

Hornbostel did not choose track. Track chose Hornbostel.

He won Big Ten titles at 880 yards, one mile, and the mile relay, and ran for two Big Ten championship teams in cross-country. He placed eleventh individually when the Hoosiers won the national AAU cross-country title at Ypsilanti, Michigan, in 1931, before there was an NCAA championship.

As a sophomore in 1932, Hornbostel won the first of his three NCAA titles in the 800 meters. He helped Indiana to its only NCAA team championship in track, setting a meet record of 1:52.7 at Chicago. That Hoosiers team included Ivan Fuqua, an Olympic relay gold medalist who finished second in the 400; pole vault winner Bryce Beecher; and Henry Brocksmith, second in the mile and two-mile.

That victory qualified twenty-year-old Hornbostel for the Olympic Trials in Los Angeles, where he finished second to Eddie Genung to make the team. At the LA Olympics, Hornbostel won his heat in 1:52.4 and beat Canada's Alex Wilson, the eventual silver medalist. Tommy Hampson of Great Britain set a world record of 1:49.7 to win the gold medal, followed by Wilson in 1:49.9. Hornbostel was sixth in 1:52.7.

In the 1933 NCAA meet at Chicago, Hornbostel repeated as champion, beating mile winner Glenn Cunningham of Kansas by inches. Hornbostel tied the 880-yard world record of 1:50.9, set the previous year by Ben Eastman, the Olympic silver medalist at 400 meters. (The time was equivalent to 1:50.3 for 800 meters, thus inferior to Hampson's world record.)

In 1934, Hornbostel prefaced a strong season by becoming outstanding performer of New York's indoor Millrose Games and winning the national AAU title at 1,000 meters. At the Princeton Invitational on June 16, Hornbostel lost the race and his 880-yard world record to Eastman's 1:49.8. Hornbostel's time was 1:50.7, also under the previous record. He won his third NCAA title a week later at Los Angeles, clocking 1:51.9 for 880 yards. Only other half-milers to have won three outdoor NCAA titles are Pittsburgh's John Woodruff (1937–39) and Tennessee's Tony Parilla (1992–94).

Hornbostel's first postcollegiate season, 1935, featured a repeat of the Wanamaker Award from the Millrose Games. He first won the 1,000-yard run in 2:13.0, one second off the world indoor record, then an hour later set a world indoor record

Charles Hornbostel
Courtesy of Indiana University Athletics.

of 1:11.3 for 600 yards. That broke the ten-year-old record of 1:11.6 held by Alan Helfrich.

Favorites in the 1936 Olympic Trials at Randalls Island, New York, were Woodruff, then a Pittsburgh freshman, and NCAA champion Charles Beetham of Ohio State. The 800-meter final was tumultuous. Southern California's Ross Bush led through 400 in a slowish 55.6. Beetham, who had beaten Woodruff in the AAU a week before, fell with 300 meters left in a collision with Indiana's Marmaduke Hobbs. That allowed Michigan State's Abraham Rosenkantz to make a break, but he was soon overtaken. Woodruff won in 1:51.0, with Hornbostel closing fast in 1:51.3 to finish second, just as he did in 1932.

Hornbostel was the first Hoosier to run in two Olympics. In Berlin, he was involved in another peculiar 800-meter final. Woodruff, boxed in at 300 meters, came to a complete stop and allowed all other runners to pass him. He moved to the outside and began passing everyone until he claimed the lead at 400. Canada's Philip Edwards went ahead on the backstretch before Woodruff reclaimed the lead in the last curve.

Woodruff won the gold medal in 1:52.9, followed by Italy's Mario Lanzi in 1:53.3 and Edwards in 1:53.6. Hornbostel was fifth in 1:54.6. Woodruff, Jesse Owens, and two other black athletes came away with eight gold medals, debunking Adolf Hitler's theories of Aryan racial supremacy. (Woodruff later served in World War II and Korea, rising to the rank of lieutenant colonel. He died in 2007 at age ninety two. He is buried in his wife's family plot at Crown Hill Cemetery, Indianapolis, section 46, lot 86.)

Here is one way to end a track and field career: set two world records in one day. Eleven days after his Olympic race, that is what Hornbostel did.

In an August 15 dual meet against the British Empire, he was on US foursomes that set world records of 7:35.8 in the two-mile relay and 17:17.2 in the four-mile relay. Hornbostel retired with bests of 1:50.7 for 880 yards (1934), 3:57.8 for 1,500 meters (1932), and 4:15.1 for one mile (1933). He earned a master's in business administration from Harvard and in 1947 joined the Financial Executives Institute, the professional association of corporate chief financial offers. He was the institute's first full-time president, serving from 1971 to 1978. He died from Parkinson's disease on January 13, 1989, at age seventy-seven.

One of Hornbostel's children, Karen Hornbostel, was a four-time masters national champion in road cycling and received the 2003 Lance Armstrong Spirit of Survivorship award. After fighting breast cancer for thirteen years, she died in 2006 at age fifty-four. The Karen Hornbostel Memorial Time Trial Series was started in her name in Colorado.

Don Lash, 1936.
IU Archives P0040355.

Don Lash
1936

A Full Life: World Record Holder, FBI Agent, Civic Leader

DON LASH WAS A RUNNER AHEAD OF HIS TIME.
 Before sports science became developed, he had his pulse rate and blood count measured for physiology research. Before athletes could openly earn income from track and field, he saved half his expense money by riding coach class on train

trips to invitational meets. That's how he paid his way through Indiana University. Before his athletic peak, World War II intervened.

Circumstances prevented Lash from more prominence. Even so, *Sports Illustrated* in 1988 labeled him America's first great distance runner. He became known as "The Iron Man of Indiana."

If ahead of his time, he was from a different time. As a boy, he plowed fields with a one-horse plow and was educated in a one-room schoolhouse. He became a track star at Auburn High School, which had no track. He trained in a neighboring pasture and by going up and down stairs in the school building. He discovered his talent while chasing rabbits on his grandfather's farm.

"I had ten or twelve young rabbits in a cage. I liked to run. But I had a good dog, too," Lash said.

He was born August 15, 1912, in Bluffton, Indiana, the son of a man who came to Indiana on an "orphan train" from Boston in 1898. His father, Brandon, was a foundry worker in Auburn. In summer months, the Lashes rented a muck farm, raising potatoes, onions, and celery. Lash also delivered newspapers to contribute to the family income.

He was profoundly influenced by his mother, Pearl, a devoted Christian, and maternal grandfather, Daniel Landis, a Church of the Brethren preacher as well as a farmer. One incident at his grandfather's home changed the direction of his life. As described in Lash's autobiography, he saw a bright light in his bedroom in a house that was without electricity or other lights. The light moved back and forth, scaring the boy, who yelled for Grandpa.

"He, of course, got up, lighted a lamp, and came up the stairs," Lash wrote. "By the time he got upstairs, the light disappeared. There was no explanation for it, except that I have always believed that God was telling me that I was a chosen one of His."

His high school coach, Zeke Young, thought Lash should choose football or basketball, two sports in which older brother Charles excelled. Lash liked basketball more than football, but running most of all. The coach once challenged Lash to keep up with Fort Wayne South Side's Perry Zahn, then the top cross-country runner in the state. Lash did keep up, then beat him.

As a senior in 1933, he won the mile at the state meet in 4:30.5, a victory that effectively launched his running career. He headed to IU with all the money his father had in his pocket: $4.75. Lash was charged $2 for the ride to Bloomington. There were no athletic scholarships, so he told Coach Billy Hayes he would have to go home. Hayes paid him $10 to water his lawn, then arranged for Lash to get a job mopping at women's dormitories. Delta Chi fraternity offered him a bed. He earned an additional $10 a week passing out samples of Beech Nut chewing gum at dorms and Greek houses.

Freshmen were ineligible for college competition, but he ran in the national AAU cross-country meet in 1933 and finished third. Lash, in his autobiography, said he never lost again in cross-country. The Big Ten, during the Depression, did not hold a championship while he was in college, so the Hoosier harriers concentrated on the AAU meet. They went 1-2-3-4-5 for a perfect score of 15 in 1936. Lash won seven consecutive titles from 1934 to 1940, a record that lasted until Pat Porter won eight in a row from 1982 to 1989.

Lash won eight Big Ten track titles, sweeping the outdoor mile and two-mile in 1935, 1936, and 1937. In 1936, he was so fit that he was invited to Princeton, New Jersey, for a June 13 meet featuring stars of the era. He was aiming at the world record of 8:59.6 set in 1931 by Finland's Paavo Nurmi, a nine-time Olympic gold medalist who set twenty-two world records. A cold spring rain left Lash with doubts.

Hayes told Lash, "Instead of slowing you down, the rain might keep you cool." Hayes watched, stopwatch in hand, as Lash lowered the world record to 8:58.4, doing so on Nurmi's thirty-ninth birthday. Lash ran evenly with miles of 4:26.9 and 4:31.5. The only other Americans to set world records at that distance were Jim Beatty in 1962 and Bob Schul in 1964.

A week later, Lash set a meet record of 14:58.5 in the 5,000 meters at the NCAA Championships, leading a 1-2-4 Hoosier finish that included Tom Deckard and Jim Smith. In the Olympic Trials, also at Princeton, Lash secured a trip to Berlin by winning the 10,000 meters in 31:06.9, breaking the American record by seventeen seconds.

In the 5,000, held nine days later, Lash built a lead through two miles but then slowed, causing spectators to wonder if he was succumbing to the heat. He had dropped back in an attempt to help Deckard make the team. Lash's sprint finish allowed him to overtake nineteen-year-old Louis Zamperini of Torrance, California, with both timed in 15:04.2. Deckard was third, also making it to Berlin. Zamperini became the subject of *Unbroken*, a biography and movie about his experience as a runner, Japanese prisoner of war, and evangelist.

Lash's chance to win an Olympic medal was lost at sea. The SS *Manhattan*, a luxury liner, took ten days to cross the Atlantic Ocean. Because of the motion of the sea and fearing shin splits, he did not run during the trip and gained ten pounds. Worse, his events were scheduled soon after arrival. He finished eighth in the 10,000 and thirteenth in the 5,000. He consoled himself with the thought that he would try again in 1940. World War II canceled those Olympics, and also those of 1944.

"Thus my dream to win an Olympic gold medal vanished," Lash wrote.

That would have changed his life. Witnessing German chancellor Adolf Hitler on a daily basis did change his life.

"I saw those people rise when he would come into the stadium, and they were just like stiff pokers with their hands out saluting him," Lash said in a 1992 interview. "I realized that he was more like a god to them than a leader of a country. When I got back and realized what he was really trying to do, I got into the FBI... I knew that we didn't want Nazism and so I was very devoted in my work."

After the Olympics, Lash remained devoted to running. In 1937, he broke another Nurmi world record, running the indoor two-mile on February 13 at Boston in 8:58.0—two tenths faster than the Finn's twelve-year-old record. At the Penn

Relays, he anchored Indiana to a world record of 17:16.1 in the four-mile relay. In a June 19 return to Princeton, Lash was edged by Archie San Romani in a mile, both timed in 4:07.2. That made them the second- and third-fastest milers in history, behind Glenn Cunningham's 1934 world record of 4:06.7.

In 1938, Lash joined the Indiana State Police and won the Sullivan Award as the nation's outstanding amateur athlete. In 1939, he set an American indoor record of 14:30.9 in the 5,000 meters February 25 at New York. That was nearly as fast as Nurmi ever ran outdoors (14:28.2) and within seven seconds of the world indoor record (14:23.2) set in 1925 by another Finn, Ville Ritola. Lash might have broken that record at New York on March 31, 1940, running an indoor three-mile in 13:55.0—equivalent to 14:25.1 for the longer 5,000 meters. He won the last of his twelve national titles that year at age twenty-eight.

In 1941, he hung up his spikes and joined the FBI. He said he was assigned to cases in which agents thought a suspect might flee on foot so that he could catch them. His twenty-one-year career in the FBI included stops in Atlanta, Detroit, Birmingham, Abilene, and Indianapolis.

One of his earliest cases nearly jeopardized his career. Agents searched the Atlanta motel room of a German believed to be a spy. Against orders not to leave a trace, Lash grabbed a black notebook and fled with it. The FBI feared the spy would be tipped off to surveillance. The notebook turned out to have names and addresses of other spies. The next day, Japanese warplanes bombed Pearl Harbor, the United States declared war, and the new agent was vindicated.

Lash retired from the FBI in 1962. He had bought sixty acres near Turkey Run State Park in Marshall, Indiana, and started a youth camp. The camp was sold to the Fellowship of Christian Athletes (FCA), and Lash became a regional director and fund raiser for the FCA. He was also an IU trustee and elected to five terms (1973–82) as a Republican member of the Indiana House of Representatives. He went into real estate in Rockville, Indiana, and was a fund raiser for hospitals and other civic improvements.

One of his sons, Russell, of Howe High School in Indianapolis, was a state mile champion in 1957 and 1958 and in cross-country in 1957. He followed his father into the FBI.

Don Lash's life would have been extraordinary if he had never been an athlete or an Olympian. He was one of the twenty-five charter members of IU's Athletics Hall of Fame and belongs to the National Track and Field Hall of Fame.

He died September 14, 1994, of spinal cancer in Terre Haute, Indiana, at the age of eighty-two. He is buried in Rush Creek Cemetery, near Tangier in Parke County. Don Lash Park in Auburn is named for him.

He dictated part of his autobiography from his deathbed to his widow, Margaret. In the preface, Lash said athletics gave him confidence to try things that others might have thought impossible. His life motto: "The older I become, the more I am convinced that true happiness comes from helping others."

Ivan Fuqua
Courtesy of Indiana
University Athletics.

Ivan Fuqua
1932

Hoosiers' First Gold Medalist Survived a Car Crash

IVAN FUQUA, THE FIRST OLYMPIC GOLD MEDALIST IN INDIANA UNIVERSITY history, nearly did not make it to the 1932 Los Angeles Games.

One of three cars carrying the Hoosiers' track and field team to that year's Drake Relays overturned twice in an accident near Sullivan, Indiana, about thirty miles from Fuqua's hometown of Brazil. In the car were coach Billy Hayes and six athletes, among them Fuqua and Charles Hornbostel, two future Olympians. The athletes received only cuts and bruises, and all were competing a week later. But the incident impaired Fuqua just as he was rounding into shape. He began the season with a pulled muscle and then endured a short illness.

The Hoosiers went on to win their only NCAA track team championship in 1932, beating second-place Ohio State 56–49¾ at Chicago's Stagg Field. Hornbostel tied the NCAA record of 1:52.7 in winning the 880-yard run. Fuqua, then a sophomore, was second in the 440 to Notre Dame's Alex Wilson, a Canadian who went on to win Olympic silver in the 800 meters and bronze in the 400.

In the Olympic Trials at Stanford, Fuqua narrowly qualified for the 400-meter final. Three per semifinal advanced, plus the next fastest—and that was Fuqua, in 48.7. He was fifth in the final in 47.6, and he was chosen for the team competing at the Olympics three weeks later.

In Los Angeles, the Olympic village did not have amenities of the twenty-first century. Fuqua said athletes were lodged in what looked like huts.

"There were four of us in each room," he said. "They were little shacks, really, just a place to sleep. And all the events were held right around the coliseum area. We hung around there all day giving out autographs."

The Americans set a world record of 3:11.8 in the first heat of the 4×400 relay. They didn't use 400-meter silver medalist Ben Eastman in the final, but Fuqua affirmed his selection with a 47.1 leadoff leg, fast enough to have won a bronze medal in the 400 meters. Fuqua, Ed Ablowich (47.6), Karl Warner (47.3), and Olympic champion Bill Carr (46.2) lowered that to 3:08.2. It was a world record that stood for twenty years, until broken by Jamaica at the 1952 Helsinki Olympics.

"That was the fastest I'd ever run," Fuqua said. "We couldn't believe we had actually won the gold medal. We felt we would win. It was just a question of whether we would get the world record. We were stunned and, of course, elated."

Fuqua's gold medal came two days before his twenty-third birthday. His welcome home to Indiana included a one-hundred-car escort, parade, and public reception in Brazil.

He was born August 9, 1909, in Decatur, Illinois. After his family moved to Brazil, he became a high school track star. As a freshman, he ran on a mile relay team that won at Indiana's state meet in 3:29.6, which lasted forty-four years as a school record. As a junior and senior, he scored enough points by himself for Brazil to finish second in the state meet—still the highest in school history—behind Gary Froebel.

At the 1929 state meet, Fuqua won the 440, long jump, and 220-yard low hurdles and anchored the winning mile relay. He remains the only boy in Indiana to have won four titles in the same state meet. He followed that at the national scholastic meet with a national record of 24.7 in the low hurdles and a meet record of 49.4 in the 440.

In 1930, he set his second and third national records—9.7 for 100 yards at the Kokomo Relays, then 21.6 in winning the 220 at the national scholastic meet. He lowered the 440 state record to 48.8.

He was so ambitious that, while still in high school, he hitchhiked to Denver for the 1929 national AAU meet. His preparation was to take a job cleaning the stadium for the meet, and all he had to show for his trip was a sunburn.

Fuqua's peak seasons came after the Los Angeles Olympics. Some accounts credit him with an indoor world record at 600 yards. He was second in the NCAA 440 in 1933 and 1934 behind LSU's Glenn Hardin, who became the 1936 Olympic champion in the 400-meter hurdles and whose world record stood for nineteen years. Fuqua won national AAU 440s in 1933 and 1934, and he ranked third in the world both years. His best 440 time was 47.3 (equivalent to 47.0 for 400 meters).

He had hoped to compete in the 1936 Berlin Olympics but was ruled ineligible because he was a coach making $2,000 a year and considered a professional. There was no question about his status in 1932.

"We were certainly amateurs, that's for sure," Fuqua said. "They gave us seven dollars a week for laundry and fed us. And we were lucky to have pants and shoes."

Fuqua has joked he was kidnapped rather than recruited to IU. Another IU student from Brazil told him he was going to the university, packed his car, and drove him to Bloomington for enrollment. The driver, George Craig, went on to become governor of Indiana from 1953 to 1957. Fuqua was a football letterman in 1931 but concentrated on track thereafter.

After graduation, he became track coach at Connecticut State (now the University of Connecticut). He joined the navy during World War II and was discharged in 1946 with the rank of lieutenant commander. Regrettably, his gold medal was stolen while he was in the military. He served as Brown University's track coach from 1947 until his retirement in 1974. He later became manager and co-owner of a Rhode Island beach club.

He died January 14, 1994, in Providence, Rhode Island, at the age of eighty-four. Some of Fuqua's memorabilia is displayed at the Clay County Historical Society. He belongs to the Indiana Track, Rhode Island Heritage, and Helms Athletic Foundation Halls of Fame.

Leroy Samse
1904

First Medalist Set Vault World Record

LEROY SAMSE OF KOKOMO, INDIANA, STARTED OUT AS A GYMNAST AND TUMbler. But he finished second in the pole vault at the 1902 high school state meet, and when he arrived at Indiana University, coach Jim Horne knew he had an athlete with potential in track and field. Horne taught Samse the "shifting-hand" technique, which was new to the pole vault. A childhood accident had cost Samse the sight in one eye, making his subsequent achievements more amazing.

The Big Ten—then the Western Intercollegiate Conference—featured many of the world's top pole vaulters. In 1903, Michigan's Charles Dvorak vaulted 11 feet, 9 inches, just under the world record. In 1904, Stanford's Norman Dole came to the conference meet (then open to nonmembers) holding the world record of 12–1½. Dole won at 11–6, beating Samse. But a week later at a meet in St. Louis, Samse vaulted 11–9 to beat Dole.

"Had the Hoosier been fresh, he would have cleared 12 feet," the *St. Louis Globe-Democrat* reported.

On September 3, 1904, also at St. Louis, the gold medal went to Dvorak, with an Olympic record of 11–6. Samse took the silver medal, winning a jump-off involving four vaulters all clearing eleven feet.

Samse became the Hoosiers' first Olympic medalist, albeit barely. Hoosier hurdler Thad Shideler also won a silver medal, but later that day.

Afterward, Samse received offers to perform on the trapeze in the circus but turned them down. He did not want to turn pro while still in college. His patience was rewarded. In the conference meet at Evanston, Illinois, on June 2, 1906, he set

LeRoy Samse, 1906.
IU Archives P0082957.

a world record of 12-4⅞. That broke the record of 12-3 set three days earlier by A. C. Gilbert of Yale. (Gilbert won the gold medal in 1908, financed medical school working as a magician, and is best known for inventing the Erector Set, a popular toy of the era.)

Introduction of fiberglass and carbon fiber poles changed the event in the 1950s. In 2009, IU organized the Leroy Samse Invitational, an informal meet in which vaulters used nonbending poles similar to Samse's. Jeff Coover won with a clearance of twelve feet, so the meet record is still considered to be Samse's.

After college, Samse joined a touring circus acrobatic group that performed in county fairs. He also dabbled in vaudeville. Most of his career was spent as a physical education instructor in Chicago and Los Angeles, and he retired in 1946.

Samse, who was born September 13, 1883, in Kokomo, died May 1, 1956, in Sherman Oaks, California. He was inducted into the Indiana Track Hall of Fame in 1982 and Howard County Sports Hall of Fame in 2008.

Lilly King
Courtesy of Indiana University Athletics.

Lilly King
2016

Outspoken and Never to Be Outdone

GEOPOLITICAL TENSION BETWEEN THE UNITED STATES AND SOVIET UNION, called the Cold War, essentially ended in 1991. A quarter century later, one swimmer heated it up again. Lilly King was not trying to do so. Lilly was being Lilly.

At the 2016 Olympic Games in Rio de Janeiro, the favorites in the women's 100-meter breaststroke were the nineteen-year-old Indiana University swimmer and Yulia Efimova of Russia. Efimova, the reigning world champion, had been banned from the Olympics for having served a previous doping suspension. She appealed to the Court of Arbitration for Sport because she had already served a ban. It was such a confusing scenario that Efimova didn't appear on Rio start lists posted hours before the preliminaries. Out of the Olympics, then in. Out, back in.

After winning a semifinal, Efimova waved her index finger, apparently in response to King doing so earlier. King watched on a TV monitor and wagged her finger back at the screen. King did not realize NBC had a camera on her in the ready room, but it likely would not have mattered. That was "authentic Lil," said Mark King, her father.

"There are a lot of people who really love Lil, and there are some people it rubs them the wrong way," he said. "It's just the way she is."

After posting the fastest semifinal (by .02), King said in an interview with NBC: "You wave your finger number one and you've been caught drug cheating? I'm not a fan."

So it was on. The match-up recalled other United States versus Russia showdowns, everything from *Rocky IV* and the 1980 Miracle on Ice to chess masters Bobby Fischer and Boris Spassky. Indeed, it resembled the Rocky movie right down to the dialogue.

"We wanted to break her," said the Hoosiers' Ray Looze, one of the Team USA coaches. It was Ivan Drago who famously told Rocky: "I must break you."

King used tactical and psychological ploys to win the gold medal in 1:04.93, an Olympic record. Efimova was silver medalist in 1:05.50. Katie Meili, another American, took bronze in 1:05.69.

King became the first native Hoosier woman to win an individual medal in swimming since Fort Wayne breaststroker Sharon Wichman at Mexico City in 1968. King was the first American to win gold in the 100 breaststroke since 2000.

In the ready room, King was the last to arrive, as if this were another race instead of her first Olympic final. As other finalists sat, King paced.

"I wanted her to have to see me," King said of Efimova.

Looze said he had never seen such audacity in such a moment. It was a "total mind game," he said.

The coach said analytics personnel from USA Swimming looked at Efimova's races for data on how others had beaten her. Efimova is a strong closer. King had not lost a 100 breaststroke race since she was beaten by Efimova on December 4, 2015, in the winter national championships at Federal Way, Washington.

King went out so fast in the first fifty meters, 30.22 seconds, that Efimova was pulled to 30.70—or more than a second faster than the Russian's first fifty meters from the semifinal. That pace was intended to tire Efimova, but it left King vulnerable.

"She had to drop the hammer, after dropping the hammer," Looze said.

The Hoosier swimmer told her coach she thought she would be caught at seventy-five meters. Instead, King extended her lead.

"Efimova, she broke her," Looze said. "And Lilly likes that kind of stuff."

Lillia King was born February 10, 1997, in Evansville, Indiana, to Mark and Ginny King. Her father ran track and cross-country for Indiana State, and her mother was a swimmer for Eastern Kentucky and Illinois State.

At various stages of her youth, Lilly participated in track, cross-country, and gymnastics. She really wanted to swim, though. She wanted to when she was six, but her mother didn't think she was ready. So the daughter stayed mad all summer. At seven, Lilly became a swimmer.

When she was eleven, she qualified for the age-group state meet in the 50-meter breaststroke. She finished last. Then came a growth spurt, adding inches to a frame that became five foot nine. She made it back to state, albeit ranking fourth or fifth place after prelims. Didn't matter. She told her parents she would win.

"She was just so crazy confident," her mother said.

And Lilly did win state.

In Evansville, it is difficult—some would say impossible—to become an elite swimmer. There is one public indoor pool, Lloyd Pool. It has eight lanes, six for lap swimming. The two other lanes are too shallow.

Of the seven high schools in town, six train there. High schoolers are confined to four lanes, shared among as many as three dozen swimmers. Traffic? Lilly was undaunted.

"Sometimes, she would even tell me, 'If we've got to put seven kids in the lane here today, I'll swim around them. Don't worry. It'll be fine,'" said Dave Baumeyer, her coach at Reitz High School.

Her club team was Newburgh Sea Creatures, where she swam summers for Aaron Opell, a former IU swimmer. She often raced brother Alex, who is one year older and went on to swim for Michigan.

She never won a high school state title until she was a senior, in 2015. There was reason for that. Champion in 2013 and 2014 was Bethany Galat, who nearly made the Olympic team in 2016 and who beat King to win a silver medal at the 2017 World Championships.

Besides, no single defeat could discourage King. That was underscored in January 2014 when the high school coach asked about her day.

"It's good," she replied. "Guess what? I've got one less person to beat to go to the Olympics. Rebecca Soni retired today."

Soni, then twenty-six, had won six medals at the 2008 and 2012 Olympics and set seven world records. King was not in that orbit. It was that crazy confidence talking.

She was making her mark, though, and not only in Indiana. At the Pan Pacific Junior Championships in August 2014 in Maui, she won gold medals in the 100-meter breaststroke and 4×100 medley relay, both in meet records. At the 2015 World University Games in Gwangju, South Korea, she won silver in the 100 breaststroke and bronze in the relay.

In between, in February 2015, she won her first high school state titles—in the 100-yard breaststroke and 200-yard individual medley. Notably, those were the only events not won by swimmers from Carmel, whose girls team that year was arguably the best in high school history.

Everyone knew King would become faster and stronger in a college environment of more yardage, weightlifting, and competition. She intended to go out of state, perhaps to Texas, Tennessee, or Florida.

However, Looze was on her doorstep the first morning he could visit prospects. On her recruiting trip, she said, IU "felt like home." Looze simply out-recruited everyone else, she added. She was a "transformative athlete," Looze said.

"I thought, 'This girl is really special. She's got the goods,'" Looze said. "She has the competitiveness. She has very large hands and feet in relation to her body. She's super flexible. And then she's just lightning quick. She's very fast. I knew once we started training all those God-given talents, we'd see her take off."

She did.

At those winter nationals, where she was beaten by Efimova in the 100-meter breaststroke, she won the 200 for her first national championship. That presaged a college season in which she swept the breaststrokes at Big Ten and NCAA meets. In the NCAAs at Atlanta, she became the first woman under 57 seconds in the 100-yard breaststroke, clocking 56.85 for an American record. She lowered her own record of 57.15 from heats. She set another American record in the 200 breaststroke, 2:03.59, bettering the 2:04.06 by Notre Dame's Emma Reaney from 2014.

King's records were effectively world records—they were fastest ever—but formal world records are not recognized at yard distances. She said she was developing an "almost obnoxious confidence" heading into the Olympic Trials. It was warranted.

In the trials at Omaha, Nebraska, she doubled up again, winning 100- and 200-meter breaststrokes. Her time of 1:05.20 in the 100 was the fastest by an American in three years. Her confidence was influencing her parents, who secured lodging in Rio even before their daughter formally made the team. Fundraisers were held around Evansville to defray the Kings' travel costs.

Of course, nothing could have prepared Lilly, or her parents, for the firestorm in Rio. It wasn't as if the breaststroker was picking on Efimova specifically. King's antidoping stance was long-standing. She was a stickler for the rules. That was underscored when she was among athletes to speak at a White House antidoping summit October 31, 2018.

Once at a high school meet, there was smoothie bar set up for swimmers. King looked at the ingredients, saw something not approved by the FDA, and declined. She would not take decongestants for a cold, and only ibuprofen for pain relief.

"She won't even eat a poppy seed muffin," her mother said.

After the Olympic final, King described the experience as "incredible," and especially the fact that she did it clean. She races as she lives: putting it out there, no holding back.

"The pressure is going to be on, but especially for standing up for what I believe is right, I felt that I needed to perform even better tonight than I have in the past," King said.

King and Efimova did not shake hands after the race or before the medal ceremony, although they posed together for a photo. In a tense, fifteen-minute news conference, Efimova was visibly strained. Asked if she thought it was mean of the Americans not to congratulate her, the Russian said she understood. King said she was "in the moment" and celebrating with Meili.

"Also, if I had been in Yulia's position, I would not have wanted to be congratulated by someone who wasn't speaking highly of me," King said. "So, if she wished to be congratulated, I apologize. She had a fantastic swim, and I always look forward to racing her."

Efimova burst into tears after the news conference, eliciting some sympathy in the process. Not from Looze. He said it was "a travesty" that Efimova was on the podium at all.

"I do believe it was good versus evil. I really stand by that," the Hoosiers coach said.

Russian reporters chased after King at three o'clock in the morning, attempting to ask again why she didn't congratulate Efimova. There was a cascade of Twitter backlash on King, but most of it was in Russian, Looze said, "so she didn't understand it." King's Twitter followers, who numbered four hundred in March and ten thousand before the Olympic final, soon exceeded twenty-one thousand. (Two years later, she had forty thousand.)

Her Olympics were not over. Unsurprisingly, she did not make the final of the 200 breaststroke, finishing seventh in her semifinal in 2:24.59. (Efimova won the silver medal.)

Also unsurprisingly, King won another gold medal, swimming breaststroke leg in the 4×100 medley relay. It was the one thousandth gold medal won by the United States at the Olympic Games.

Each of the women had already won individual medals in Rio: Kathleen Baker, silver in backstroke, 59.00; King, gold in breaststroke, 1:05.70; Dana Vollmer, bronze in butterfly, 56.00, and Simone Manuel, gold in freestyle, 52.43.

Total time was 3:53.13. Australia won the silver medal and Denmark bronze. The Americans were in fourth after the opening leg, and King pushed them ahead to stay. Still, her time was the slowest of four 100 breaststrokes in Rio and nearly a second slower than Efimova's 1:04.98.

King became the seventh IU swimmer to win as many as two golds in a single Olympics, and the second woman. No Hoosier had done so since Jim Montgomery forty years before. The six others are all in the International Swimming Hall of Fame.

"To think that a little less than a year ago she was nowhere near this level is mind-boggling," Looze said. "Lilly was part of one of the best Olympic swimming teams in the history of the Games."

The United States finished with as many swim golds (sixteen) as in 2012 and two more medals overall (thirty-three).

Returning home to celebrity status was unsettling at times. She was besieged with fan mail and requests for autographs and appearances. The Evansville Otters had her throw out the first pitch at a baseball game. People asked for photos, and she spent an hour signing autographs.

A cousin she had never met sent her a present: a belt he had received in Afghanistan, featuring the old Soviet hammer and sickle on the buckle. Afghans wore the buckle upside down, the cousin explained, to symbolize beating the Russians.

Post-Olympic letdowns are common, and King was hit hard. School was hard. Celebrity was annoying. Racing was dull. Practice was drudgery.

She was called into a winter meeting with coaches to discuss poor grades. Turns out those grades were symptomatic of a larger issue.

She talked. She sobbed. She lost it. In doing so, she won back her life.

"So I think once I let it all out, I was a lot better," she said. "Most of my teammates knew what was going on. I'm pretty good at hiding things when they're not quite right."

It was so hard to do normal activities in her hometown—go to the grocery store or eat at a restaurant—that she considered wearing a wig to disguise herself. Her likeness was on a bingo card at a fall festival, so people purposely looked for her. When in Evansville now, she said, she looks at the ground so that no one will recognize her. After an initial wave of attention on campus, she walked around without interruption.

King didn't characterize her condition as depression but said she did not feel like herself. She credited one of her roommates, Abby Fleck, a former high school teammate, for improving her mood.

"I don't know what I'd do without her," King said.

First-semester grades—she said her average was 2.5, despite a reduced load—were not the only indication something was wrong. She was beaten in the 100-meter breaststroke, her signature event, in December's short course World Championships at Windsor, Ontario. She made fundamental mistakes and told Looze she didn't want to lose *that* way again.

She came away from that meet with a gold medal in the 50-meter breaststroke and three relay golds, but the defeat was humbling. Asked whether it was mistake for her to swim there at all, Looze said he would not change anything. King wanted to go, and sometimes it's good to lose, he said. Besides, she loves to race.

"She gets bored easily," Looze said. "You've got to keep that carrot out in front of her."

Out of the pool, King raised her second-semester grades to 3.4. In the pool, she was a better version of herself.

Dryland training and a better diet allowed her to trim body fat by 1.5 percent. She looked leaner. She became faster in 2017, breaking her American records in the 100-yard breaststroke (Big Ten) and 200-yard breaststroke (NCAAs).

Oddly, she received pushback on social media after she asserted world records were next. After two Olympic gold medals, uh, what other goals would there be?

"It's like the logical next step," King said. "I guess it's easy to make a lot of people mad."

The step before that was to qualify for the World Championships, set for Budapest, Hungary. She did so by winning the 50-, 100- and 200-meter breaststrokes at the USA Championships in Indianapolis. Her time of 1:04.95 in the 100 was just .02 off that from Rio.

Encores can be difficult, especially for an athlete as decorated as King. Yet in Budapest, she exceeded Rio, coming away with four gold medals, all in world records. Her first event was the 100 breaststroke, in which she had a rematch with Efimova. The Russian actually went into the worlds with a faster time than King.

"The rivalry is definitely there. I don't think it's going away anytime soon," King said. "Obviously, it's very awkward between the two of us. We're competitors. We don't like each other too much."

The day before the final, in the warmup pool, King and Efimova kept swimming in each other's lane as the mental warfare resumed. Even the Russian coach walked on the pool deck to stand right by Looze, again a member of the American staff.

On the starting blocks, King looked to her left and stared at Efimova in the adjacent lane. Then the Hoosier went out and executed another race plan crafted by a USA Swimming consultant.

King crushed Efimova for the gold medal, winning so emphatically that teammate Meili pushed Efimova to bronze. King's time of 1:04.13 broke the world record of 1:04.35 set by Lithuania's Ruta Meilutyte at the 2013 World Championships in Barcelona, and also the American record of 1:04.45 set by Jessica Hardy in 2013.

"While it's great winning every race, it's nice not knowing what's going to happen," King said. "I love that component of our rivalry."

King conceded she was "freaking out" when she arrived at the pool. All she demonstrated was that she is a breaststroking freak.

The next day, she was the only female breaststroker in the final of the mixed medley relay, a new event. Her 1:04.15 leg helped the United States set a world record of 3:38.56 for her second gold medal.

Four days later, she won two more golds. She lowered the world record in the 50 breaststroke to 29.40, and contributed a 1:04.48 leg to the team that set a world record of 3:51.55 in the women's medley relay. King and Efimova hung on the lane divider after the 50 breaststroke and smiled together.

"I mean, obviously, we're not best friends. We're rivals," King said. "But I've always had a good time racing her. We've definitely been a lot more civil than we were last year, so I've enjoyed that."

King narrowly missed a fifth medal, finishing fourth in the 200 breaststroke. Efimova's time was 2:19.64 to beat another native Hoosier, Galat, who won the silver medal. King missed bronze by .18.

King's four golds were the most at a major championship by an IU swimmer since Mark Spitz's seven at the 1972 Olympics. Jim Montgomery won three at the 1976 Olympics and Charlie Hickox three at the 1968 Olympics. King became the first Hoosier to set a world record in an individual event since Montgomery in the 100-meter freestyle in 1976.

"The relay records were kind of the cherry on top," she said. "The individual records were definitely something I was looking forward to since Rio."

The following year, 2018, she won third consecutive NCAA titles in both breaststrokes, breaking her American records. Her time of 56.25 for 100 yards bettered her 56.30 from the 2017 Big Ten meet. She became the first to break 2:03 for 200 yards, lowering that to 2:02.60. In the 2018 long course season, King repeated as national champion in 50- and 100-meter breaststrokes.

Some of King's peers—Missy Franklin, Simone Manuel, Katie Ledecky—did not use all their college eligibility before turning pro. King could have gone that way, too. The decision cost her earnings, notably $60,000 in world record bonuses. The NCAA does allow Olympic athletes to keep medal money from the US Olympic Committee and national governing bodies, and King earned more than $100,000 from the Olympics.

"I signed on for four years," she said. "I didn't sign on for three. I didn't sign on for two and then decide to go pro. I signed on for four. Kept my word."

As a senior, she made a lifetime memory at the Big Ten Championships. Not only did she become the first woman under 56 seconds in the 100-yard breaststroke, lowering the American record to 55.88. The underdog Hoosiers, in their own pool, won their first Big Ten team title since 2011.

"It was incredible to see the girls all come together like they did," King said.

She had expressed doubt she could break her American record in her final college meet, the NCAAs at Austin, Texas. No one should underestimate Lilly King. Not even Lilly King.

She further lowered the 100 breaststroke record to 55.73, completing a four-year NCAA sweep. After she won the 200 in 2:02.90—just .30 off her record from the year before—she held up four fingers on each hand, signifying her double quadruple. She said she did not feel good in warm-ups and credited teammates for cheering from the pool deck.

"Before the race, I was like, 'I better not mess this up.' My last one," she said.

Brendan Hansen is the only other breaststroker, male or female, to go 8-of-8 in NCAA finals. King's eight individual titles are most ever by a female Big Ten swimmer and exceeded by just five women in history.

Her collegiate success carried over to another golden summer.

She won three gold medals and a silver at the 2019 World Championships in Gwangju, South Korea, repeating in the 50- and 100-meter breaststrokes (29.84) and 1:04.93) and 4×100 medley relay. She was denied a fourth, in the mixed medley relay, by .02, and a possible fifth, in the 200 breaststroke, by a controversial disqualification in the heats. She had some solace in being on the team that broke the world record from 2017 in the medley relay.

Then it was back to Bloomington in the fall to resume student teaching in physical education classes. It was all buildup to a return to the Olympics. Heading into 2020, she had amassed sixteen American records and was unbeaten in the inaugural season of the pro International Swimming League. King was committed to becoming the first woman to repeat as gold medalist in the 100-meter breaststroke, and she made another commitment as well.

"When I have a problem, I tell somebody about it," she said. "Try not to bottle things up."

Cody Miller
Courtesy of Indiana University Athletics.

Cody Miller
2016

No Glitz, Just Grit, out of Las Vegas

LIFE IS FULL OF CROSSROADS, AND CODY MILLER HAD TO NAVIGATE MANY. He was born with pectus excavatum, or sunken chest. That is an inconvenience if you are, say, a gymnast. He is a swimmer. How is a guy supposed to breathe?

He is not only a swimmer but a breaststroker. Top breaststrokers are six foot three to six foot five, and Miller is five foot ten. Yet Miller takes longer and fewer strokes than anyone. He was not destined to thrive in a so-called country club sport. He was raised in Las Vegas by a single mother—and that is the short version. His sister, Catie, also a swimmer, said the two children raised themselves.

"He could have gone one way or the other in high school," said Ray Looze, his coach at Indiana University. "Either on the streets, or what he's doing in the pool now."

There was a reason for Miller's exuberance after winning a bronze medal in the 100-meter breaststroke at the 2016 Rio Olympics. He set an American record of 58.87 seconds, breaking the mark of longtime nemesis Kevin Cordes, who finished fourth. Miller was third behind the world record of British gold medalist Adam Peaty, and he became the first American swimmer out of IU in forty years to win an individual medal.

Miller looked at the scoreboard, punched the water, and shouted, "Yes! Yes! Yes! Yes!" For so long, the answer to a question about his Olympic dream would have been an emphatic no. "That celebration... to my dying day, that will be something I'll never forget," Looze said.

Miller was born January 9, 1992, in Billings, Montana. His mother, Debbie, could not swim and wanted her children to learn.

Cody turned out to be gifted at breaststroke, in which he set records and was ranked first in the nation as early as age ten. He acknowledged breaststroke is "the stepchild of swimming," difficult to master and reliant on technique.

He was cocky, sometimes angry, and had little structure at home. His father, Craig, a former Canadian minor league hockey player, developed dependencies on alcohol and prescription drugs. He lost jobs. Their home was foreclosed, and Miller, his mother, and his sister bounced around.

Miller did not divulge his private struggles until after the Olympics, when he was interviewed by Pat Forde of Yahoo! Sports.

"My dad was not a bad guy," Miller said. "I definitely have good qualities I got from him. But I always remember him drinking. Always, always drinking. We did everything we possibly could to help him for as long as we could. He went to rehab twice. But he didn't want any of it."

Swimming supplied structure. Miller's club, the Sandpipers, had two coaches, Ron Aitken and Chris Barber, who were willing to mentor him. Also, swimming helped Miller broaden his chest and develop his rib cage. He became a junior national champion, set national age-group records and was selected to the USA junior team.

Aitken used to swim against Looze, and the two have been friends for years. Miller was recruited by college powers Texas and Southern California but decided to link up with Looze. In Bloomington, he had a support system previously unknown. He told one of the volunteer coaches, Ali DeWitt, he had never had a hot breakfast before. It was all cereal and bagels. And Miller was good, if not future-Olympian good. From 2011 to 2014, he won eight individual Big Ten titles, including a four-year sweep of the 200-yard breaststroke. He finished seventh in the 200-meter individual medley at the 2012 Olympic Trials and came away from the 2013 World University Games with a relay bronze medal.

In his senior year, he finished second to Cordes in the 200-yard breaststroke at the NCAA Championships and sixth in the 100-yard breaststroke. The Olympic Trials were more than two years away, and he did not want to end his swim career.

There was money in the sport—most of it going to Michael Phelps—and some swimmers who could genuinely call themselves pro athletes. Miller was a wannabe.

"That summer was a make-or-break summer for me," he said.

To support himself, he worked at swim camps, washed cars, sold PlayStations on eBay, and spent twelve hours detailing a coach's motorcycle. He ate a steady diet of peanut butter and jelly.

"Living cheap, dude. Living cheap," he said.

To be eligible for funding that goes to those on the national team, Miller needed to post a time among the top ten in the world. He did more than that. He unexpectedly became national champion in the 100-meter breaststroke at Irvine, California. He was the only one in the race under one minute (59.91).

"That changed my life. That allowed me to totally dedicate my life to swimming," Miller said.

Looze said the way Miller carried himself, the way he spoke, the way he practiced, it all changed. That one minute in the pool would reverberate for a lifetime.

"It rarely happens that way," Looze said. "It's usually a gradual process. For him, it was that moment."

Later in 2014, Miller won two relay medals at the short course World Championships and twice broke the American record in the 50-yard breaststroke, lowering the mark to 23.91 and 23.61 in a meet at Edmond, Oklahoma.

In 2015, in his first long course World Championships, he won a gold medal as part of the Americans' 4×100 medley relay team at Kazan, Russia. In semifinals of the 100-meter breaststroke, he was ninth in 59.86, or one spot from the final.

He discovered he had some physical advantages. In tests at the US Olympic Training Center in Colorado Springs, Colorado, he was "the most symmetrical swimmer they'd ever seen," Miller said. Swimmers in most strokes favor one side because they breathe to one side. He was not pigeon-toed, nor did his knees bend inward, both common for breaststrokers.

Who else had researchers seen with such symmetry? Michael Phelps.

Miller's buildup to 2016 was underscored in the Duel in the Pool, a mid-December 2015 meet matching the United States against Europe at Indianapolis. To the astonishment of coaches, Miller not only won the 100- and 200-meter breaststrokes, he set short course American records in both.

First up was the 200, in which he beat world-record holder Daniel Gyurta of Hungary and clipped .05 off Cordes's American record, clocking 2:02.33. US coach Jack Bauerle of Georgia said not until that morning was Cordes taken out of the lineup. Team USA wanted Cordes fresh for the breaststroke leg of the 4×100 medley relay because relays were so important: seven points for first, zero for second.

So in went Miller as the number three breaststroker . . . and down went the American record.

"Good coaching there, huh?" Bauerle joked. "We had him as number four."

Miller said he had envisioned a time of 2:02.

"I've been coming up here for years," he said of the natatorium there. "Some of my best races have been in this pool. It means a lot."

He repeated his victory a day later, winning the 100 breaststroke in 56.43, under Cordes's 2013 mark of 56.88.

In the week leading up to the meet, Miller had received a couple of voice mails from his father. The swimmer decided not to listen, trying to stay focused and avoid an upsetting exchange.

On Christmas Day 2015, Miller was with family in his mother's home state of Montana. Debbie's phone rang with a call from an area code in San Diego, where Craig Miller was living. The call went to voice mail, and the message was from a police detective asking for a call back. Cody called. His father had been found dead, homeless and shoeless outside an office building. Suspected cause of death was accidental overdose of drugs and alcohol. Craig Miller was fifty-nine.

Cody said he acted strong for his mother. He did not feel so strong. "Everything just went numb," he said, "except for that horrible pit in my stomach." He said he broke down the next day, listening to the voice mails. It would be the last time he heard his father's voice.

For someone so young, Miller had endured grief previously. The night before his first NCAA championship, as a freshman, he took a call in his Minneapolis hotel room from a former teammate in Las Vegas. Their friend and former teammate, Jay Sirat, had been found dead in his mother's garage, hanging himself with an electrical cord. The death was attributed to an addiction to bath salts.

A year later, a week before the 2012 Olympic Trials, Miller received another call. Another former club teammate was dead. Yung C. "Andrew" Chin, an Air Force Academy student, had shot himself with a shotgun while home on summer leave.

Miller managed to reach finals in both 200 breaststroke and 200 individual medley in those 2012 trials at Omaha, Nebraska. In 2016, death was intruding again as he prepared for another Olympic quest.

He arranged for his father's cremation and paid for it. Ashes were sent to one of Craig's brothers in Winnipeg, Manitoba. Then he met with Looze and another coach, Mike Westphal, to tell them what happened.

"He was raw," Looze said. "I've not seen him like that. He's a tough dude, takes a lot to get any sort of emotion out of him. That was a really, really rough meeting."

Miller had committed himself to making the Olympic team, and he would see it through. He had given up junk food, soda, ice cream. It was lights out by 9:30, every night.

He did not have to win at the Olympic Trials, but he would have to finish in the top two. In semifinals, Cordes set an American record of 58.94, and Miller was second-fastest, 59.09. That didn't count for Rio, though.

In the final, Miller was fourth through fifty meters, and he chided himself for gliding to the finish. But the scoreboard was a relief: first, Cordes, 59.18; second, Miller, 59.26. The long shot from Las Vegas had made it.

"It's very surreal," Miller said afterward.

The Hoosiers had three male swimmers on the US team at Montreal in 1976—Jim Montgomery, Gary Hall, Charlie Keating—but none since then. Now, Cody Miller could add his name.

Making the team was one thing. Medaling was another.

Peaty, the world record holder, was an overwhelming favorite. Cameron van der Burgh, the 2012 gold medalist and former world record holder, was formidable. And, of course, there was Cordes.

To win a medal, Looze told Miller, he would have to beat his American teammate. At the Olympics, Miller made it through heats and semifinals, reaching the final as a number two seed. Peaty set a world record of 57.55 in the heats and followed with 57.62 in a semifinal, but the next four were separated by .28.

Peaty set another world record, lowering it to 57.13. Van der Burgh took silver in 58.69. Happiest bronze medalist ever: Cody Miller.

"You never think something like this is going to happen until it finally does," Miller said. "I have a lot of people to thank. Everyone back home, all my coaches, my family.

"To be in a heat like that, it was no doubt probably the fastest heat of 100 breaststroke ever, and for me to get my hand on the wall and win a medal for my country, I honestly can't describe how it feels. I'm so happy. I'm feeling good. That was something."

Miller became the Hoosiers' first US Olympic medalist in swimming in forty years. That celebration did not end his Olympics, nor his swimming career. Ryan Murphy (backstroke world record), Miller, Phelps (butterfly), and Nathan Adrian (freestyle) won gold in the 4×100 medley relay, setting an Olympic record of 3:27.95.

On September 9, 2017, Miller married DeWitt, who had become his fiancée. She was by then a schoolteacher in Martinsville, Indiana. They shared a love of Star Wars, Marvel Comics, and Harry Potter.

"Harry was an orphan. I could relate to that," Miller said.

He made it back to the World Championships in 2017, held in Budapest, Hungary, and finished fifth in the 100 breaststroke behind Peaty (gold) and Cordes (silver). Miller swam in prelims of the 4×100 medley relay and picked up another gold.

He built a strong social media presence via Twitter. The self-described nerd and movie buff attracted more than fifty thousand subscribers to his YouTube channel for vlog posts.

In 2018, he developed knee pain and tore a meniscus six weeks before summer nationals. He finished fifth in the 100 breaststroke at Irvine—site of his breakthrough four years before—and thus did not qualify for the 2019 World Championships or for top-tier funding from USA Swimming. He subsequently underwent procedures on both knees in which surgeons removed clotted blood that was suffocating tendons. He represented Team USA in the 2019 Pan American Games at Lima, Peru, winning a silver medal in the 100 breaststroke.

"Someone said to me recently that when things don't go your way and when things get hard, you can either choose to let that affect you and make things worse.

Or let those things become scars that become a part of the fibers that make you stronger," Miller said. "And that is most certainly the way I've handled all of my darker moments in my life. All of my failures, everything, I've always found a way to come out of it and be better and stronger and learn from those things. I honestly believe as humans, we grow and gain strength through our struggles. Struggle breeds strength, and struggle breeds who we are."

Miller had mettle, and the medal to prove it.

Blake Pieroni
2016

Rio Was Prelude, Not Finale

BLAKE PIERONI MIGHT HAVE BECOME A FOOTBALL PLAYER OR BASEBALL slugger. He had the power. But as a twelve-year-old, he watched his idol, Michael Phelps, swim to eight gold medals at the 2008 Beijing Olympics.

"That was pretty impactful," he said.

Pieroni resolved to swim in the Olympics himself. It was surprising to many that he did so eight years later.

Coming off his sophomore season at Indiana University, he was ranked twenty-third in the 100-meter freestyle ahead of the 2016 Olympic Trials, with six selected for the relay team. He made it, competed in preliminaries of the 4×100 freestyle relay at Rio de Janeiro, and was rewarded with a gold medal. Pieroni became the first American male swimmer from IU to win Olympic gold in forty years. Days later, Cody Miller added to that list in the 4×100 medley relay.

The Olympics are the pinnacle for most swimmers. They were an intermediate step for Pieroni.

Over the next two seasons, he earned eight relay world medals, won his first world and US titles, led the Hoosiers to their highest NCAA team finish in forty-three years and set two American records. You want more swimming history? He became the first to swim two hundred yards in less than 1 minute, 30 seconds.

Pieroni was born November 15, 1995, in Crown Point, Indiana, and grew up in nearby Valparaiso. He tried the usual sports—football, baseball, soccer—before qualifying for junior national meets. That made it easier to concentrate on swimming, especially after he arrived at Chesterton High School.

"I've always loved swimming," he said. "I never felt like I was giving up a lot when I decided to just do swimming."

He was a three-time state champion in the 100-yard freestyle, and his time of 43.37 was best in the nation for a high schooler in 2014. He led Chesterton to a

Blake Pieroni
Courtesy of Indiana University Athletics.

mythical national championship that year, swimming on two relay teams that set national public school records. His first international experience came in the 2013 World Junior Championships at Dubai, where he was on a team winning a bronze medal in the 4×200-meter freestyle relay.

"It was on an entirely different level," he said.

After living in Indiana all his life, he wanted to experience something else. Moreover, his father, Christopher, had been a Purdue swimmer. So Pieroni looked at Auburn, Arizona, and Wisconsin for college. But Miller influenced Pieroni, who stayed in the state after all. Pieroni's decision represented "a major breakthrough" in recruiting, Indiana coach Ray Looze said.

After high school, Pieroni enrolled at IU early and trained in Bloomington over the summer. During the 2014 USA Championships, he twice broke the school record in the 100-meter freestyle, clocking 49.90 in prelims and 49.69 in the final. That was historic because the previous record—49.99 by Jim Montgomery at the 1976 Montreal Olympics—was the first time ever under 50 seconds.

"I had never heard of Jim Montgomery," Pieroni said. "The coaches told me he was the first man to break 50 seconds. I was like, 'How is that still the record at IU from 1970-something?'"

He won silver medals in the 100- and 200-meter freestyles later that summer in the Junior Pan Pacific meet at Kihei, Hawaii, and finished fourth in the 200-yard freestyle at the 2015 NCAAs as a freshman.

Over time, his training was enhanced in an environment that he said "kind of breeds from itself." He was around swimmers such as Olympic gold medalists Miller and Lilly King and pro Zane Grothe. Pieroni paid more attention to diet, nutrition, sleep, rest, and recovery. In a sport in which elite male sprinters are six foot four or taller, he is six foot one.

"He's not the biggest guy out there," Looze said. "He really shows up in the big moments."

In 2016, Pieroni won the first of what would become three successive Big Ten sweeps of the 100- and 200-yard freestyles. Still, finishing eighth in the 200 free and tenth in the 100 free at the NCAAs did not project the twenty-year-old as a contender for the Olympic team.

That was especially so after he finished twelfth in semifinals of the 200-meter freestyle, in which he was seeded sixth, during the Olympic Trials at Omaha, Nebraska. He still had the 100 freestyle left.

"I had nothing to lose for the 100 free. The only thing that I could lose was another bad swim," he said.

Pieroni came to the trials with a school record of 49.48, nowhere near fast enough to make the Olympic team. He improved in every round: 49.39, 49.07, 48.78. He finished sixth, and he was Rio-bound. Looze called it "an electric swim." Pieroni changed strategy, breathing on every stroke of the first fifty meters, allowing him a faster second fifty. The final ten meters, he did not take a breath.

"It took a long time to set in, to realize that I would be an Olympian," said Pieroni, who was tattooed with Olympic rings afterward. "At the time, I was just in shock for a while. I didn't really believe it for months maybe."

In Rio, he swam a 48.39 third leg in prelims of the 4×100 freestyle relay, in which the Americans' time of 3:12.38 trailed Russia's 3:12.04. In the final, Caeleb Dressel, Phelps, Ryan Held, and Nathan Adrian won gold in 3:09.92.

Because Pieroni swam prelims, he came away with a gold medal. He said he went into his race with a "one-and-done kind of mentality," knowing he likely would not be in the final. "Being in this atmosphere is everything I could ask for," he said.

Four months after Rio, he won three relay medals in the short course World Championships at Windsor, Ontario. He nearly won an individual bronze, finishing fourth in the 100-meter freestyle.

In 2017, he led the Hoosiers to their first Big Ten team title since 2006. In the NCAAs at Indianapolis, he tied for second in the 200-yard freestyle behind Texas's Townley Haas. Three months later, also in Indianapolis, he was second to Haas in the 200-meter freestyle to make the team for the World Championships. At the worlds in Budapest, Hungary, Pieroni won two golds and one silver in relays.

All of that prefaced what turned out to be his finest season. In 2018, Pieroni led Indiana to a repeat Big Ten title and highest NCAA finish (third) since 1975, set an American record in the 200-yard freestyle, and won his first US championship.

In the 4×200-yard freestyle relay at NCAAs, he led off the Hoosiers in 1:29.63, the first time ever under 1:30. Haas, the 2017 world silver medalist, reclaimed the record to win the 200 freestyle in 1:29.50. Pieroni clocked 1:30.23 to repeat as runner-up. He swam a 40.62 anchor leg for a team that won the 4×100 medley relay, representing Indiana's first NCAA relay victory since 1977.

In four days at NCAAs, he raced thirteen times and earned seven All-America certificates. He did not win two individual titles, as teammate Ian Finnerty did, but was the force behind a Hoosier renaissance. Texas won for the fourth year in a row, outscoring California 449–437½. The Hoosiers scored 422 in the closest three-team race since 1983.

"They're fearless. They remind me of the 1980 US Olympic hockey team," Looze said.

In his first nationals as a pro, Pieroni surged over the closing twenty meters to score an upset victory in the 100-meter freestyle at Irvine, California. He beat the reigning world champion, Dressel, and 2012 Olympic champion, Adrian. Pieroni was first in 48.08, Adrian second in 48.25, and Haas third in 48.30.

Pieroni was active on the 2018 World Cup circuit from September through November 2018, finishing fifth in men's standings. He won six of seven 200-meter freestyle races. He tied Ian Crocker's fourteen-year-old American record with a time of 46.25 in the 200 freestyle (short course meters) on October 5 at Budapest. In winning the 200 freestyle November 17 at Singapore, his time of 1:41.15 came within .07 of Ryan Lochte's eight-year-old American record.

In the December 2018 short course World Championships at Hangzhou, China, the Hoosier came away with three golds, including the 200 freestyle in 1:41.49. In the 2019 long course worlds at Gwangju, South Korea, he finished fourth in the 100 freestyle, or .06 from bronze. He earned three medals in relays, including gold in the 4×100 freestyle relay with Zach Apple, who was coming off his senior season at IU.

Not since the 1970s had two IU swimmers been on the same foursome winning gold at a major championship. Jim Montgomery and John Murphy were in the 4×100 freestyle relay at the 1975 worlds in Cali, Colombia. Mark Spitz teamed with Murphy in the 4×100 free relay and with Mike Stamm in the 4×100 medley relay at the 1972 Munich Olympics.

Pieroni's interests are not confined to the pool. He is a longtime animal lover—his parents' five-acre property includes three horses, four cats, two dogs, chickens, and a parrot—and enjoys paintball and poker. He goes snowboarding and skiing in Colorado and Utah, too, although he might delay those activities until he retires from elite swimming.

Reaching one Olympics turned out to be less than satisfying. Pieroni aimed for Tokyo 2020, and maybe Paris 2024. He said Rio 2016 cannot be the last great thing he does in swimming.

"Something happened after the Olympics," he said. "I was so much more motivated and had so much more confidence. I've had crazy motivation ever since, just want to get better."

Gary Hall, 1969.
IU Archives P0028290.

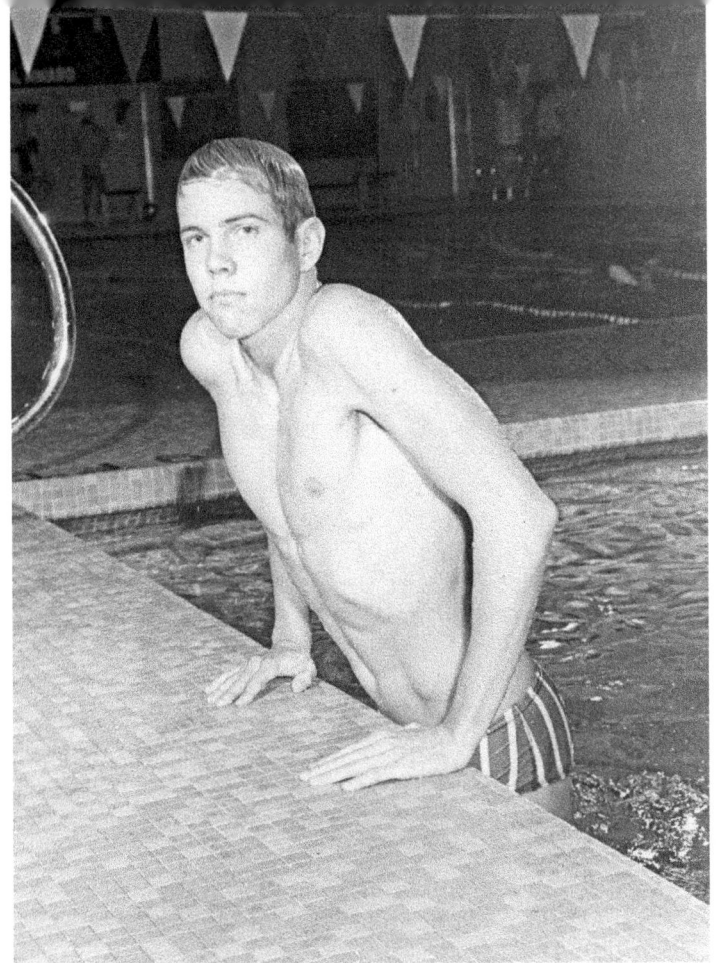

Gary Hall
1968, 1972, 1976

Three Olympics, Three Events, Three Medals

GARY HALL WAS A TEEN PHENOM, MEDALIST AT TWO OLYMPICS, TEN-TIME world record holder, and two-time world swimmer of the year.

Heading into 1976, none of that mattered. Hall had not trained for nine months. He had effectively retired after 1973, a year in which he led Indiana to the last of six consecutive NCAA championships.

"Usually, when you hung it up after college, that was it," he said.

In 1975, he was coaxed into returning to the pool by Charlie Hickox, a former Indiana teammate who edged Hall for the gold medal in the 400-meter individual medley at the 1968 Mexico City Olympics. Hickox was going to law school and Hall to medical school. Hall was training for one hour four times a week, and he was father of Gary Jr., a six-month-old son. Hall said Hickox "tricked" him into competing in the April national championships at Cincinnati. "I ended up going three best times," Hall recalled.

He won the 100-yard butterfly and was encouraged to go for a third Olympics. He reasoned that he retained some speed, and weight training was making him stronger. What could he do if he really trained?

Medical school made that impossible. He did not resume regular workouts until the following January. He became ill and abandoned twice-a-day training because "it was killing me."

Hall likely would not have entered the 1976 nationals if the meet had not been in Long Beach, California, near his hometown. He tied for sixteenth in preliminaries of the 100-yard butterfly, then lost a swim-off. Here he was, less than two months before the Olympic Trials, and he could not even make a consolation final.

"It was like a rude awakening," Hall said. "I went home and worked hard and put that race out of my mind."

In the trials, also in Long Beach, he was fourth-fastest in prelims and needed to be top three in the final to reach a third Olympics. Joe Bottom finished first in 54.97, followed by Hall in 55.05 and Matt Vogel in 55.25. In triumph, Hall held his twenty-one-month-old son high above his head, twenty years before Gary Jr. ascended his own Olympic podium. A photo of them at the pool became one of the most famous sports photos of the era.

Gary Sr. had been barely seventeen at his first Olympics, and now he was going back at age twenty-four. Moreover, he was elected American flag bearer at the opening ceremony in Montreal. No other swimmer would do so until Michael Phelps in 2016.

"To me, that was more important than winning the gold medal," Hall said.

Hall was captain of a men's swimming team that won twelve of thirteen gold medals, twenty-seven of a possible thirty-five medals, set world records in eleven events, and achieved 1-2-3 sweeps in five. Hall attributed it all to the psychological ploys by Doc Counsilman, his coach at Indiana.

"Nothing could be explained on a physical basis," Hall said. "It was an emotionally charged team. It led us to compete at a level beyond what we thought we were capable of."

Vogel, of Fort Wayne, Indiana, won the 100-meter butterfly in 54.35, just 0.08 off the world record set by Mark Spitz at the 1972 Munich Olympics. Joe Bottom and Hall were second and third in 54.50 and 54.65. Hall said he was leading for ninety meters. If he hadn't decided to "go for it," Hall said, there would have been no bronze medal.

"I was on the podium, and I was happy," he said. "I did the time I wanted to do. I didn't win, but I did my best effort."

Because Hall did not win an Olympic gold medal, he might be omitted from a list of greatest swimmers of all time. Yet consider that Hall set world records in four events and both individual medleys, medaled in three Olympics in three different events, and joined Spitz as the first collegians to win at least one event a year on teams winning four straight NCAA championships. The first 200-point swimmers in NCAA history were Spitz with 218 points and Hall with 214½.

Hall was born August 7, 1951, in Fayetteville, North Carolina. He was raised in Garden Grove, California, playing the usual sports like basketball and baseball. By age six or seven, he was a swimmer. He liked shooting hoops, but...

"I was kind of a runt," he said.

He was close to quitting swimming altogether at age thirteen. He was five foot five, 115 pounds. Then he grew two or three inches and gained twenty-five pounds, and he was on his way.

He was coached at Anaheim High School by Jon Urbanchek, who coached at Michigan from 1984 to 2006 and won thirteen Big Ten team titles. But Hall said his next coach was a math teacher who knew nothing about swimming, and he said, "I thought my career would end there." Not for someone as devoted as Hall. He had a reputation for swimming twice a day for his club team, then sneaking into the pool at the Disneyland Hotel for a third workout.

Hall linked up with a new coach, the innovative Flip Darr, at Rancho Alamitos High School. Darr later coached Shirley Babashoff and other swimmers who earned a total of nine Olympic medals.

Heading into the 1968 Olympic Trials at Los Angeles, Hall's club coach was Don Gambril, hall-of-famer. Hall was second-slowest qualifier in both the 400-meter individual medley and 200 butterfly. The events were on the same day, so Hall picked the IM on a coin flip. In a morning prelim, Hall chopped seven seconds off his previous best. Gambril was so stunned that he dropped his stopwatch on the pool deck, breaking the crystal. Hall cut off two more seconds in the final and finished third, making the team.

"But I was just happy to be there," Hall said. "My whole life I was thinking '72 would really be my Olympics."

He also made the 1968 team in the 200 backstroke by finishing third. He recalled being one of five high school swimmers on the men's Olympic team, and all but one chose Indiana for college. Training camp was at the high altitude of Colorado Springs in an attempt to prepare for Mexico City's elevation. Swimmers were lodged at the Broadmoor Hotel dormitory, usually reserved for figure skaters. Hall said it was a cliquish, fragmented team. Moreover, it was his first international experience, and men's and women's teams had no interaction.

"For being my first time, it was something I was blown away by," Hall said. "It was every man for himself."

American swimmers dominated at Mexico City but could have performed better, Hall said. Hickox and Hall swam side by side for virtually the entire 400 IM, with Hickox winning in 4:48.4 to Hall's 4:48.7. Hall was fourth in the 200 backstroke, a distant 1.7 seconds from bronze. Hall was also blown away by Counsilman, and there was little question he would become a Hoosier. Hall said he was not impressed by high-pressure recruiting tactics, and he was attracted by the coach's personality and scientific approach.

That Indiana had scored a recruiting coup was underscored when Hall, who had just turned eighteen, won three titles and set four world records (two in the 400 IM) in the August 1969 nationals at Louisville, Kentucky. So Hall was a world swimmer of the year before he was an NCAA champion.

He was world swimmer of the year again in 1970, beating out Spitz. At the 1970 nationals, Hall scored an upset victory in the 200-meter butterfly over Spitz, who had set a world record of 2:05.4 in morning prelims. Hall lowered that to 2:05.0 in the final.

Hall won three NCAA titles in 1971 and two in 1972, leading the Hoosiers to their fourth and fifth successive team trophies. In 1971, as sophomore, he swam in five events—including twice in relays—and each time swam the distance faster than anyone in history. That performance ranks next to Spitz's 1972 Munich Olympics "as the two greatest meets any swimmer ever has had," according to Counsilman.

Hall credited Counsilman for creating a culture fostering excellence. Indiana swimmers would break American records in practice. The coach was funny but demanding, analytical but relational. In this sport, Hall said, Counsilman "is regarded almost like a deity, a god." Despite assembling a team of superstars—in summer 1970, IU swimmers held nine of twelve recognized world records—Counsilman "made everyone feel like a teacher's pet," Hall said.

As much as Spitz, who went on to win a record seven gold medals, Munich was supposed to belong to Hall. Indeed, the two were roommates at NCAA Championships, a pairing that worked because they raced in different events. That changed in Munich because they opposed each other in the 200-meter butterfly. That wasn't the best event for Hall, who had set world records of 2:09.30 and 4:03.81 in the 200 and 400 IMs on successive days during the Olympic Trials at Chicago.

The 200 butterfly was the first Munich final for Spitz, who broke his own world record with a time of 2:00.70. Hall won silver, but far behind in 2:02.86. That turned out to be his only podium there. In retrospect, Hall said, he should have conceded to Spitz. The 400 IM was next, and Hall could not regroup.

"I lost my confidence in the 400 IM," he said. "I just swam a terrible prelim. I didn't sleep well, I didn't have it. Biggest event of my life, and I didn't have it. I destroyed myself."

Sweden's Gunnar Larsson won 400 IM gold in 4:31.98, the same time as the United States' Tim McKee, who was declared silver medalist by two thousandths of a second (0.002). (Thereafter, rules were changed so that same times to a hundredth were a tie.) Both swimmers were more than a second slower than the world record set by Hall, who was fifth in 4:37.38.

Hall had not lost a 400 IM since Mexico City. The slow prelim left him panicky. "That's what I could never understand. Why that day?" he said. "When I made the last turn, I knew it was over. I think I was fifth. Tears were flowing from my eyes the whole last lap."

Hall did not medal in the 200 IM, either, finishing fourth in 2:08.49—but under his world record from the Olympic Trials. Larsson took gold in 2:07.17. The Swede was going to win, Hall said, no matter what. If he'd been told before the Olympics that he would break his world record, Hall would have been satisfied. Yet the scar from the 400 IM remains.

"Every other race I swam in the Olympics, almost across the board, was the best race I could have done," Hall said.

He could have retired after the 1973 NCAAs. He had already set ten world records and twenty-three American records, won seven NCAA titles, and medaled in two Olympics. A career as an eye surgeon awaited.

A case could be made that Hall is the greatest swimmer never to have won Olympic gold. It would have meant a lot, he said, but he is content with what he did achieve. We all hate to lose, he said.

"But at the same time, as a person, we all have to learn to lose at something," Hall said. "And there's a valuable lesson, even at the Olympics. Even though it's an amazing glory and honor to win at the Olympics, not having done that left me hungrier for life. I looked back and thought maybe that wasn't such a bad thing. It left that little bit of drive inside me. I wanted to go and achieve that gold medal in something.

"Winning life's gold medal... how do you balance yourself in life? I think that's for God to decide. It's not about being the best at anything. It's about being good at a lot of things and being balanced in your life."

Hall married Mary Keating, whose father, Charles Keating Jr., was convicted (later overturned) in the saving and loans scandals of the 1990s. Hall's son, Gary Jr., won ten medals at the 1996, 2000, and 2004 Olympics. Often cited by the NCAA as a model student-athlete, Gary Sr. became an ophthalmologist in Phoenix.

After retiring from his medical practice, Hall continued to compete in triathlons and swimming events. He moved to the Florida Keys to help direct The Race Club, designed to train elite swimmers, and conduct swimming camps. He maintained residences in Islamorada, Florida, and Coronado, California.

Jim Montgomery
1976

Barrier Breaker

AT AGE FOURTEEN, JIM MONTGOMERY COULD NOT HAVE ENVISIONED WHAT a fateful decision this would be.

Jim Pettinger, his age-group coach in Madison, Wisconsin, told him he could go places if he concentrated on swimming. That meant giving up football, basketball, and baseball. No more ice hockey, water skiing, snow skiing, or golf, either.

So Montgomery focused on swimming. The coach was prescient.

The sport took the swimmer to places beyond Indiana University and the medals podium. It transported him to World Championships in Yugoslavia, Colombia, and Germany. It made him something of an immortal, considering he became the first man ever under fifty seconds in the 100-meter freestyle. That was akin to Roger Bannister's 1954 feat of becoming the first to run a sub-four-minute mile. Montgomery broke four individual world records and was on relay teams setting seven more.

He was born January 24, 1955, in Madison. He learned to swim when he was two and started racing in summer country club meets when he was seven or eight. He swam for the Madison Downtown YMCA from ages nine to fourteen, competing only in winter. That's when he switched over to Pettinger at the Badger Dolphin Swim Club. At Madison East High School, he won six state titles. At eighteen, before he even represented the Hoosiers, he won a then-record five gold medals in the 1973 World Championships at Belgrade. He won the 100- and 200-meter freestyles and was on three winning relay teams.

Although Montgomery was a splendid sight churning through the water—"He'll get up high and plane water like a speedboat," Tennessee coach Ray Bussard said—he was downright scary in the starting blocks.

Jim Montgomery, 1974.
IU Archives P0028378.

"He could intimidate," Indiana coach Doc Counsilman said. "He was six-six, 212, and he'd tell the swimmer beside him, 'I'm going to beat the hell out of you.' Jim was probably the greatest competitor I ever had."

And, the coach added, "the meanest."

As an Indiana freshman, Montgomery was NCAA champion in the 200-yard freestyle and two relays and was on two more champion relays the next year. In

1975, he lowered the world record in the 100-meter freestyle to 51.12 in the heats, although he was just bronze medalist in the World Championships at Cali. But the next month, he lowered the record—again—to 50.59 at the AAU Championships.

The year of Jim Montgomery was 1976.

First, he won Big Ten and NCAA titles in the 100- and 200-yard freestyles. He made the Olympic team in the 100- and 200-meter freestyles, winning the former in 50.95 after a 50.79 prelim at the Olympic Trials. Then he became a key figure on one of the greatest teams ever assembled—any country, any sport, any era.

The 1976 US swim team was as ascendant as the 1992 basketball Dream Team. American men won twelve of thirteen gold medals at Montreal, twenty-seven of a possible thirty-five medals (77 percent), set world records in eleven events and achieved 1-2-3 sweeps in five. Team USA coach was Counsilman, then fifty-five. As renowned as he was as an innovator and scientist, he was also a psychologist. "He's the smartest guy I've ever known in my entire life," Montgomery said. "Just sheer brain power. And he had a sense of humor."

At the end of the Olympic Trials in Long Beach, California, Counsilman called all men on the team together. The scene must have resembled one from the movie *Miracle*, when Herb Brooks, coach of the 1980 Olympic hockey team, asked the players, "Who are you playing for?" Finally, one player replied satisfactorily, "United States of America."

College rivalries, especially between Southern California and Indiana, were intense in 1970s swimming. Counsilman intervened. If we all pull for each other, he told the Trojans and Hoosiers and everyone else, we can all swim faster. Because we are not going to Montreal to win medals, the coach said. We are going to win *all* the medals.

"He just put it right on the plate," Montgomery said. "'We're going to absolutely dominate. That's my goal, and that's my goal for you guys.'"

The swimmers were energized, but Counsilman was only beginning motivational ploys. He announced there would not be one head coach, but three. He assigned eight swimmers to himself and eight to each of two assistant coaches, George Haines and Don Gambril.

It is difficult to peak for the trials and again for the Olympics, but something unexplainable happened during team training camp. The swimmers were growing closer, and they were growing faster.

"That's the only team I've been on that everybody sacrificed their individual self and really put the team first," Montgomery said.

In Montreal, Counsilman had a team meeting before each night's finals in his room, across the street from the pool. The message was the same: we are sweeping every event tonight. "One, two, three!" the swimmers shouted.

The coach reached into a closet and brought out two objects: a flag and a broom. Swimmers walked arm-in-arm, led by a flag carrier, chanting, "Sweep, sweep, sweep."

The first final was the 200-meter butterfly, in which East Germany's Roger Pyttel held the world record of 1:59.63, becoming the first ever under two minutes. One-two-three was out of the question. Yet Michael Bruner won the gold medal, lowering the world record to 1:59.23. American teammates Steven Gregg and Bill Forrester were second and third.

"We all looked at each other and thought, 'My God! He's right. We can do it,'" former IU swimmer Gary Hall said. "It was one sweep after another."

Montgomery won gold medals in the 4×200 freestyle and 4×100 medley relays, both in world records. In the 200 freestyle—another sweep—he was bronze medalist behind Bruce Furniss, who set a world record of 1:50.29, and USC's John Naber, who had won the 100 backstroke an hour earlier.

On the last of eight days of swimming came Montgomery's signature event, the 100-meter freestyle. By then, he was feeling tattered around the edges.

"Mentally, they were just carrying me out of there on a stretcher," he said. "It was a long time to keep it going."

In the heats, he lowered his world record to 50.39, breaking Mark Spitz's Olympic record of 51.22. In the final, Montgomery delivered his breakthrough of 49.99. It was another medal sweep, with teammates Jack Babashoff second in 50.81 and Peter Nocke third in 51.31.

"Fifty seconds was the last barrier," Counsilman said. "It's like breaking a minute, which happened fifty years ago. It has taken that long to get down [from sixty seconds to fifty], and there's no way anyone's ever going to break forty."

At that moment, Montgomery said, he did not consider 49.99 a big deal. He just wanted to win. Counsilman approached him and said the landmark achievement would mean more to him later than it did in the moment.

"And he was exactly right," Montgomery said.

Thereafter, Olympic swimming events were limited to two per country. Never again will there be the same three flags raised at a swimming medal ceremony. It is perhaps a moot point. Swimming has expanded, featuring more participating nations. Eighteen countries won swim medals in 2016, compared with eight in 1976.

Montgomery's world record lasted twenty days. In the AAU Championships at Philadelphia, Jonty Skinner, barred from the Olympics because of South Africa's policy of racial apartheid, lowered the mark to 49.44.

In 1977, Montgomery again won Big Ten titles in the 100- and 200-yard freestyles before finishing third and second, respectively, at the NCAAs. In the medley relay, he swam the 100-yard freestyle anchor leg in 42.51—nearly a full second under the American record of 43.49—to bring Indiana from behind. It proved to be a historic victory. It was the last of Counsilman's fifty-eight NCAA individual or relay championships, at least one a year in each of the final sixteen nationals in which the Hoosiers participated.

Montgomery pushed on toward another Olympics, winning bronze in the 100-meter freestyle and gold in the 400 free relay in the 1978 World Championships at West Berlin. He teamed with Babashoff, Rowdy Gaines, and David McCagg for a time of 3:19.74 in the last of his world records.

Then the United States boycotted the 1980 Moscow Games, so Montreal was Montgomery's only Olympics. Because he had registered as a masters swimmer, rules at the time made him ineligible for trials picking the team for the 1984 Los Angeles Olympics.

He began participating in open-water races and won the 2.4-mile Waikiki Roughwater Ocean swim in 1986. As a masters swimmer, he won fourteen world championships, including a 1994 return to the Montreal pool where he won his three Olympic golds.

Montgomery founded a Dallas masters swimming program in 1981 and was US Masters Swimming coach of the year in 2002. He was a consultant to those designing aquatics facilities and coached a high school team in Addison, Texas. He was active in Dallas 2012, a group attempting to bring the Olympics to Texas. In 2016, he launched the Jim Montgomery Swim School.

He was inducted into the International Swimming Hall of Fame in 1986. He and his wife, Diane, have five children.

Mark Spitz, 1972.
© *Bloomington Herald Times.*
IU Archives P0041935.

Mark Spitz
1968, 1972

Perfect Seven in Munich

HE HAD THE GOLD MEDALS, THE GOOD LOOKS, THE ICONIC *SPORTS ILLUS-trated* cover, the million-dollar endorsements. Mark Spitz had it all in 1972.

There were moments less than four years before, however, when he had none of it. The so-called world's greatest swimmer had flamed out at the 1968 Mexico City Olympics, leaving without an individual gold medal. American teammates openly rooted against him.

Spitz, who was about to enter college, had planned to decompress after that October's Olympics and enroll somewhere in January. His intended destination, Stanford, had rejected his application. He committed instead to Long Beach State, which had won the 1968 NCAA Division II championship and was coached by Don Gambril, who was close to the Spitz family. Spitz had reservations about the pick—he never signed a national letter of intent—but neither did he actively look at other universities.

In December, Spitz toured South America with other American Olympians, including a teammate from the Santa Clara Swim Club, Mitch Ivey. Ivey wanted to transfer from Stanford, and the school he spoke about most was Indiana. Spitz remembered the camaraderie of Indiana swimmers from the pre-Olympics camp but did not know a lot about coach Don Counsilman. There was no internet, no Twitter. The Hoosiers were coming off their first NCAA team title, and Spitz had heard others elaborate about Counsilman's research and innovation. The coach's book that became the sport's bible, *The Science of Swimming*, was not published until 1968.

Coincidentally, Spitz's flight back from South America included a layover in Miami, and the Hoosiers were training nearby in Fort Lauderdale. He showed up at Counsilman's hotel room, telling the coach he had decided to go to Indiana. Counsilman, dumbfounded, told Spitz to discuss it with Gambril. The IU coach also said he needed to submit an application and asked that he take the ACT entrance exam again so there would be no accusation of impropriety.

Make no mistake, though. Counsilman knew what he was getting. "Mark is the greatest natural swimmer I've ever seen," the coach once said.

On Spitz's arrival home, his parents, Arnold and Lenore, were angry with their son. They talked about it in a hospital room while awaiting Mark's scheduled tonsillectomy. The swimmer made his case: the positive vibe of IU swimmers, full scholarship (Long Beach offered a partial one), improved chances of dental school, respect for Counsilman's methods, ease he felt around the coach. When the conversation ended, his parents agreed the decision showed maturity.

Spitz flew to Bloomington to take the ACT in mid-January on the same weekend Joe Namath and the New York Jets upset the Baltimore Colts in the Super Bowl, changing the NFL. Change was coming to college swimming, too. There was a scare when the Californian slipped on an icy sidewalk and landed flat on his back, but Spitz was undeterred. He was coming to Indiana. A week before Spitz was to be at Long Beach, he called Gambril and told him. It is hard to comprehend, especially a half-century later: the greatest athlete in IU history was not actively recruited by IU.

"It was kind of fluky that he ended up at Indiana," said Gary Hall, a Californian who would become Spitz's college teammate.

Hoosier swimmers had mixed feelings about Spitz. As team cocaptain Fred Southwood put it, if he couldn't get along with people he had known all his life, how would he adjust to new teammates in a new place? Counsilman made it clear to all: give Spitz benefit of the doubt and judge him on what he does at Indiana, not on reputation.

Hall first met Spitz at an age-group meet years before. With the newcomer, the Indiana team remained close-knit. There would be no berating or criticism of each other, and especially not of Spitz.

"Doc didn't put up with any of that," Hall said.

Counsilman had a gift for assembling talented swimmers and making each one "feel like a teacher's pet," Hall said. If Spitz needed special treatment, the coach was willing to accommodate that. For instance, before each practice, Spitz would stick his toes in the water and complain it was too cold. He would stall on deck until Counsilman took off his belt and chased him around the pool, through the stands, and back into the water.

Hall and Spitz roomed with each other at NCAA Championships. They weren't in the same events anyway, and there was no tension.

"He could be difficult," Hall said. "But in that way, we all said, 'Ah, that's Mark.'" Spitz and other swimmers often ended up at Counsilman's house for meals or study time. Hall recalled the coach locking Spitz in a room and checking on him every half hour. It was open house. Spitz became friends with his roommate, Canadian swimmer George Smith, and joined a fraternity. He sneaked a beer or two, and Counsilman pretended not to know.

Spitz said the coach did not help much with his strokes but with his outlook. For years, Spitz said, he had been told he was stupid. When he started beating all comers in swimming, he compensated by becoming cocky. Simply put, Counsilman made Spitz feel good.

"When he came to me, his self-image was pretty low, and I felt he didn't have a true picture of himself," Counsilman said. "He felt very competent athletically, but he didn't think he was very smart because some people had told him he wasn't. And he didn't feel competent socially."

It would be no exaggeration to suggest Counsilman saved Spitz's swimming career. Or at least allowed Spitz to fulfill his considerable potential. After all, Spitz was a national champion by age sixteen and set his first world record when he was seventeen.

"I went through an identity crisis," Spitz said. "The things that happened [at IU] enabled me to stay in swimming and keep going four years after Mexico City. I don't think Doc received enough recognition for that."

Spitz finished his career with nine gold, one silver, and one bronze medal from two Olympic Games; five golds from the 1967 Pan American Games; thirty-three world records; thirty-eight American records; twenty-four national AAU titles; and eight NCAA titles. He won the 1971 Sullivan Award as America's top amateur athlete and was a three-time world swimmer of the year (1967, 1971, 1972).

Before Counsilman, Spitz's main influences were Santa Clara Swim Club coach George Haines and his father. The swimmer was born to Jewish parents on February 8, 1950, in Modesto, California. His father's family was from Hungary and his mother's from Russia. When Spitz was two, his family moved to Honolulu, where he swam at Waikiki Beach. The family returned to California when he was six. When he was eight, he was enrolled in a swim program at the Sacramento YMCA. By age ten, he was working out for ninety minutes a day and setting age-group records.

Arnold Spitz was tough, aggressive, and direct. He eventually became operations manager for Schnitzer Steel Products in Oakland, a large scrap-metal firm. Before there were terms such as *helicopter parent* or *soccer mom*, his father relentlessly and unapologetically pushed his precocious son.

"If I pushed Mark, it was part of his development," the father once told *Sports Illustrated*. "And you know why I pushed him? Because he was so great, that's why. I can't believe a parent would say, 'Honey, if you're tired, you don't have to go to work out.' A child who has his parents behind him can govern his time, know there's a time to work and a time to play. If the parent isn't behind the child, there can be nothing outstanding, and it's not really a sacrifice. It's love.

"Swimming isn't everything," Arnold Spitz continued. "Winning is."

When Mark was nine, his father took him to the Arden Hills Swim Club near Sacramento so he could be coached by Sherm Chavoor, whose career landed him in the International Swimming Hall of Fame. In 1961, the family moved to Walnut Creek, California, near Oakland. Spitz went from one program to another until Chavoor recommended that the boy go to George Haines of the Santa Clara Swim Club, which was a forty-mile drive from their house. Mother and son arose at five o'clock each morning to attend workouts until the family relocated to Santa Clara.

"That was the turning point in my life," Spitz said. "That was the point where I really went into swimming for a business, where I decided that I wanted to be good, to be somebody." His ascent was dizzying:

- 1964, age fourteen: first AAU nationals
- 1965: first Maccabiah Games in Israel
- 1966: first national title, in 100-meter butterfly, beating world-record holder Luis Nacolao of Argentina, a Santa Clara teammate; comes within four-tenths of a second of a world record in the 1,500-meter freestyle; sets national high school records in 100-yard butterfly and 200-yard individual medley
- 1967: at seventeen, leads a Santa Clara High School team that was designated the best ever by *Swimming World* magazine, breaks seven world records in three and a half months, and wins five Pan Am golds at Winnipeg, Manitoba

Spitz was a club teammate of Don Schollander, hero of the 1964 Tokyo Olympics with four gold medals. Spitz aimed to surpass Schollander's achievements, and in doing so irritated the older swimmer by always moving to train in a lane next to him.

"I got a secret charge knowing that I had the capacity to exasperate him," Spitz said.

In 1967, he did more than exasperate Schollander. In an obscure meet at San Leandro, California, he humiliated him. It was the Don Schollander 400 Freestyle Challenge, and Spitz approached the race so cavalierly that he wore two swimsuits. Afterward, Haines excitedly rushed to Spitz to tell him his time, 4:10.6. Spitz said the well-beaten Schollander was "dumbfounded" by the teenager's first world record. Haines stoked the rivalry, increasing friction between the two swimmers.

"I'll never forget it," Spitz said of his first world record. "I remember the warmth of the sun, how the air and chlorinated water smelled. I remember every lap of that swim."

Spitz lost that world record nine days later to France's Alain Mosconi, then regained it July 7 with a time of 4:08.8 at the Santa Clara Invitational. On his first trip with the US senior team, Spitz set world records in the 100- and 200-meter butterfly en route to five golds in Winnipeg. Spitz lowered the American record in the 100 butterfly again October 7 in West Berlin.

Out of the pool, Spitz acted his age. He was boastful and immature. Older teammates resented him. He endured anti-Jewish taunts and was spat at, scratched, elbowed, and kicked in the groin. The rift perhaps contributed to his humbling Olympics the next year. Spitz's father blamed Haines for being so aloof that he was oblivious to the intraclub tension. Haines attributed it to jealously and dismissed the conflict.

"I'll say this for Mark; whenever he said he could so something, he could do it," Haines said.

The Olympic year, which was Spitz's senior year of high school, started auspiciously enough.

In February, he set one American record in the 200-yard butterfly and swam on a medley relay team that set another. In March, he traveled to Germany and was unbeaten there, including an 800-meter freestyle faster than the world record. In May, in the Central Coast Section meet at Cupertino, he broke Schollander's national high school record in the 200-yard freestyle by seven-tenths of a second, won the 100 butterfly, and took a full second off the 100 freestyle national record to lead off a relay. *Swimming World* magazine posited that Santa Clara High School could have finished fifth in the NCAA.

Spitz began long course season by setting his third world record in the 400-meter freestyle. In the AAU Championships at Lincoln, Nebraska, he scored an upset victory in the 200 freestyle over Schollander, who had not lost the race at nationals since 1962. He won his signature 100 butterfly but was upset in the 200 fly by Carl Robie, the 1964 Olympic silver medalist. In the 100 freestyle, Spitz again beat Schollander, 53.6 to 53.7.

Heading into the Olympic Trials, the question was not whether Spitz would make the US team but how many events he would swim and medals he could win. Even given the 7,300-foot altitude at Mexico City, coach and swimmer reasoned that five or six gold medals were possible.

"Maybe we tried to do too much, but I don't think so," Haines said. "The only thing I worried about was him being so young and whether the pressure would get to him. I think it probably did."

The Olympic Trials, held in Long Beach, did not reveal any warning signs. Spitz began by setting a world record of 55.6 in the 100 butterfly and beat Doug Russell, who held the record for five weeks in 1967 before Spitz broke it. After a day off, Spitz won again, coming from behind to take the 200 fly in 2:05.9, or just 0.2 off his own world record.

There was delay in announcement of results of the 100 freestyle because electronic touch pads were unreliable and decisions were left to judges. Zac Zorn tied Ken Walsh's world record of 52.6, followed by Walsh in 53.1. Spitz was third in 53.3, ahead of Schollander, whose shocking fifth-place finish left him with just two Mexico City events.

After the trials, Spitz's Olympic schedule guaranteed him five races, and possibly a sixth. Spitz supposedly did not forecast his gold-medal haul. Haines did: "Personally, I think he can swim them all." News media pounced on the pronouncement, and headlines reflected the bold prediction.

The United States had a pre-Olympics training camp at the Air Force Academy, where the 7,258-foot altitude in Colorado Springs, Colorado, mimicked that of

Mexico City. Given all that happened there, maybe the eighteen-year-old Spitz had little chance for a breakthrough Olympics. Tonsillitis knocked him out of the first thirteen practices, which was the important hard training. The team was cliquish and divisive. Hall, who became Spitz's college teammate, said Spitz "responded really negatively" to condescending comments from older swimmers.

Another incident reflected how bad things had become. On the eve of Spitz's first Olympic race, coach Don Gambril told him and other swimmers to shave arms and legs, as is customary. The only bathtub in the dormitory belonged to William Lippman, chairman of the US Olympic swimming and diving committee. He had assigned himself the only room with a tub and TV. Swimmers began congregating there, so Lippman padlocked the door. Gambril broke the lock so that swimmers could use the tub. Spitz went last, so he was caught when an indignant Lippman returned to the room. Spitz attempted to explain, but the team leader berated him as if he were a burglar.

The slights at training camp, shock of a student massacre before the Olympics, black power demonstration in Olympic Stadium, and lack of any friends on the team all combined to depress Spitz. Yet he kept his thoughts to himself.

All that notwithstanding, he earned a gold medal in his first Olympic race. He swam the fastest 100-meter relay leg (52.7) as the United States set a world record of 3:31.7 in the 4×100 freestyle relay.

After advancing through trials and semifinals of the 100 freestyle the next day, Spitz was set for the eight-man final. It turned out to be disappointing not only for him, but for Team USA, which featured the two men sharing the world record—Zorn, twenty-one, and Walsh, twenty-three. Zorn started fast but faded to eighth. Michael Wenden, an eighteen-year-old Australian, lowered the world record to 52.2 with the biggest victory margin at the Olympics in forty years. Walsh took silver in 52.8 and Spitz bronze in 53.0.

The outcome of 100 butterfly was devastating to the eighteen-year-old Californian. Not only did he own the world record, but Spitz had beaten Russell in nine previous races, always by coming from behind. This time, Russell did not start as fast as he usually did, allowing Spitz to touch first at fifty meters. The three Americans—Spitz, Russell, and Ross Wales—were virtually even with twenty-five meters left.

"When I got to the middle of the pool, coming home in the last fifty, I knew was going to win," Russell said.

Russell took gold in an Olympic record of 55.9, followed by Spitz in 56.4 and Wales in 57.2. Spitz could not believe he had lost.

"When the ceremony was over, someone had to nudge me to get off the podium. I felt like the loneliest person on earth," Spitz said.

The night grew worse. His time on the third leg of the 4×200 freestyle was nearly five seconds slower than his swim-off at the Olympic Trials, leaving it to

Schollander to hold off Wenden and allow the United States to win gold over Australia. Teammates were angry Spitz had not given up his relay spot to someone else, costing them an Olympic or world record.

After eight swims in five days, Spitz had three days to regroup before the 200 butterfly, in which he held the world record. It did not help. Spitz made the final but finished last. Robie, relegated to silver in 1964, upgraded to gold.

For Spitz, Mexico meant misery. There was no six-gold haul. Just two relay golds plus an individual silver and bronze. He offered no excuses.

"I can just be disappointed in myself," he said. "I didn't swim up to my potential. I had the worst meet of my life."

If that timing could not have been worse, timing could not have been better for Spitz thereafter. He arrived in college just as freshman eligibility was being reinstated. He was joining a developing dynasty. He would be in the shelter of an Indiana program for the four years leading up to the next Olympics, training with world-class swimmers under an innovative coach.

Spitz had a mentor in Counsilman, who talked to him about things other than swimming, like photography and stereos. Spitz worked a few hours a week in Counsilman's shop, assembling pace clocks that the coach had invented and was selling nationwide. The extra cash allowed Spitz to cover his losses in card games. It even helped that one of the Hoosier swimmers, Ronnie Jacks, a Canadian, was able to make Spitz feel included by teasing him.

Even better? Spitz's first NCAA Championships was in Bloomington, before a celebratory crowd at Royer Pool. The toughest part of the 1969 buildup for Counsilman was limiting his squad, under a new rule, to eighteen. Didn't matter. Indiana scored in every event, piled up 427 points, and won by 121 over runner-up Southern California—each a record for the NCAAs. Charlie Hickox, a triple gold medalist at Mexico City, won two events and Spitz three. Counsilman asserted it was the greatest college team in history.

"No team ever had two swimmers like that, because there never were two swimmers like them," the coach said.

Spitz first won the 500-yard freestyle over Hans Fassnacht, a German representing Long Beach State, the school he had spurned. Spitz's time was just off the American record he and Fassnacht had shared from the heats. Spitz followed with another American record, 1:39.5 in the 200 freestyle, to break the mark he had set in high school. In the 4×200 freestyle relay, he trailed by three body lengths to start the anchor leg and nearly overtook USC, which set an American record. Spitz's third win was the first of his four NCAA titles in the 100 butterfly, beating Olympic teammate Wales.

Councilman said Spitz began fighting for the team as much as did for himself. When the jubilant Hoosiers went off the diving board, Spitz jumped along with everybody else. The Hoosiers had it easy enough in the Big Ten a year later, winning their tenth straight conference title in the home pool. But the 1970 NCAAs revisited all of Spitz's anxieties: high altitude and Doug Russell. The meet's location was Salt Lake City, which is 4,226 feet above sea level—not as high as Mexico City, but enough to revive bad memories.

Spitz was second and third in the 50- and 200-yard freestyles, respectively. Those weren't the races that worried him. The one that did was the 100 butterfly, in which he was matched against Russell, who won Olympic gold in Spitz's signature event. Russell, of Texas-Arlington, had skipped the 1969 college season. Spitz had skipped the previous year's AAU nationals. So this would be their first meeting since Mexico City.

As the fly finalists approached the starting blocks, the Hoosiers began chanting, "Let's go, Spitz-O!" The rival USC swimmers started, "Let's go Russell!" In the compressed space of a natatorium, even with a high ceiling, it was like living in surround sound. USC coach Peter Daland recalled few races with as much excitement. Spitz clenched his fists so tightly that he had difficulty opening them for his strokes. He false-started, he said, because his hands cramped up. He conceded he was also trying to "ice" Russell as a football coach would do to an opponent's kicker. Russell allowed later that he was tense from two years of pent-up emotion.

Russell reverted to his usual strategy, leading from the start. He remained in front when both touched the wall at seventy-five yards, but Spitz was gaining. The Hoosier did to Russell as Russell had done to him in Mexico City, waiting to make his move until the closing strokes. Spitz touched first, barely, in 49.82.

"I have a lot of respect for Russell. But he never broke my records, and to me the best swimmer is the most consistent one," Spitz said afterward. "This was very satisfying to me, because I proved to myself I could beat him. I can't forget losing, and I never will. My worst moment was at the Olympics, and my best, maybe, was tonight."

In the 1970 AAU nationals at Los Angeles, he was disappointed not to race Russell in the 100-meter butterfly but won anyway, missing his world record by a half-second with a time of 56.12. He won the 200 freestyle the next day, then surprised himself by setting world records in prelims of both 200 butterfly and 100 freestyle. He lost in both finals, but it had not been a serious summer for him.

The differences between Counsilman, who kept meticulous training logs, and Spitz, who loathed practice, were sometimes comical. When Hoosier swimmers played water polo in the fall to stay in shape, Spitz virtually disappeared for three months. In December, when dual meets began, he would finally show up.

One year, no sooner did he arrive at the pool than he wanted to leave. He had not been in the water since August. Counsilman, exasperated, agreed to let him leave if he could break 50 seconds in the 100-yard butterfly. At the time, the American record was 49.1, and only two men had ever broken 50 seconds. Spitz went out and clocked 49.6. He was Usain Bolt in a Speedo. "And we're all going, 'Oh my God. That's a time what would've won the NCAAs!'" Hall recalled. "Mark just said, 'I'll see ya later, guys,' and he was outta there."

The 1971 college season proceeded without incident—the Hoosiers were unbeaten in dual meets, streaking toward what would become 140 straight victories, and won the Big Ten by a record 276 points—until the NCAA Championships. Spitz had always been a hypochondriac, but this time he was correct—he was sick. On the flight to Ames, Iowa, for the NCAAs, his coach noticed a red blotch on Spitz's neck. With one Hoosier swimmer recovering from German measles, Counsilman figured that's what Spitz had contracted. So the coach concocted a ruse intended to persuade Spitz he was fine. When the Hoosiers arrived at their hotel, Counsilman ordered everyone to shave down immediately, a day earlier than usual. After Spitz finished, he noticed a red spot on his chest. He was pale, and his joints ached. He told Counsilman, who replied it was nothing but razor rash.

Spitz began by finishing fourth in the 50-yard freestyle, but he subsequently won the 200 and 100 butterfly races. He somehow ignored obvious signs of illness—splotches, shivers, aches—and helped Indiana win a fourth straight team title. On the flight home, Counsilman told Spitz he thought it was indeed the measles. Spitz laughed about it later but vowed not to trust his coach for medical diagnoses.

With the Olympics a year away, summer of 1971 took on more significance. At the AAU nationals in Houston, Spitz prefaced what he would accomplish in Munich. He swam to a historic four victories, setting world records in both the 100- and 200-meter butterfly. It didn't even matter that he told reporters the pool was "the worst I've ever competed in."

He then traveled to Europe with a US team—there were no World Championships until 1973—and twice lowered the world record in the 200-meter freestyle. *Swimming World* chose him world swimmer of the year, and he won the Sullivan Award over world-record hurdler Rod Milburn as the nation's outstanding amateur athlete.

During Spitz's senior year, he learned he had been admitted to IU's dental school, and he continued to enjoy a brotherhood with teammates and fraternity parties as a member of Phi Kappa Psi. Much like 1971, the 1972 college season was routine enough. The Hoosiers extended their streak in duals and won the Big Ten championship by 250 points. In Big Ten and NCAA meets, Indiana was seven-of-seven since Spitz arrived.

The NCAAs, held at the US Military Academy in West Point, New York, would be no runaway. Spitz placed third in the 50-yard freestyle before winning the 200 butterfly by an astounding four-second margin, setting an NCAA and American record of 1:46.89. Before Spitz's signature 100 butterfly, Counsilman predicted a time in the 48s. In a race in which no one had ever broken 49 seconds, Spitz became the first under 48. His time of 47.98 set another American and NCAA record. In the 4×100 free relay, his anchor leg carried the Hoosiers to fourth place and secured the team championship over USC, 370–351.

The Olympic Trials were August 2–6 in an outdoor pool near Chicago's O'Hare International Airport. It was a poor facility by modern standards, only three and a half feet at the shallow end. Deeper pools reduce waves and thus enhance times.

Not that times were the issue: top three places to Munich, fourth out of luck. Timetable was more appropriate for Spitz than in 1968, accommodating his four best events: 100 and 200 freestyle and butterfly.

Up first was the 200 fly, the most grueling. Robin Backhaus, a seventeen-year-old from Riverside, California, broke Spitz's American record with a time of 2:03.84 in the fourth heat. In the next heat, Spitz reclaimed the world record with a time of 2:01.87. He lowered it again in the final, clocking 2:01.53 to beat Backhaus and IU teammate Hall.

Prelims of the 200 freestyle were so fast that USC's Frank Heckl, winner of six golds at the previous year's Pan American Games (in Spitz's absence), was tenth and failed to make the eight-man final. Spitz won in 1:53.58, just .08 off his world record but only .21 ahead of UCLA's Steve Genter. In the 100 fly, Spitz lowered the world record for a fifth and sixth time, to 54.68 in prelims and 54.56 in the final.

"I lost it in 1968 when I was the world record holder, and it just wasn't going to happen again," he said.

He capped his four-for-four trials by winning the 100 freestyle, giving him a shot at seven golds in Munich, including three relays. He set a world record of 51.47 in prelims and won the final in 51.91, tying his pretrials world record.

Buildup to the Olympics in 1972 was nothing like 1968. Training camp, held at West Point, was two weeks instead of five. Spitz had allies in six Indiana teammates. He had split from his former coach, Haines, and was more self-assured under Counsilman and Chavoor, who had reunited with Spitz. That the Olympics had been entrusted to Germany, whose Nazi regime slaughtered Jews during World War II, was a coincidence not lost on Spitz. These Olympics were the largest yet, featuring a record 7,173 athletes from 121 nations. From the beginning, the hosts' emphasis was on a peaceful Games, and the swimmer was able to concentrate on the races, not his religion or ethnicity.

Everyone else was concentrating on his moustache. He had intended to shave it off until a chance encounter. Days before the opening ceremony, eager to test the ambient light of evening hours (when finals would be contested), he approached the Russian team and asked to get in the pool for ten minutes of its allotted training. Lane 1 was cleared for the American. The Russians asked if he was going to shave his moustache.

"And I don't know what prompted me to say this, but I stroked my moustache and said, 'This moustache deflects the water away from my mouth and allows me to get a lot lower and more streamlined in the stroke and therefore less likely to swallow water, and it allows me to swim faster and helped me break a couple of world records last month,'" Spitz said. "It was utter nonsense." But by 1973, the Russian men's swimming team had, according to Spitz, all grown moustaches.

The 200-meter butterfly was Spitz's least favorite event, but he talked himself into thinking it was best to swim that first. US coach Peter Daland of USC suggested the 200 fly would set a tone for the entire team. Spitz conceded winning could springboard him into history, and losing could derail him as it had done four years before. This Mark Spitz was no bullied schoolboy, however. He had the presence of mind to close the sliding door separating the adjoining rooms between himself and Hall, his roommate during college road meets and a top contender in the 200 butterfly.

"I didn't want to censor myself around Gary, and I didn't want to wonder about what he was doing," Spitz said. "My focus for that race was intense."

Hall said he understood. The fact that Indiana teammates like Hall actually did understand made all the difference in Spitz's life and career.

In the 200 fly, Hall, Backhaus, and Spitz took turns setting the Olympic record in heats 1, 2, and 4. The final was never in doubt. At fifty meters, Spitz already led by three-fourths of a body length. He lowered the world record to 2:00.70, a time so fast that even Hall, accustomed to Spitzian feats, was astounded. In an era in which world records fell regularly, this one lasted nearly four years.

"I never thought anyone would be around two minutes flat," Hall said. Hall was second and Backhaus third, completing an American sweep. With the hard one out of the way, Spitz had another sweep in mind.

That night, he won another gold medal with another world record, 3:26.42 in the 4×100 freestyle relay. Ominously, Jerry Heidenreich's third leg (50.78) was faster than Spitz's anchor (50.91).

Prerace drama involving Spitz's next event, the 200 freestyle, was not about him but about rival Steve Genter. The UCLA swimmer developed a collapsed lung on the charter flight to Munich. Five days before Genter's Olympic debut, he had surgery that allowed the lung to expand to normal. At risk to his own health, he rehabbed all night and was able to raise his right arm, despite the thirteen stitches. American doctors were able to override their German counterparts, and Genter was released from the hospital.

It was little short of a miracle that Genter's prelim time was only .13 behind Spitz's 1:55.29. In the final, Spitz led through fifty meters but was overtaken by Genter at the midpoint and still trailed at 150. Genter's stitches had ripped open at the second turn, but not until twenty-five meters remained did Spitz pass him for good. Spitz lowered the world record for a fourth time, to 1:52.78, and beat Genter by nearly a full second. It was Spitz's third gold in two days, overcoming Genter's against-all-odds swim. Spitz bluntly stated he "had the ability to turn up the speed whenever I needed to," and Genter did not contradict him.

"All I can say is, if my lung had not collapsed, Mark would have had to swim a little faster to get the gold medal," Genter said.

The postceremony drama was nearly as intense as that of the prerace. Spitz grabbed his worn Adidas shoes without having time to slip them on, and then, holding the shoes, waved at fans from the medals podium. The Russians complained Spitz was endorsing the shoes in violation of amateurism, and he was called in front of the International Olympic Committee's eligibility committee. Such an incident would be unthinkable in a modern era in which even college swimmers retain medal money, but it was a serious issue at the time. The IOC cleared him of any wrongdoing.

After a day off, Spitz had two gold-medal chances August 31—in the 100 butterfly and 4×200 freestyle relay. His fly nemesis, Russell, had retired after the 1970 NCAAs. But there was ample competition: East Germany's Roland Matthes, better known for backstroke; Canada's Bruce Robertson, who equaled Spitz's time in prelims; and the other Americans, Heidenreich and Dave Edgar. Edgar started fastest but was overtaken at the turn by Spitz, who built a lead of half a body length. Spitz lowered the world record for the seventh time, to 54.27, followed by Robertson and Heidenreich. It was Spitz's fourth gold, tying Schollander's record.

In the 4×200 freestyle relay, the Americans led off with Spitz's Indiana teammate, John Kinsella, who was slightly behind Russia. The United States trailed West Germany through two legs, but Genter's 1:52.72 third leg gave anchorman Spitz a lead of more than two body lengths. Genter's split was fastest of the race, even faster than Spitz's world record (albeit with a rolling start). The final time of 7:35.78 broke the world record by an astounding eight seconds. Silver medalist West Germany was also under the former record and lost by six seconds.

Four days. Five gold medals. Five world records.

After nine races in four days, Spitz's load would be light thereafter: three 100 freestyles and leg of the 4×100 medley relay over four days. Time off made him fretful, though. What if he lost in the 100 free? Better to be six-for-six, right? Heidenreich was fast enough to beat him, and Spitz knew it. After he told Daland he might not swim the 100 freestyle, the American coach approached Chavoor, coach of the women's team. Essentially, Chavoor told Spitz he would be "chicken" if he did not swim. That was unacceptable.

In prelims and semifinals, Heidenreich and Australia's Wenden, the defending Olympic champion, were both faster than Spitz. Yet in the 100 freestyle final, in contrast to his anxiety in the ready room of four years before, Spitz sensed the others were worried about him. He called it an execution chamber.

"Every time I left that room, they died, I won a gold medal, and my load got lighter," he said. "I was also very aware of the fact that every time I swam a race, it would be the last time I swam that event."

Spitz had held back in earlier swims. Not now. He was ahead as early as fifteen meters, leading at the turn over Heidenreich and the Soviet Union's Vladimir Bure. The Russian drifted to the right side of lane 2 to take advantage of Spitz's draft. Spitz moved to the center of lane 3 to foil that tactic. He lost rhythm near the end but reached the wall a half-stroke ahead of Heidenreich. Wenden, having over-trained in Australia, was fifth. Spitz's time was 51.22, making it six-for-six in world records. His six gold medals set a record for most by any athlete in any sport, surpassing the five by Italy's Nedo Nadi in fencing at the 1920 Antwerp Olympics.

Heidenreich, who took silver in 51.65, was disconsolate. Winning this gold had been a life's ambition ever since his parents moved the family from Terre Haute,

Indiana, to Texas so he could swim year-round. Heidenrich won four medals in Munich, two of them gold in relays, in a career so decorated that he wound up in the International Swimming Hall of Fame. Heidenrich, at age fifty-two, committed suicide in 2002 a year after suffering a stroke.

Spitz and Heidenreich shared the pool once more, in the climactic 4×100 medley relay. Matthes tied the world record in the opening 100 backstroke to give East Germany a lead over Mike Stamm, another Hoosiers teammate of Spitz. But silver medalist Tom Bruce put the Americans in front before Spitz's butterfly leg, and Heidenreich's freestyle anchor completed a world record of 3:48.16.

It was finished. Seven races. Seven gold medals. Seven world records.

Michael Phelps's eight golds at Beijing in 2008 eclipsed Spitz's record. When it comes to dominance, a case could be made Spitz's achievement was greater. Spitz's closest race in Munich was in the 100 freestyle, in which the margin was .42. Phelps famously won the 100 butterfly by .01, lunging at the finish, and took gold in the 4×100 freestyle relay because of Jason Lezak's for-the-ages anchor.

Spitz was taken to dinner at the Kafer-Schanke restaurant that evening by a *Sports Illustrated* writer and photographer. There was murmur among the diners when the Olympic hero walked in at about nine thirty. Spitz was dropped off at Olympic Village at about two o'clock in the morning, about two hours and one hundred yards from what became the darkest episode in Olympic history.

Spitz showed up hours later, at 8:00 a.m., a Tuesday, for a news conference that went on as scheduled. The room was set up to accommodate about three hundred, but one thousand journalists showed up. An Olympic official announced what had happened overnight. Eight Palestinian terrorists broke into the Olympic Village and took over the building where Israeli athletes were housed. Spitz was totally unprepared to answer questions about the terrorists. Security officers stood in front of him at the press conference, which ended quickly.

Yet few still understood the gravity of the situation, including many of the athletes. Spitz was taken in a van back to the Olympic Village, where eight guards were stationed near his apartment. German organizers urged him to leave the country immediately, for his own safety, so he packed, waited in a small room with Chavoor, and watched the news on TV. Spitz was one of five Indiana swimmers housed in a four-room, second-floor apartment about a block from the Israelis' Building 31. Within minutes after Spitz left for his flight, even the Mark Spitz nametag was torn off the door.

"They didn't take any chances," said John Murphy, one of the IU swimmers housed along with Spitz. "They cleaned out everything referring to Mark."

When Spitz arrived at his London hotel that evening, a standoff at a military airport had not yet concluded. Two Israelis had been killed in the invasion by the Black September group, and all nine Israeli hostages, along with seven Palestinians, were killed in a gunfight with West German police. Spitz did not know the fate of the hostages until reading a newspaper the next morning. Because he had been encouraged to leave the country, he could not even attend the memorial service.

Spitz could reflect on the tragedy privately, but public demands nearly overwhelmed the twenty-two-year-old. He became the first athlete to make a large post-Olympics impact on corporate America, earning endorsements estimated at $5 million. Signing with the William Morris Agency, the world's largest theatrical agency, proved to be astute. A photograph of the mustachioed Spitz, posing in a red-white-and-blue swimsuit with seven gold medals hanging from his neck, became the most popular-selling sports poster ever. He appeared on television specials with Bob Hope, Bill Cosby, and Sonny and Cher, but Hollywood was not interested.

After the Olympics, he began dating Suzy Weiner, the daughter of one of his father's business associates. He wed Weiner, a UCLA theater student and part-time model, and they had two sons, Matthew and Justin. Spitz has had an eclectic résumé, working as stockbroker, real estate entrepreneur, corporate spokesman, and motivational speaker.

He failed in a high-profile attempt to make a comeback and qualify for the 1992 Olympics in the 100-meter butterfly. He lost 1991 match races against Tom Jager and Matt Biondi in the 50-meter butterfly, although the forty-one-year-old acquitted himself better than is perhaps remembered. Spitz's time of 26.51 in the 50 fly would have beaten the masters world record in his age group by more than a half-second. In the end, he did not qualify for the Olympic Trials.

He remained outspoken, claiming it was "demeaning" not to be invited to the 2008 Olympics, where Phelps aimed at his record medal haul. He has also chided FINA, the world governing body for aquatic sports, and the International Olympic Committee for not being serious about doping.

In September 2019, he announced he had been diagnosed with atrial fibrillation, or an irregular heartbeat. Spitz worked with doctors to manage the condition.

"After competing at that level, I never imagined that I would be diagnosed with a heart condition like this one," he posted on social media. "I feel lucky that I was able to catch this before it put me at serious risk for other heart complications. I look forward to spreading awareness about AFib as I learn more about this condition and live with my own diagnosis."

If Spitz could be criticized for anything, it is for being a perfectionist. That is what he learned in California, and that is what he nurtured in Indiana. That is who he was in Munich: a perfect seven.

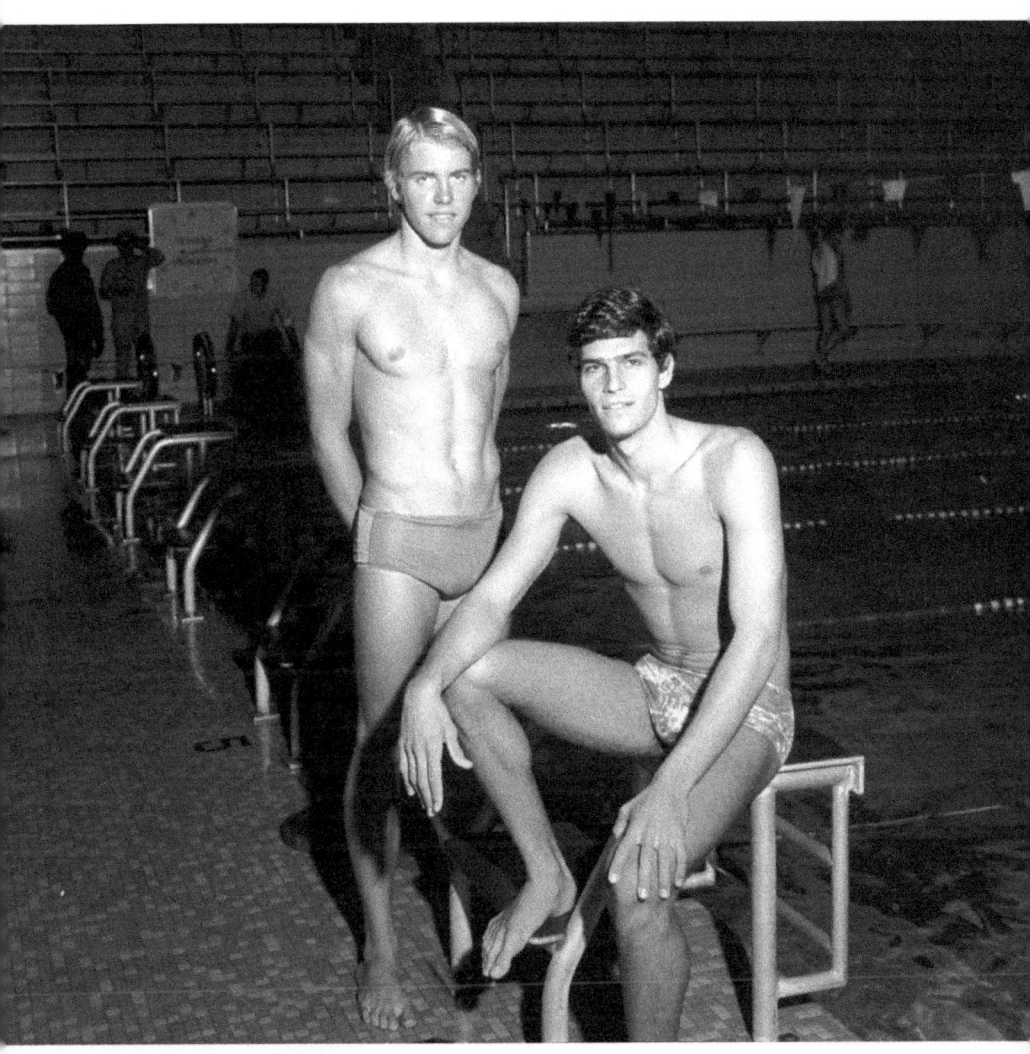

Gary Hall and Mark Spitz (*right*), 1973.
IU Archives P0052391

Mike Stamm
1972

San Diego Surf to Munich Podium

RECRUITING HAS ALWAYS BEEN UNPREDICTABLE, IRRESPECTIVE OF SPORT or era. For instance, Indiana University lured swimmer Mike Stamm, a six-foot-three San Diego surfer, to cornfield country in an unconventional way. He was impressed by the revolving door in the Indiana Memorial Union.

"I had never seen one except in the movies," he said. "When I first went through, I got in the same compartment with another guy."

Of course, there was more to it than that. Stamm liked Hoosiers coach Don Counsilman, and Mike Troy was Stamm's club coach. Troy became Counsilman's first individual Olympic gold medalist in 1960.

Michael Eugene Stamm was born August 6, 1952, in San Pedro, California, and attended Crawford High School in San Diego. He might have a more prominent place in the sport if his career had not coincided with that of his Indiana teammate, Mark Spitz, and East Germany's Roland Matthes, who won eight Olympic medals, set sixteen world records, and was unbeaten in backstroke from 1967 to 1974. Stamm was on IU teams that won six consecutive NCAA championships. He won seven individual Big Ten titles and swept both NCAA backstrokes in 1973. He remains the last San Diego swimmer to win an individual Olympic medal.

Stamm set a world record even before he competed for the Hoosiers, lowering the 200-meter backstroke mark to 2:06.3 at Los Angeles on August 20, 1970. Matthes broke that with a time of 2:06.1 three weeks later and held onto the world record until 1976.

Stamm was runner-up in both backstrokes at NCAA meets in 1971 and 1972. Even though he once held that world record, he was unspectacular in the 1972 Olympic Trials at Chicago's Portage Park. He was second to Mitch Ivey in the 100 backstroke and third behind Ivey and Alexander McKee in the 200 backstroke. In the 200, Stamm finished two-tenths of a second ahead of Indiana teammate Gary Hall for

Mike Stamm, 1970.
IU Archives P0028421.

the third and final Olympic berth. Stamm was six-tenths ahead of sixteen-year-old John Naber, who won four gold medals at Montreal four years later.

At the Munich Olympics, Stamm peaked perfectly, winning two silver medals. Matthes set an Olympic record of 56.58 in winning the 100 backstroke, followed by Stamm in 57.70. (Coincidentally, Matthes had beaten another Indiana swimmer, Charlie Hickox, to win gold in 1968.) Matthes then equaled his world record of 2:02.82 in the 200 backstroke, followed by Stamm in 2:04.09. Stamm swam backstroke on the 4×100 medley relay team that supplied Spitz with his seventh gold medal of that Olympics.

Swimming events ended the night before the massacre of eleven Israeli athletes by Palestinian terrorists.

"It affected the whole atmosphere of the village, which is insulated," Stamm said. "The bubble over the village was broken."

He had perhaps his best season in 1973. He swept both NCAA backstrokes, helping the Hoosiers to a sixth successive team title, and the last year in which they were national champions. He took a silver medal behind Matthes in the inaugural World Championships at Belgrade and another 4×100 medley relay gold.

Stamm's senior season of 1974 was anticlimactic. At the NCAAs, he was sixth in the 100-yard backstroke, in which he was defending champion. Southern California ended the Hoosiers' six-year reign by one point, 339–338. He failed in an attempt to make it to another Olympics in 1976.

He has had an eclectic postswimming career. After graduating from IU, he was a catering service waiter, a sandwich maker in a deli, a head valet for a Saudi Arabian prince, a lifeguard, and an owner of an art store.

"I wanted to experience life a little bit," he said. "I had that beach mentality." He wears studs in both earlobes, with rushing water tattooed on his right forearm and flickering fire on his left.

He entered culinary school in 1980 and found cooking was his calling.

"I found out chefs are like me—goofy, crazy, creative," Stamm said. "And cooking was like swimming; it's all about the training. It's repetitive. When the dish goes out, that's like the race. You can still do everything right and fail."

His occupation led him to the Society of St. Vincent de Paul in Oakland, California, where he taught men and women from low income or substance abuse backgrounds to become cooks.

John Kinsella, 1970.
IU Archives P0028344.

John Kinsella
1968, 1972

"The Machine" Changed Swim Culture

JOHN KINSELLA HAD A TOUGH ACT TO FOLLOW: HIMSELF.

His nickname was "The Machine" for his capacity to push himself in training, lap after lap, mile after mile, day after day. Of course, no one is a machine, even one chosen as the United States' greatest amateur athlete at age eighteen. John Kinsella had his triumphs and travails.

It was bad timing that his greatest season was 1970, in between Olympics, when he became the second-youngest man ever to win the AAU's Sullivan Award. (Youngest was Olympic decathlon gold medalist Bob Mathias, also eighteen, in 1948.)

Just before Kinsella enrolled at Indiana University in 1970, he set world records of 4:02.8 in the 400-meter freestyle on August 20 and 15:57.1 in the 1,500-meter freestyle on August 23, both in the national championships at Los Angeles. He became the first under 16 minutes. Those were his only individual world records, and he set nine American records.

At Indiana, he won both the 500-yard and 1,650-yard freestyles for NCAA team champions in 1971, 1972, and 1973. Before that, as a sixteen-year-old high schooler, he won a silver medal in the 1,500-meter freestyle at the 1968 Olympics in Mexico City.

Kinsella had an influence on teammates that extended beyond races he won, records he set, or points he scored. He "changed the whole attitude in workouts," said Gary Hall, world swimmer of the year in 1969 and 1970. "He's so much better in practice than any swimmer I've ever known."

The Hoosiers once trailed Ohio State midway through a dual meet when many of their top swimmers were absent. As soon as Kinsella left the water after winning the 1,000-yard freestyle, Counsilman asked him about swimming the next event. It was the 200-yard freestyle. "I've never lost a meet in high school," Kinsella said, "and I'm not going to lose now."

Kinsella won, and so did the Hoosiers, whose dual-meet streak eventually reached 140 in a row. Kinsella was born August 26, 1952, in Oak Park, Illinois. He grew to be big for his age, and tireless. His first swim coach, Dixson Keyser of the Hinsdale (Illinois) Golf Club, told the ten-year-old Kinsella's parents that their son would make an Olympic team by his fifteenth birthday and become one of the world's greatest swimmers.

"We knew he [the coach] didn't drink," said Kinsella's father, John Sr. "We thought he'd lost his mind."

The youth's talent was nurtured by Don Watson at Hinsdale Central High School. The coach grew up swimming alongside Doc Counsilman at the St. Louis YMCA and was once his assistant. Watson's Hinsdale teams produced four Olympians, three world record holders, and won twelve consecutive state titles. Although Kinsella was a state sprint champion as a high school sophomore, he became a distance swimmer under Watson.

"He took to it easily," Watson said. "He enjoyed the work. Many distance swimmers aren't willing to pay the price it takes to get to the Olympics. John was."

Heading into 1968, Watson believed Kinsella not only could make the US team but win a medal. In workouts, Kinsella often swam faster than eventual gold medalist Mike Burton.

The sixteen-year-old called the experience "scary." He was away from home for five months to train at altitude in Colorado, and he developed dysentery in Mexico

City. He said he felt apprehensive and disconnected. Olympic coach George Haines changed that.

"He had a very commanding presence, and right before the race, he put a hand on my shoulder and told me, 'You've put an awful lot of work into this moment. Don't waste the opportunity. Make the most of it,'" Kinsella recalled.

Burton won gold in the 1,500 freestyle in 16:38.9, an Olympic record but 30 seconds off the world record, given the 7,300-foot altitude. Kinsella took silver in 16:57.3.

On his return to Illinois, Kinsella was presented with a key to the city of Oak Brook, and Hinsdale Central honored him with a school assembly. The attention made him uneasy, as if he were being placed on a pedestal he did not seek. Everything was, well, different.

"It was tough with my peers, and tough scholastically," he said. "My homework had slid by the wayside. It was flattering but a very stressful time. I got mono later that year and basically was run down most of the year." However, former teammate and close friend Gary Ferraro said Kinsella was not alienated from the rest of the team, that he did not have an insufferable ego.

The swimmer went from one powerhouse, Hinsdale Central, to another, Indiana. There was little question Kinsella would choose the Hoosiers, although Counsilman fretted that the swimmer would go to Southern California. The Indiana coach remembered the exchange.

Kinsella: "Doc, I've made up my mind, but before I tell you, I want you to know that we'll always be friends."

Councilman (swallowing hard): "Oh, so then you've decided on USC?"

Kinsella: "No, I'm coming to Indiana. I just wanted to shake you up."

Late in summer 1970, just before Kinsella enrolled, Indiana might have had on campus the greatest team in history—in any sport.

Kinsella had just set two world records. There were certified world records in twelve individual events, and IU swimmers held nine of those in a twenty-day span from late August to early September. It was the peak of a nineteen-year period in which at least one world record always was held by a present, past, or future Hoosier. Going by times, a dual meet matching the Hoosiers against the rest of the world would have gone down to the last relay.

Kinsella had a strong relationship with his coach, as many teammates did. Counsilman eased monotony of training by tossing jelly beans as rewards, chasing them around the pool deck with a belt, and telling bad jokes. Before the last day of one particular NCAA Championships, the Hoosiers were tense because they had such a small lead over USC. Counsilman did not deliver a pep talk but more zingers.

Kinsella was once surprised when Counsilman visited his room. Several Hoosiers had transported cases of Coors beer, which was then available only in the West, back to campus from a nationals in Dallas.

"Without a word, Doc goes over, sits on the case of beer and talks to us about what he came to talk to us about," Kinsella said. "You knew he knew what was going on."

Kinsella's epic national meet of 1970 was followed by a poor one in 1971, and struggles continued into 1972. He found it difficult to train as hard. USC was a threat to Indiana at the NCAAs, and Kinsella had the pressure of being in the opening event, the 500-yard freestyle. He delivered victory in 4:24.50, an American record, and set the Hoosiers on a path toward a fifth consecutive team championship.

The 1972 Olympic Trials were home, in Chicago . . . and Kinsella proceeded to have one of the worst meets of his life. He was fourth and fifth in the 400- and 1,500-meter freestyles, respectively, failing to make it to Munich in either event. He was fourth in the 200 freestyle to qualify for the 800 free relay, in which he led off the team that set a world record and supplied Mark Spitz the fifth of his seven gold medals.

Kinsella speculated that being taken off a weightlifting program by Counsilman hurt his stamina. The coach said he and Watson should have shielded him from hometown pressures. Kinsella's friend, Ferraro, said he might have burned himself out.

Kinsella's college career ended ignominiously. In the 1974 NCAA Championships at Long Beach, USC ended Indiana's six-year reign by one point, 339–338. The Hoosiers had a series of judging decisions go against them, were disqualified in a relay, and diver Gary James was subjected to heckling by the pro-USC crowd.

Kinsella, a six-time NCAA champion, finished seventh, sixth, and sixth in the 200, 500, and 1,650 freestyles. He said he ate less than he should have, instead taking fructose tablets, a regimen designed by Counsilman. It was ill-advised to try something like that at the NCAAs, making for an unsatisfying ending to Kinsella's college career.

"Disappointing, to say the least," he said. "It's not like I can't sleep at night, but when someone brings it up, there's a twinge of regret."

He was not yet through with swimming, becoming a world professional champion in marathon races. He won swims across the English Channel, Lake Ontario, and elsewhere. In six marathon swims in 1978, he won them all and earned $43,000. For that, he earned induction into both the International Swimming and Marathon Swimming Halls of Fame.

In 1982, he pleaded no contest to charges that he failed to file income tax returns in 1975, 1976, and 1977. He had earned a total of $50,000 in those years. Initially ordered to serve twelve weekends in jail and pay a $30,000 fine, a judge reduced the sentence to probation.

"It was a tough time," Kinsella said. "The case took so long, and the financial drain with the lawyers was so great. The experience had a good side, though, as far as maturity. At twenty-two, I was less mature in the ways of the world than some of my contemporaries. I`d been training and focusing on swimming four to five hours a day, six days a week, for a long time."

He attended Harvard business school and became an investment officer, institutional broker, and financial adviser in the Chicago area. He said he did not miss swimming when he first stopped, then became bored by a sedentary life. He began jogging in addition to swimming, and he tried triathlon.

Open water events weren't added to the Olympic program until 2004, or Kinsella might have kept going and won a medal in 1976. He once had no peer as a marathon swimmer. At his peak, he was, well, a machine.

"I get a lot of satisfaction out of being in good physical condition, but the most gratifying thing is that last hundred meters, when you know you're going to make it," Kinsella said. "You know you've surmounted the challenge and you're going to finish. You've got that dock ahead of you, and you touch it and feel your whole body relax. You can stand on solid ground."

Charlie Hickcox
1968

From School without a Pool to Record Rampage

THE PHONY THREAT THAT CHARLIE HICKCOX USED TO MAKE TO COACH DOC Counsilman is that he would abandon swimming and go out for football at Indiana.
"I'll probably get something broken the first day," Hickcox once said. "But at least I'll have had the satisfaction of trying. And maybe I'll make a great flanker."
We will never know whether Hickcox, six foot four and barely 175 pounds, would have been a great flanker. We know he was a multisport athlete. And a great swimmer. In one fourteen-month stretch of 1967 and 1968, he set eight world records.
In a 1969 interview, Counsilman said, "I think he's the best all-around swimmer of all time."
Inexplicably—other than he competed in just one Olympic Games—Hickcox goes missing from lists of the greatest swimmers of all time. In the aftermath of Mexico City 1968, he did not receive recognition that he might have after, say, winning three gold medals at the 2016 Olympics. He became the first to win two golds in individual medleys, indicative of all-around swimming. His three golds were then second-most ever by a male swimmer, trailing Don Schollander's four from Tokyo 1964. And Hickcox was 1968 world swimmer of the year.
The television spotlight did not shine as brightly on Olympians then as it does now. That Olympic team was not invited to the White House, as it was in 1964. The inattention bothered Hickcox, as it bothered Counsilman.
"Of course, Indiana swimming hasn't gotten the recognition," the coach said in a 1969 interview. "We're just out of the mainstream, I guess, and there is a different trend in writing to look for the Joe Namaths. The old hero image has changed."
Hickcox was better known on campus for coaching the Phi Delta Theta cycling team that raced in the Little 500 than he was for swimming. He conceded he was upset about the perceived snubs and nearly quit swimming with a year of college eligibility left. He said perhaps he did not talk enough, except about his coach.

Charlie Hickcox, 1966.
IU Archives P0028301.

"I build up antagonisms and I get mad sometimes, but I forget that, too," Hickcox said. "I'm just an easygoing guy. I've had a good time all my life just playing around and having a good time."

Charles Buchanan Hickcox was born February 6, 1947, in Phoenix. He played basketball and tennis at Washington High School there. The school had no pool, so he trained at Phoenix and Paradise Valley country clubs. When, at age thirteen, he showed up for training with sister Mary Sue, she was welcomed. He was skinny.

"Get lost, kid," was the coach's response.

Undeterred, the skinny kid kept at it and began winning at age-group meets. Paradise Valley coach Joe Phillips changed Hickcox's strokes, but the young swimmer adapted "without any reluctance." Hickcox was a natural backstroker but ultimately mastered all strokes.

At seventeen, he showed what he was capable of at the 1964 Olympic Trials. He finished seventh in the 200-meter butterfly. (Coincidentally, that is the event in which Michael Phelps made his first Olympic team in 2000 at age fifteen.) Hickcox was seemingly headed for the University of Arizona until persuaded by Counsilman to choose Indiana.

"He was good, but he was so raw. His turns were agonizing," Counsilman said. "I thought he'd kill himself going into the wall. But he worked, I'll tell you. After about two months, I guess he started believing in me."

Hickcox had the ability "to *punish* himself," Counsilman said.

In his sophomore year, Hickcox won both backstrokes at the 1967 NCAA Championships, beating Michigan State's Gary Dilley, who had been unbeaten in collegiate meets. Stanford won the team title for the first time, and Indiana finished third.

The following summer, Hickcox won seven international medals, six of them gold. The silver came in the 200-meter backstroke in the Pan American Games at Winnipeg, Manitoba. He finished behind Canada's Ralph Hutton, who won six medals in his home country. Hickcox won the 100 backstroke in 1:01.19 and teamed with Schollander, Greg Charlton, and seventeen-year-old Mark Spitz for gold in the 4×200 freestyle relay.

In a span of four days, August 28–31, Hickcox set four world records at the World University Games in Tokyo, including two in the 100 backstroke (59.3 and 59.1). He came away with four gold medals, two in the backstrokes and two in relays.

Yet 1967 merely prefaced a 1968 in which he became the Hoosiers' first world swimmer of the year.

In an attempt to improve Hickcox's breaststroke—his weakness in the individual medley—Counsilman developed an odd solution. The coach nailed two pieces of wood stuck together at an angle with a shoe nailed on top, and he asked Hickcox to wear them. Counsilman theorized that a tight Achilles tendon inhibits proper leg kick in the breaststroke, and this was supposed to remedy that. The shoes "looked like a crocodile with its mouth open," Hickcox said. He walked up and down the halls each night, prompting derisive humor from fraternity brothers.

The joke was on Hickcox's rivals. On the first day of the NCAAs, he set an American record in prelims of the 200-yard individual medley, then lowered it to 1:52.56 in the final. Those crocs worked.

"When Charlie finished that swim," Counsilman said, "I looked down at my watch, blinked, and nearly fell in the pool."

Hickcox set another record in prelims of the 100-yard backstroke and tied it in the final. On the last day, he won the 200 backstroke by nearly two seconds. *Sports Illustrated* referred to him as "a tall, lean, intense fellow with deep-set eyes" and reported, "After each win he bobbed up out of the pool, fist clenched, jaw set and fire in his eyes. He not only won his races, he aroused the entire Indiana team."

The Hoosiers scored a record 346 points, 93 more than runner-up Yale, to secure their first NCAA championship. In 1990, when Counsilman retired and reflected on his career, he said that first title might have been the highest point.

"Charlie was responsible for that one," Counsilman said.

At the 1968 Olympic Trials, Hickcox set world records in the 200 and 400 IMs—2:10.6 and 4:39.0—and won the 100 backstroke in 59.7. After six weeks of altitude training in Colorado Springs, the American swimmers headed for Mexico City's 7,300-foot elevation.

He won his first gold in the 200 IM, setting an Olympic record of 2:12.0 and leading a 1-2-3 sweep by Americans. That oxygen debt was an issue was underscored by bronze medalist John Ferris, who wobbled and clutched his stomach as he marched to the podium for the medal ceremony. Finally, after warning the gold medalist, Ferris fainted in the direction of Hickcox, who held him at semi-attention through the final bars of "The Star-Spangled Banner."

That was not the only out-of-pool oddity.

"After each event, we would have to go and lie down on a cot in some little back room while a Mexican medical guy sprinkled sugar into our open mouths," Hickcox said. "It was supposed to make you bounce back quickly or something. But mostly he sprinkled sugar into our eyes."

In Hickcox's case, maybe it was gold dust.

He went on to win the 400 IM in a stroke-for-stroke duel with seventeen-year-old Gary Hall, who would later become his Indiana teammate. Hickcox touched in 4:48.4 to Hall's 4:48.7. Despite a world record by East Germany's Roland Matthes on the backstroke leadoff, Hickcox won a third gold in the 4×100 medley relay. He teamed with IU breaststroker Don McKenzie, Doug Russell, and Ken Walsh for 3:54.9, the eighth and last world record by Hickcox. He was silver medalist in the 100 backstroke behind Matthes.

Mexico was momentous for the Hoosiers, who won seven gold medals, six silvers, and four bronzes in aquatic sports. Their total was exceeded by only seven nations—for all sports.

After those Games, Hickcox married Olympic teammate Lesley Bush, the diver who won a gold medal in 1964. The couple later divorced.

Hickcox welcomed Spitz to the Bloomington campus in January 1969, going as far as throwing a luncheon in his honor. Spitz was supposed to be a breakout star in Mexico City but instead came away with no individual gold medals. Spitz's own teammates were angered by him and rooted against him.

With two superstars, 1969 Indiana was one of the greatest college swim teams ever assembled. In their home Royer Pool, the Hoosiers outscored runner-up Southern California 427–306 at the NCAA Championships. Spitz, a freshman, won three events. Hickcox, a senior, won two and placed second in a third. That loss by Hickcox was his only one in eight individual NCAA finals.

In the 200-yard IM, Hickcox defeated Michigan's Juan Bello, an Olympian from Peru who had upset him in the Big Ten meet. In the 100 backstroke, Hickcox missed two turns, banged into lane markers throughout the last lap, and was beaten by Stanford's Fred Haywood, 52.44 to 52.46. Hickcox atoned for that in the 200 backstroke, the last individual swim of his career, by winning in an American record of 1:53.6.

"I wanted to set the record for Doc," Hickcox said, "especially after last night."

He proved to be as versatile out of the water as he was in it. He graduated from law school at Kentucky State but spent most of the rest of his life in his native Phoenix. He was a coach, TV commentator, and commercial real estate developer. He headed the Feldman-Hickcox Company, a firm based in Scottsdale, Arizona. He also volunteered his time visiting schools, youth groups, juvenile detention centers, and prisons to share his story and encourage others.

He had six children from two marriages. He died from cancer on June 15, 2010, in San Diego. He was sixty-three. He is a member of the International Swimming, Arizona Sports, and IU Halls of Fame.

"My soapbox was that I wasn't the greatest, that I had been blessed and that I had very solid people behind me," Hickcox said in 1987. "I'm one of those people who tries to do a very good job, with a lot of integrity, and I understand it's just not about me."

Don McKenzie
1968

A Little Tequila Never Hurt Anyone

DON MCKENZIE WAS BORN IN HOLLYWOOD BUT WAS FAR FROM A STAR heading into the Olympic year of 1968. He did help the Indiana Hoosiers win their first NCAA team championship in swimming and diving that year, finishing fourth in the 100- and 200-yard breaststrokes. McKenzie headed to Long Beach, California, for the Olympic Trials, and somehow he knew that wouldn't be the end of it.

His roommate, soon-to-be national hero Charlie Hickcox, packed his biggest suitcase because he knew he would be going straight from the trials to altitude training camp at Colorado Springs. He would need that many clothes. McKenzie? His trunk was bigger. McKenzie was a capable swimmer but had never won a national championship. Nor a significant title of any kind, really.

"Don, why are you packing such a big trunk?" Hickcox asked.

"Well, after I win the trials, isn't training camp for six weeks?" McKenzie responded.

McKenzie won the trials in the 100-meter breaststroke, beating Indiana teammate Dave Perkowski, who was third, and former Hoosier Dan Jastremski, the former world record holder who finished fifth. After that, it was on to Colorado Springs and then Mexico City.

Despite his Long Beach victory, McKenzie remained an afterthought at the Olympics. The world record holder was the Soviet Union's Nikolai Pankin. Another Russian, Vladimir Kosinsky, was also a top contender. Pankin won one semifinal in 1:08.1. Koskinsky beat McKenzie in another semifinal, 1:07.9 to 1:08.1. In the final, McKenzie drew lane 3, with the two Russians on his left in lanes 4 and 5.

Don McKenzie

The Russians appeared to be headed for gold and silver until the closing twenty meters, when McKenzie's surge sent him past both. The twenty-one-year-old Hoosier set an Olympic record of 1:07.7, followed by Kosinsky and Pankin. McKenzie earned a second gold medal in the 4×100 medley relay, teaming with Hickcox, Douglas Russell, and Kenneth Walsh for a world record of 3:56.5. (Through 2016, the United States has never lost that relay at an Olympics.)

Many American athletes contracted diarrhea—referred to as "Montezuma's revenge"—but McKenzie remained healthy for the duration of the Olympics. Toward the end, an Olympic teammate, former IU swimmer Gary Hall Sr., asked for the secret. McKenzie reached down in the cabinet next to his bed and pulled out a bottle of Mexican tequila.

"I just took a shot of this every night before bed," McKenzie said. "I figured it would kill anything."

Donald Ward McKenzie was born May 11, 1947. He attended Grant High School in Los Angeles and Los Angeles Valley Junior College before joining coach Doc Counsilman's swimming program.

At the 1969 NCAA Championships in Bloomington, McKenzie helped the Hoosiers to a repeat team title by setting an American record of 58.3 in the 100-yard breaststroke. He led a 1-2-4 finish by the Hoosiers, who scored a record 427 points. He had a full head of blond hair when he stood on the podium after winning at Mexico City. But before those NCAAs, he shaved his head.

"Besides, I don't go for this long hair anyway," he said at the time.

After leaving IU, he graduated from US Naval Officer Candidate School and became a Nevada real estate investor. As president of Practice Management Services, he created and supported computer software for medical, dental, and small businesses. He was an avid masters swimmer and never lost his competitive fire.

In 1998, he set a masters national record in the 100-yard breaststroke with a time of 1:01.02—just three seconds slower than he swam twenty-nine years earlier and a record that stood until 2010.

In 1997, he was persuaded by Hall to participate in a 4×50-meter medley relay race with other men in their 50s pitted against the US Olympic women's team. The men had lost a similar race the year before, but without McKenzie on breaststroke. Amanda Beard was not available for the women's team, so South African's Penny Heyns filled in on breaststroke.

In a tribute to McKenzie posted on the US Masters Swimming website, Hall wrote, "It took three of us to zip up the full bodysuit Don put on for the relay, two to pull in the material while he sucked in his gut and one of us to zip it up. It was worth the effort. Swimming the 'old-fashioned' breaststroke, head up, flat as a pancake, Don split 30.5 (meters!!!) and caught Penny."

Hall swam evenly against Misty Hyman, and former Hoosier Jim Montgomery touched out Jenny Thompson on the freestyle anchor leg.

"We didn't get any medals for this 'special' race, but if we had, we would have all given them to Don," Hall wrote. "From Mexico City to that relay in Phoenix, Don had never really changed. He was one of the fiercest competitors our sport has ever known."

McKenzie died from a brain tumor on December 3, 2008. He was sixty-one. He belongs to the International Swimming, IU, and Los Angeles Valley College Halls of Fame.

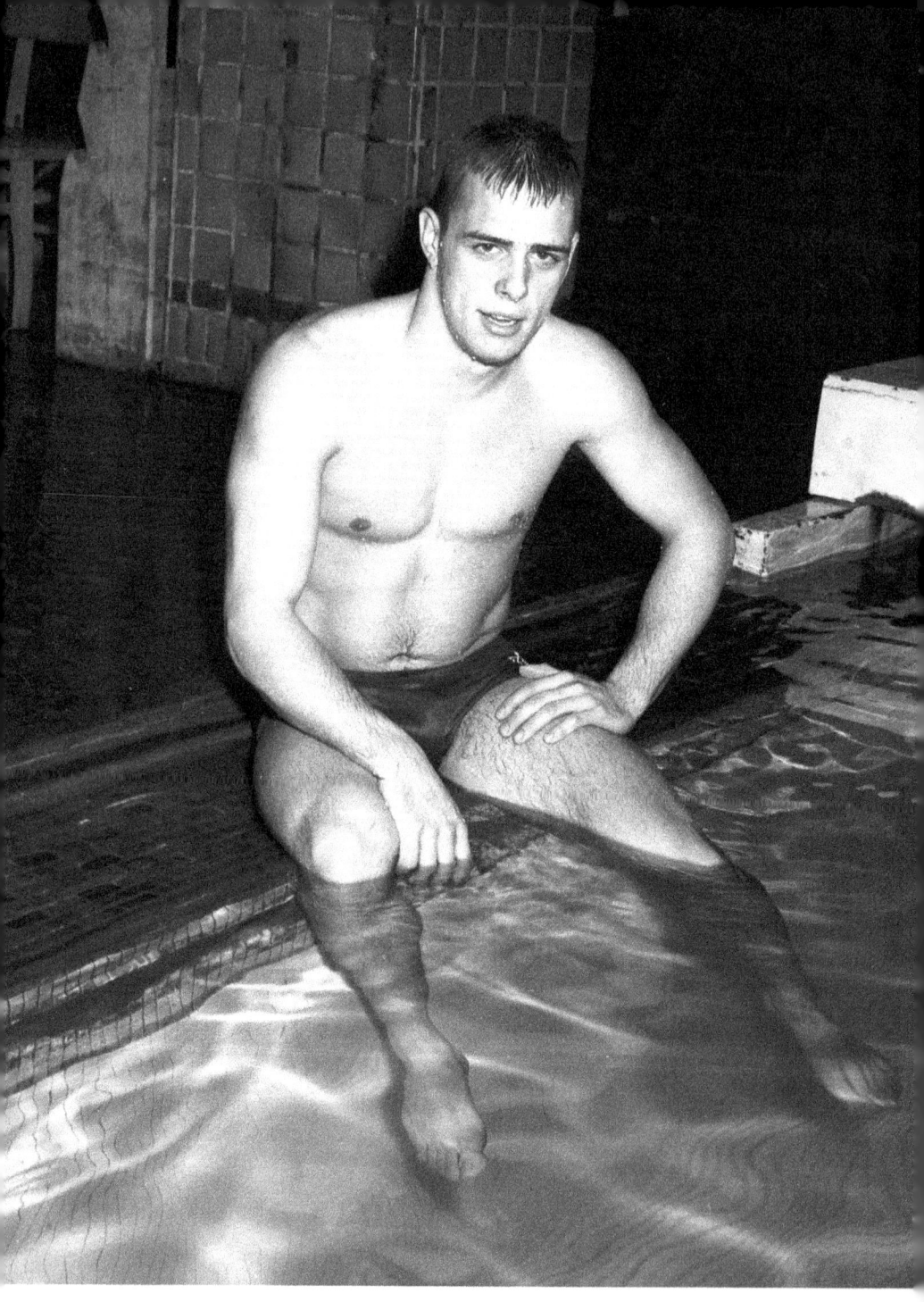

Chet Jastremski, 1960.
IU Archives P0021231.

Chet Jastremski
1964, 1968

Future Physician Reinvented Breaststroke

NO ONE EVER HAD A MORE WRETCHED OLYMPIC HISTORY THAN SWIMMER Chet Jastremski. "Chet the Jet" revolutionized the breaststroke, set nine world records, nearly made four Olympic teams... and had one bronze medal to show for it.

He kept it in a desk drawer in his Bloomington home. Moreover, he never won an NCAA title because Indiana University was on probation in all sports while he was enrolled.

Yet consider this:

Far more swimmers have gold medals than have appeared on covers of *Sports Illustrated*. Jastremski was on the cover of the January 29, 1962, edition of the magazine. He was then "beyond argument the best swimmer in the world," writer Arlie Schardt asserted. Three other Hoosiers—Charlie Hickcox, Gary Hall, and Mark Spitz—have been designated world swimmers of the year by *Swimming World*. But *Swimming World* didn't introduce that honor until 1964.

So again, timing was against Jastremski after his seminal season of 1961. He shall be remembered as the swimmer who took breaststroke from dial-up to wireless speed. He abandoned convention, the frog kick, for a whip kick. That reduced drag and led to times thought to be impossible using breaststroke.

"Arguably, you could put him right behind Mark Spitz as one of the greatest who ever swam for us," Hoosiers coach Ray Looze said.

Jastremski's Olympic misfortunes were such that they would have elicited lawsuits and sports talk outrage if occurring during the 2000s:

- In 1956, when he was fifteen, he finished first in the 200-meter breaststroke at the Olympic Trials in Detroit, not far from his Toledo, Ohio, home. In a disputed ruling, he was disqualified for an improper turn. Maddeningly, a swimmer who moved into Jastremski's slot was also on the water polo team and, when there was a scheduling conflict in Melbourne, the swimmer skipped his heat to compete in water polo. Jastremski was told an official at the far end of the pool accused him of the illegal turn.

"I was upset but not really bitter," he said. "I was still in high school, so it wasn't a big deal. I just felt like I lost an opportunity. There wasn't any meanness associated with the decision. I just don't think anybody was really sure about the rule."

- In 1960, Jastremski finished second in the 200 breaststroke at the trials, also at Detroit, but was left off the team heading to Rome. The United States sent two breaststrokers, but one was to compete in the 4×100 medley relay. At the trials, Paul Hait won the 100 breaststroke (which was not then an Olympic event). So a committee selected Hait over Jastremski. Bill Mulliken won Olympic gold in 2:37.4, and a year later Jastremski was nine seconds faster than that. Hait finished eighth in Rome. The Hoosier swimmer said the decision was never fully explained, not even by Indiana coach Doc Counsilman, who was in the meeting.

    "I was told by somebody that, since we already had several guys on the team from Indiana, that they might have wanted some more equity from other parts of the country. Paul was from California," Jastremski said. "Whether that is true or not, I don't know."

- In 1964, the twenty-three-year-old Jastremski was out of college and retired from swimming, studying for medical and law degrees. Retirement did not last long. He resumed training, then clocked 2:28.2 in the 200 breaststroke in the Olympic Trials at Astoria, New York, breaking his own world record from three years before. He was poised for a long-awaited gold medal but was sluggish during pre-Olympics buildup.

    Instead, Australia's Ian O'Brien won gold in Tokyo, breaking Jastremski's world record with a time of 2:27.8. The Hoosier earned bronze in 2:29.6. Years later, Counsilman told Jastremski that he probably piled on too much mileage before the Olympics.

    "We trained so hard during that time that we were very tired. He thought that maybe the distance training broke me down," Jastremski said.

- In 1968, having finished medical school, he made another comeback and finished fifth in both breaststrokes at the Olympic Trials. He traveled to Mexico City as an alternate, and in the meantime kept getting faster. In prelims of the 4×100 medley relay, his leg turned out to be faster than the 1:07.7 by the Hoosiers' Don McKenzie in winning a gold medal. Under today's rules, that relay swim would have earned Jastremski a gold medal, too. Then, only finalists were awarded medals.

"I had just graduated from medical school and there was not enough time to train before the trials," Jastremski said. "I only had eight weeks."

- In 1972, he made a third comeback at age thirty-one. By then, he was married, a father of three children, and finishing a four-year commitment as an army flight surgeon. He spent one year of residency at a base in Texas and three at West Point. He qualified for the Olympic Trials but did not come close to making it to Munich.

He was part of two more Olympics, serving as team physician for the United States at Montreal in 1976 and as part of a drug-testing committee at Moscow in 1980.

"There are two ways of looking at it," Jastremski said. "One is that the best in the world doesn't always win at the Olympics. He just might not be up that day. The other is that the best in the world is the guy who responds to pressure and wins the big one. Since I've never won it, I subscribe to the first view."

Chester Andrew Jastremski Jr. was born January 12, 1941, in Toledo. His father was an assistant foreman at the Champion Spark Plug Company. His mother, Gertrude, was afraid of the water and enrolled her son in a swim class at an indoor YMCA pool. Jastremski said it took him nine months to learn to swim because he cheated on his breathing.

"I'd turn my head but wouldn't take a breath. I always had to stop after ten yards," he said.

Finally, his instructor, Tom Edwards, told him, "Swim thirty yards or else." The youngster, gasping for air, swam thirty and was promoted from minnow to flying fish.

As he grew faster, Edwards asked him to be on the swim team, and Jastremski swam in his first race soon after he turned nine. His family began taking him to meets around the Midwest, going into debt to do so. His mother took courses at the University of Toledo so she could get a job teaching fourth grade and pay off the travel expenses. Meanwhile, the YMCA coach realized he had someone exceptional.

"You could see he was going to be a champion," Edwards said. "His main asset was a muscle definition far in advance of other boys that age."

As a seventh grader, Jastremski was racing, and beating, college swimmers in all four strokes. At age thirteen, he was eighth at an AAU nationals. But after Edwards left the Toledo YMCA for Kenyon College, Jastremski's progress stalled. His high school, St. Francis de Sales, had no swim team. The swimmer lacked guidance and motivation. He gave up playing double bass in a dance band, but that didn't help. Former rivals passed him. Counsilman recruited him, though, seeing something in Jastremski that no one else did.

Initially, Jastremski found it as hard to learn from Counsilman as it was from his YMCA instructor. The coach called Jastremski "a frustrated butterflyer" who was trying to avoid Ken Nakasone. His Hawaiian teammate always beat him in practice. Jastremski was "pretty lousy" sometimes, as Counsilman put it, but stayed with breaststroke as the coach continued to experiment with technique.

Counsilman's theory was to introduce short, fast arm pulls and leg kicks rather than a wide, slow motion that had been conventional. It made Jastremski look like a tugboat churning through a choppy river.

> "Doc made my stroke narrower because that cuts down water resistance," Jastremski said. "Instead of lifting the entire body to breathe, I lift my head by using only the neck, so I can ride low in the water rather than high. That avoids working against gravity and cuts down surface tension. Actually, you can go faster underwater than on the surface, so I start with a deep, sharply angled dive and take a long, underwater glide off each turn. I also take several more strokes per lap than most breaststrokers. Doc has me breathe every stroke instead of every other."

Jastremski never won an NCAA title because football violations caused Indiana to be banned from national championships in all sports in his three varsity seasons (1961, 1962, 1963). There was no stopping his 1961 record spree, though.

From July 2 to August 20—beginning in Chicago and later in Tokyo, Osaka, and Los Angeles—he lowered the world record six times in the 100-meter breaststroke, twice in the 200 and once in the 4×100 medley relay. He trimmed the record in the 100 from 1:11.4 to 1:07.5. He was on the *Sports Illustrated* cover a few months later.

"That was a great thing, and I really enjoyed the experience," he said. "But, by the year after, I was largely ignored. There wasn't much emphasis on swimming then. The interest was in professional sports."

Jastremski showed what could have been in two Big Ten meets. In 1962, his winning times in the 100- and 200-yard breaststrokes were 1:01.7 and 2:13.7. Winning NCAA times were 1:01.7 (by Michigan's Richard Nelson, who was beaten by Jastremski in the Big Ten) and 2:16.8. A year later, Jastremski's times were 1:00.9 and 2:13.2, compared with 1:02.2 and 2:17.0 for the NCAA champions.

Besides his nine individual world records (and three in relays), he finished his career with a gold medal from the 1963 Pan American Games, twenty-one American records (four in relays), and sixteen national AAU titles. He was the first to swim the 100-yard breaststroke in less than a minute.

He practiced family medicine in Bloomington from 1972 until 1979, when he had to give it up because of pain from rheumatoid arthritis. He taught kinesiology at IU and served as women's swim coach for the Hoosiers for five years, then reopened his family medical practice in 1991. He kept his world-record certificates in a wood-bound book that even his three children and five stepchildren never saw until late in his life. His son, Kelly Jastremski, said his father's empathy made him adored by swimmers and patients alike.

"As a coach, he would always try and create situations that inspired people," said Kelly, a dentist and former swimmer. "He was the type of person that would push you, but he wouldn't belittle you. He wanted to make you feel as good as you can be."

He had the gift when people came into his office of making them feel good just by his disposition regardless of their condition, whether it was with a joke or really showing a lot of caring and empathy for their situation. He was a huge inspiration for me for the things I've chosen to do.

His grandson, Logan Jastremski, added to the family legacy when he swam for Bloomington South's winning 200-yard freestyle relay team at the 2012 high school state meet. Jastremski's grandson went on to swim for the Hoosiers.

Chet Jastremski was inducted into the International Swimming Hall of Fame in 1977, IU's Hall of Fame in 1983 and National Polish-American Hall of Fame in 2007. He died May 3, 2014, in Bloomington.

Kathy Ellis
1964

Four Medals as a Seventeen-Year-Old

IF SHE HAD BEEN BORN IN ANOTHER ERA, KATHY ELLIS MIGHT HAVE BEEN A three-time Olympian and collected multiple medals. But she is not at all resentful about the opportunities she had.

"Oh, gosh no," she said. "It was a different time. It was a really different time."

As a seventeen-year-old, she came away from the 1964 Tokyo Olympics with four medals, including golds (and world records) in anchoring two relays. It was such a different time that Ellis said she was the second-oldest swimmer on the US team.

She won a bronze in the 100-meter freestyle from an outside lane, qualifying seventh for the final. Ellis said that was not as great of an achievement as it sounds because she was conserving energy in her semifinal.

"I miscalculated a little bit, is the truth of why I was in an outside lane," she said. "And almost didn't get in there."

The gold medalist was Australia's Dawn Fraser, then twenty-seven. Weeks earlier, Fraser had been injured in a car collision that killed her mother. She became the first swimmer of either gender to win the same event at three successive Olympics. Fraser set an Olympic record of 59.5 seconds, followed by Americans Sharon Stouder and Ellis in 59.9 and 1:00.8, respectively. Stouder won gold in the 100 butterfly, with Ellis again claiming bronze.

Ellis said the Olympics is "something that stays with you" and that she continued to be asked about her experience a half century later. Publicity for the Olympics was much less then, she said. She remembers the "architecturally beautiful" aquatics venue in Japan.

"The basketball arena was next to it. It seemed kind of hysterical to us, being from Indiana," Ellis said.

Kathy Ellis
Courtesy of Indiana Swimming.

Ellis was a prodigy at the Indianapolis Athletic Club, winning her first national title as a fourteen-year-old in 1961. She later shifted to the Riviera Club in Indianapolis.

In 1963, she won a gold medal in the 100 butterfly and bronze in the 100 freestyle in the Pan American Games at São Paulo, Brazil. Ellis's sister, Maddie, also won a gold at the Pan Am Games and barely missed making the Olympic team.

Later in 1963, Ellis set a world record of 1:06.5 in the 100 butterfly at the nationals. That led to her first encounter with famed Olympic broadcaster Jim McKay of ABC.

"I set my world record and afterwards, it's High Point, North Carolina. You know how girls are, and he looked at me, I just set a world record, and he asked, 'Is that lipstick you have on?' I don't know what to say," Ellis said.

In Tokyo, she and Stouder, Donna de Varona, and Pokey Watson won gold in the 4×100 freestyle relay in 4:03.8, a world record. De Varona, also seventeen, had set a world record in winning gold in the individual medley. She was a magazine cover girl even before the Olympics and later a TV trailblazer, teaming with McKay on ABC and becoming the first female network sportscaster. De Varona covered the Olympics from 1968 through 1996.

In an amateur era before allowable swim income, Title IX, and women's college sports, Ellis retired from swimming to enroll at Indiana University. She graduated from IU with a nursing degree in 1969.

"I think it's interesting when you hear people say, 'But you missed out on this, that, and the other.' No, look at what I did! I got to go to South America. I went to Japan," Ellis said.

She returned to swimming as coach at the Riveria Club and coached the men's team at Butler University. The retired nurse has two children. She and husband Charles Greer live near the Butler campus and often attend basketball games at Hinkle Fieldhouse. Ellis was inducted into the International Swimming Hall of Fame in 1991.

Fred Schmidt
1964

Human "Battleship" Rescued Astronauts Who Walked on the Moon

ATHLETES ARE ENCOURAGED TO SHOOT FOR THE MOON. FRED SCHMIDT ONCE rescued those who did just that.

The Indiana University swimmer, who won gold and bronze medals at the 1964 Olympics, became a Navy SEAL and member of an underwater demolition team. He was a lieutenant in charge of Apollo 14 and 15 recovery missions, both in 1971 in the Pacific Ocean. They were the third and fourth space missions to land men on the moon.

Frogmen assigned to pick up the astronauts were equipped with a giant syringe to ward off sharks, injecting them with carbon dioxide.

"Because he cannot swim, a shark cannot breathe, so he presents no problem," Schmidt said.

Frederick Weber Schmidt was born October 23, 1943, in Evanston, Illinois. He was a swimmer at New Trier High School of Winnetka, Illinois. In 1961, New Trier was recognized as one of the greatest high school teams of all time, holding every national high school record. At the state championships, Schmidt set an American record of 52.7 seconds in the 100-yard butterfly, breaking the record of 53.1 held by the Hoosiers' Mike Troy, an Olympic gold medalist. New Trier finished third in the AAU Championships behind Yale and IU.

At age seventeen, Schmidt set a world record of 58.6 in the 100-meter butterfly on August 20, 1961, a mark that stood until the following April. At six foot two and 182 pounds, he appeared to be all arms. His technique was so exceptional that video exists of him demonstrating butterfly to sportscaster Bud Palmer as Santa Clara Swim Club coach George Haines narrates. Adolph Kiefer, a swim equipment innovator, was the last surviving gold medalist of the 1936 Olympics. Kiefer, who died in 2017 at ninety-eight, once wrote of Schmidt, "When he goes through that water with arms plowing, he looks like a battleship."

Schmidt won his first NCAA title in 1964, in the 200-yard butterfly, and was second in the 100 butterfly. Oddly, there was no 100-meter butterfly on the program for the Tokyo Olympics. Schmidt set an American record of 2:08.0 in the 200-meter butterfly at the Olympic Trials in Astoria, New York. At the Olympics, he won a bronze medal behind Australia's Kevin Berry, who set a world record of 2:06.6 and later represented the Hoosiers.

Schmidt won gold in the 4×100 medley relay, in which the United States became the first team ever to go under four minutes, clocking a world record of 3:58.4. Thompson Mann led off with a world record of 59.6, making him the first man under one minute in the 100 backstroke. Germany and the Soviet Union were even with the United States through two legs, but Schmidt's 56.8 butterfly leg pushed the Americans far ahead. (At the time, the butterfly world record was 57.0.)

Schmidt became a real estate syndicator and head of the San Diego-based Doerring Group, a real estate investment and development company with operations in California, Arizona, Texas, and Colorado.

Fred Schmidt, 1961.
IU Archives P0021735.

Frank McKinney Jr.
1956, 1960

Pushing Forward in the Backstroke

FRANK MCKINNEY JR. WAS A PIONEERING BACKSTROKER AND FOUNDAtional figure in coach Doc Counsilman's Indiana swimming dynasty. And so much more: army intelligence officer, banker, civic leader, car collector. He even helped a Hungarian swimmer defect.

As a sixteen-year-old sophomore at Indianapolis's Cathedral High School, McKinney won two gold medals—100-meter backstroke and 4×100-meter medley relay—in the 1955 Pan American Games at Mexico City. McKinney followed that the next year by taking bronze in the 100-meter backstroke at the Melbourne Olympics.

His decision to attend Indiana helped the Hoosiers sweep past Yale as college swimming's dominant power. He was killed September 11, 1992, in midair collision of two small airplanes. He was fifty-three.

As a teenager, McKinney was the leader of a group of Indianapolis Athletic Club swimmers who won a national team championship while still in high school. Until he introduced the bent-arm technique, the conventional style of backstroke was the straight-arm used by Yoshi Oyakawa, an American who was gold medalist at the 1952 Olympics. Films shot by Counsilman of McKinney's bent-arm influenced modern backstrokes.

"There never has been a prettier backstroker," teammate Alan Somers once said. "When he swam, there was no splash."

McKinney Jr. was born November 3, 1938, the son of Frank McKinney, a national Democratic chairman whose houseguests often included Harry S. Truman. The elder McKinney also owned the Pittsburgh Pirates.

After the 1956 Olympics, McKinney was voted outstanding US male aquatics athlete by the *Los Angeles Times* and Columbus Touchdown Club. His most vivid Melbourne memory was in helping a Hungarian swimmer defect, according to an

Frank McKinney Jr., 1960.
IU Archives P0079366.

interview in *Fortune* magazine. Just before those Olympics opened, Soviet troops invaded Hungary to quell a rebellion. In the Olympic village, athletes slept on platform beds nailed to the floor. McKinney said he removed his box spring and hid the swimmer underneath. While the KGB searched, McKinney lay in bed, and the swimmer escaped.

McKinney was a fourteen-time national champion and swept Big Ten backstrokes in 1959, 1960, and 1961. His best year was perhaps 1959, when the twenty-year-old won two NCAA titles and twice set world records in the 200-meter backstroke in a fourteen-day span. That event was not on the Olympic program until 1964.

At the 1960 Rome Olympics, he won silver in the 100 backstroke behind repeat champion David Theile of Australia. Theile set an Olympic record of 1:01.9, followed by McKinney in 1:02.1. A postseason ban for football violations kept Indiana swimmers out of NCAA Championships from 1961 to 1963, so McKinney could not add to his NCAA totals.

He worked for two years as an officer in US Army Intelligence and became a banker. He advanced from assistant cashier of the First National Bank of Chicago to vice president, then president and chairman of the board of the Indianapolis-based American Fletcher Corp., a banking company his father headed from 1959 to 1968. He became president of Banc One after it bought American Fletcher. As a swimmer who once trained for two to six hours a day, McKinney said he learned time management, and he kept to an exercise routine of running, swimming, and tennis.

"You can plug into your time management anything you want," he said. "You can plan to do nothing."

He kept a small office in a downtown Indianapolis hideaway, a building that was a one-story warehouse on North Illinois Street. There he kept fourteen cars, including a 1941 four-door Cadillac that had belonged to his father. Two of the cars were the antithesis of the quiet McKinney: a bright red 1990 ZR-1 Corvette and bright red 1957 Chevy short-bed pickup truck.

McKinney's death came less than a year after the longtime Democrat turned down a Republican invitation to seek the party's nomination for governor. He was inducted into the International Swimming Hall of Fame in 1975, or ten years after he helped found the hall and served as its first treasurer. He was influential in bringing Amateur Athletic Union headquarters to Indianapolis.

Reverend Joe Wade, pastor of St. Matthew Catholic Church, was a high school classmate and spoke at McKinney's funeral.

"He had discipline, which he acquired in childhood, and he used it for the rest of his life to achieve the goals he sought," Wade said.

McKinney is buried at Crown Hill Cemetery in Indianapolis.

Mike Troy
1960

Magazine Jinx? Not This Swimmer

MIKE TROY APPEARED ON THE *SPORTS ILLUSTRATED* COVER OF AUGUST 1, 1960, ahead of the Olympic Trials. A month later, at the Rome Olympics, the nineteen-year-old swimmer became a double gold medalist.

He was invulnerable against the infamous *SI* cover jinx. Pretty good for someone who, well, was a fat kid.

Troy was barely getting started when he swam in the Olympics. He became a naval officer, decorated war veteran, successful coach, and Paralympics advocate.

Troy was three years old when his father, an Indianapolis coal dealer, died. His mother, Helen, worked as a secretary to support him and an older brother.

> "When I was twelve, there was only one way to describe me—fat," he told *Sports Illustrated* for that 1960 cover story. "That year I started swimming at an Indianapolis pool. We had a team that swam against other city pools, and I got on it, just to kid around, really. I didn't want to race. But our coach said race or quit. My first race I finished second. What a surprise! I won a red ribbon. There's never been a redder ribbon. It was my biggest thrill. Then I found out you could win medals, too. It seemed like a real deal. I've been at it ever since."

His journey took him from Our Lady of Lourdes Elementary School and Ellenberger Park pool to Scecina Memorial High School and Indianapolis Athletic Club.

In the late 1950s, the butterfly was evolving as an offshoot of the breaststroke, and Troy was revolutionizing the dolphin kick. There was only one butterfly event at the Olympics, the 200 meters, and no medley relay. Under the modern schedule, Troy might have left Rome with four golds: 100 and 200 fly, 4×100 and 4×200 freestyle relays.

From the Indianapolis Athletic Club, Troy went to Indiana University to train under Doc Counsilman. Troy had "a rare, intuitive feel for the water; instinctive

Mike Troy, 1959.
IU Archives P0021937.

reaction to push back when the pressure of water is felt on his hands," Counsilman said.

Freshmen then were not eligible for varsity sports, so Troy began his college career as a sophomore in 1959–60. Troy thought he could provoke his coach when he told Counsilman his goal in the 200-yard butterfly was 2:00.99. The record was 2:01.

Counsilman told him his time would be in the 1:57s. The swimmer was dumbfounded. "I thought, 'The man doesn't know what the record is,'" Troy said. "What the hell is wrong with him?"

Troy's time at the NCAA Championships: 1:57.4. He was the first to swim the event under two minutes.

Leading up to the Olympic Trials, Troy and other swimmers stayed for eight weeks in the house of his fraternity, Phi Kappa Psi, near campus. Their training timetable was one "that would demoralize a monk," *SI* reported.

"You want to train, but you dread that morning workout," Troy said. "I lie in bed and I hope that somehow they'll forget me. They never do. Lots of guys sleep in swimsuits so they can stay in bed longer. Sometimes they go three days without taking them off."

He set the first six ratified world records in the 200-meter butterfly. The magazine cover preceded the Olympic Trials at Detroit, where he lowered the record to 2:13.2 on August 4.

> We had the picture of the Olympic medal on the wall on our bulletin board at the pool. It was just a black-and-white photograph. There was no frame around it, just the medal. I used to say, "I'm going to the Olympics, I'm going to win a medal, I'm going to win the gold medal." I was so convinced, like Cassius Clay saying I'm the greatest there is, I kept saying to myself, "I'm going to win, I'm going to win, I'm going to win. All I have to do is go to Rome and pick it up." I envisioned in my own mind that my name was engraved on the side of that, which I thought was very thick. *Michael Francis Troy* in beautiful script, much better than I could write.

(Regrettably, in 2010, one of Troy's gold medals was stolen in Arizona.)

Troy took gold in the 200-meter butterfly in Rome, lowering his world record to 2:12.8. He won by three body lengths with a margin of victory of 1.8 seconds—exceeded only by Mark Spitz (1972) at an Olympics. Troy swam third leg in the 4×200 freestyle relay, in which the Americans set another world record (8:10.2) in overcoming Australian and Japanese teams that had dominated the event since 1955.

He finished with five Big Ten titles and was captain of the Hoosiers' 1962 team. His 1961 team won the first of Counsilman's twenty consecutive Big Ten championships. Before that, he helped the Hoosiers end Michigan's streak of thirty-three straight dual-meet victories.

A postseason ban for football violations kept Indiana swimmers out of NCAA Championships from 1961 to 1963, so his last collegiate meet was the Big Ten on March 2, 1962 (coincidentally, the day Wilt Chamberlain scored one hundred points in an NBA game). Troy's time of 52.9 in the 100-yard butterfly set an American record.

After graduating, Troy studied for a year in Switzerland, then signed up for officer's candidate school. He did not want to swim anymore until he learned underwater demolition SEAL teams earned double play for hazardous duty.

"You got to scuba dive, jump out of airplanes, ride in subs, shoot off explosives," Troy said. "It was really fun... 'til it was time for Vietnam and they started shooting real bullets at you. Then it was not so fun."

He started coaching a Navy SEALs swim team program before being deployed, then resumed coaching when he returned. In the Vietnam War, he was awarded the Silver Star for heroism.

His first club was the Coronado Navy Swimming Association, which started out with twenty-five kids and eventually produced four Olympic gold medalists, including Matt Biondi. Troy later started the Gold Medal Swim School in Chandler, Arizona, and was national director for the US swim team at the 2004 Athens Paralympics. He was chosen national teacher of the year by the United States Swim School Association in 2004. He also served as a national director for the US Paralympic swim team.

Even a half century after the Olympics, Troy continued receiving two or three letters a week, asking for autographs. He is willing to sign the *SI* cover in exchange for donations to a nonprofit supporting wounded warriors.

"When I sign autographs for kids, I sign, 'Do something great with your life,' or 'Make your parents proud,'" he said.

He died August 3, 2019, in Arizona. He was seventy-eight.

Bill Woolsey
1952, 1956

Hawaii Was Once a Hotbed for Swimming

DOC COUNSILMAN IS RIGHTFULLY CREDITED WITH BUILDING INDIANA UNIversity into a swimming power. But before Counsilman arrived on campus, a Hawaiian named Bill Woolsey helped jump-start the program.

Woolsey, who became the Hoosiers' first NCAA swim champion in 1956, was an Olympic gold medalist before he enrolled. At age seventeen, he was the youngest member of the American swim team and took gold in the 4×200-meter freestyle relay in 1952.

"I was just a kid," he said.

William Tripp Woolsey was born September 13, 1934, in Honolulu. He lived on the shoreline, and he was introduced to the water as soon as he could walk. When he was five or six, he said, he was able to go free-diving and fish with a spear and a sling. By the time he was eight or nine, he was swimming competitively.

Eventually, he was introduced to Soichi Sakamoto, a coach who was inducted into the International Swimming Hall of Fame. Sakamoto, a schoolteacher and Boy Scout scoutmaster on Maui, developed a training program that included swimming against the current of a drainage ditch. He was a US assistant coach at the

Bill Woolsey, 1956.
IU Archives P0028459.

1952 and 1956 Olympic Games. Nine swimmers with Hawaii ties competed in those two Olympics, four earning gold medals.

In 1937, Sakamoto started the Three-Year Swim Club, intending to produce swimmers for the 1940 Tokyo Olympics. The club's motto: "Olympics first and Olympics always." The 1940 Olympics were canceled because of World War II, but the club persisted. Sakamoto persuaded Woolsey to concentrate on swimming.

Woolsey, in a 2012 television interview, recalled Sakamoto's pitch.

"You play basketball?"

"Yeah."

"Quit."

"Football?"

"Yeah."

"You gotta quit."

"You surf?"

"Yes."

"Quit."

Woolsey spoke to his mother, and she agreed with the coach.

"You go down there and you swim, and give up everything," he remembered his mother saying. "And maybe that will keep you out of trouble."

Swimming got him to Astoria, New York, where he made the US team at the Olympic Trials, and then to Helsinki. He swam second leg on the 4×200 freestyle relay team that set an Olympic record of 8:31.1. Then swimming got him to Bloomington, where the coach was Robert Royer.

As a junior in 1956, Woolsey won Big Ten titles in the 220-, 440- and 1,650-yard freestyles. He added NCAA titles in the 220 and 440, helping the Hoosiers to sixth in team standings. He repeated those NCAA titles in 1957, and Indiana climbed to fourth. Also scoring for the Hoosiers were two other Hawaiians, Dick "Sonny" Tanabe and Ron Honda.

Woolsey won the 100-meter freestyle in 57.0 in the 1956 Olympic Trials at Detroit but was no match for the Australians, who swept the medals at Melbourne. He finished sixth in 57.6. He finished tenth in heats of the 400 freestyle in 4:38.2, or 0.6 from the final. Woolsey won his second Olympic medal, a silver in the 4×200 freestyle relay, far behind the Australians.

His international career continued through the 1959 Pan American Games at Chicago, where the twenty-four-year-old won a bronze medal in the 100 freestyle.

Woolsey became a learn-to-swim advocate and was dismayed when he found out so many Hawaiian children did not know how to swim in a state where water beckons. Swimming, which was once mandatory in physical education programs in schools, was phased out.

"Most of the kids want to do board surfing," Woolsey said. "But the problem is, they don't know how to swim. They can barely tread water."

Woolsey became a high school coach in Hawaii and a swimming consultant to five private schools in Japan during a career lasting a half-century. His ten-lesson *Ho'au* ("forward in the water") learn-to-swim method taught children in Hawaii and California.

"He's like a magician, turning nonswimmers into swimmers," said Keith Arakaki, assistant coach with the Hawaii Swim Club.

Before that, he helped turn prairieland Indiana into a swimming state.

Michael Hixon
Courtesy of Indiana University Athletics.

Michael Hixon
2016

From Shooting Threes to Diving for Tens

HE COULD HAVE BEEN SPIKING A FOOTBALL AFTER A MEMORIAL STADIUM touchdown or exulting after a dunk in an Assembly Hall blowout. Except Michael Hixon was not in Bloomington but five thousand miles away, in Brazil.

Why not pound your fists in the water after what opponents called a "sick" final dive?

"As soon as that dive happened," Hixon said, "I was pretty sure we were a medal lock."

The Indiana University diver teamed with Sam Dorman for a silver medal in synchronized 3-meter springboard at the 2016 Rio Olympics. The two came within 4.11 points of gold.

That was shocking enough, considering they never competed as a pair until the US trials at Indianapolis two months before. Even more so was the fact they were second to Great Britain, not the all-powerful Chinese, who had won the three other synchro events.

"It's the Olympics. Anything can happen," Dorman said.

What happened to Hixon is that he became a celebrity, at least for a few days, because of his resemblance to Zac Efron. The actor was hanging out with Olympic athletes in Rio de Janeiro, and NBC's Olympics account posted a photo of the two together on Twitter.

That was a light moment, but competition was serious for the Hoosiers. IU swimmers and divers totaled seven medals in 2016, the most since winning fifteen in 1976.

Hixon and Dorman, of Tempe, Arizona, had hoped for bad weather, and got it. They trained outdoors in preparation for the open-air Maria Lenk Aquatics Center. They coped with wind, rain, and green water caused by a failure of the pool's chemical treatment. They climbed from seventh place after two rounds. Lastly, they weathered a delay before their final dive as the Mexican team asked for a do-over.

Dorman said that helped him because it was a distraction that took his mind off diving. He went on "autopilot," as he put it. Hixon and Dorman nailed their front 4½ somersault, receiving 8.5s and 8s on a high degree of difficulty. Their score of 98.04 was the highest of any of the forty-eight dives by eight teams. You have to slap the water after that.

"I was definitely very excited and very in the moment," Hixon said.

It was at a training camp where USA Diving coaches decided to pair Dorman with Hixon. They made it work. They did so even though Dorman, who was in his first major international competition, underwent daily treatment for a herniated disk.

Jack Laugher and Chris Mears won Britain's first diving gold ever with a score of 454.32. Hixon/Dorman scored 450.34, followed by China's Cao Yuan and Qin Kai with 443.70.

In individual 3-meter, Hixon finished tenth in Rio.

He was born July 16, 1994, in Amherst, Massachusetts. He is a former basketball player whose father, David, was the Amherst College basketball coach. His mother, Mandy, a former Ohio State diver, was diving coach at UMass-Amherst and formerly coached her son. The five-foot-eight Hixon shot hoops through his freshman year of high school before concentrating on diving.

"I think basketball is great cross-training," he said, adding that he no longer played, for fear of injuring his ankles. "I have quickness, fast-twitch, explosiveness ... it's huge."

Hixon began going to his mother's diving practices instead of day care, learning to hang from his feet off the 3-meter board when he was four. Besides basketball, he also excelled in football, soccer, and lacrosse.

"He's always had a knack for sports. It's his biggest thing," said his older brother, Matthew. "He has a crazy drive when it comes to athletics and working hard. He's had amazing skill at every sport he's played. From a young age you could tell Michael had this incredible ability in terms of athleticism. He would lift himself completely horizontal on a pole with just his arms. He was always impressing older people, which I was always noticing."

Jim Matuszko, the Amherst Regional High School coach, said Hixon would have been a four-year varsity player with an "off the charts" basketball IQ. But the coach ran a trucking business and could only hold basketball practices at night. That conflicted with diving practice, and Hixon became a full-time diver.

He won the first of his nine junior national titles soon after his thirteenth birthday. In 2010, he was a bronze medalist at the Youth Olympics in Singapore. He won 1-meter bronze and synchro silver at the 2012 and 2010 World Junior Championships, respectively. Beginning in 2011, Hixon was on the national team every year.

He spent his freshman season at University of Texas, where he won NCAA 1- and 3-meter titles in 2014, before transferring to Indiana. He did so to follow Drew Johansen, the US Olympic coach in 2012 and 2016.

"It's the best decision I ever made," Hixon said. "Indiana's definitely more me. I made that move because I thought if I was to make a run at 2016, coach Johansen was the best man for the job. I thought he's exactly what I needed. He's taken my diving to another level."

Hixon did not repeat his NCAA titles in 2015 but that summer surprisingly won a bronze medal on 1-meter in the World Championships at Kazan, Russia. That was prelude to the Olympic year, in which he redshirted.

He twice was diver of the Big Ten Championships, setting a conference meet record on 1-meter in 2017. Hixon left Indiana with four Big Ten titles. In his senior year, 2018, he won the NCAAs on 1-meter and became the first male IU diver to be national champion since Mark Lenzi on 1-meter in 1990.

Hixon did not win medals at either the 2017 or 2019 World Championships. He teamed with another Hoosier diver, Andrew Capobianco, for a bronze in synchronized 3-meter in the 2019 Pan American Games at Lima, Peru.

Mark Lenzi
1992, 1996

Gold Medalist from "Out of Nowhere"

MARK LENZI WAS INSPIRED TO BECOME A DIVER AFTER WATCHING TELEvised coverage of Greg Louganis at the 1984 Olympic Games.
One problem, though. Lenzi was sixteen, far beyond the ideal age to take up such a technical sport. When Louganis was sixteen, for instance, he had already won an Olympic silver medal. But Lenzi defied convention and won an Olympic gold medal on 3-meter springboard in 1992 and followed that with a bronze in 1996.
"No one has ever learned that quick and done so much," former Indiana University coach Hobie Billingsley said.
Lenzi, five foot four and 160 pounds, was a high school wrestler in Fredricksburg, Virginia. He was so determined to be a diver that he ran away from home for a couple weeks and quit wrestling, a sport in which his father thought Lenzi could earn a college scholarship.
"It's the strangest thing," Lenzi said, "but ever since I saw the Olympics in '84, I just knew I could do it. I put my trust in God. He gave me the opportunity, and I did the best I could with it."
Fittingly, he was born on the Fourth of July in 1968, in Huntsville, Alabama. The family moved to Fredricksburg, where there was no pool at his school. So he drove an hour twice a week to train in Washington, DC. On the advice of a former Hoosier diver, Lenzi was awarded a scholarship by Indiana.
Billingsley recalled that Ron O'Brien, who coached Louganis, told Lenzi, "You're too late. And you're too rough. Take up golf."
After first watching Lenzi dive, Billingsley agreed. "He was terrible."

Mark Lenzi, 1989.
IU Archives P0030174.

Not for long. Lenzi astounded everyone, except perhaps himself, with his rapid rise. He could learn dives in one day that others took months to master. Still, clashes between coach and diver—both strong-willed—were inevitable.

"When I first met Hobie, I was a spoiled little brat," Lenzi said. "I thought everybody should do things for me and I didn't have to do anything for anyone.

"Hobie set me straight. He said you've got to carry your weight around here. He helped me grow up a lot. He kicked me in the butt when I needed it. He just said, 'You're equal with everyone else. Go out, work hard, and see what happens.'"

A lot happened.

In 1989, Lenzi swept Big Ten titles on 1-meter, 3-meter, and platform. He won two NCAA titles on 1-meter and was NCAA Diver of the Year in 1989 and '90.

After graduation, he left Bloomington to train under coach Dick Kimball in Ann Arbor, Michigan. In 1991, Lenzi won gold on 1-meter at the Pan American Games, a world championship, and became the first to score more than 100 points on a single dive. He was the first American to complete a forward 4½ somersault in competition. By 1992, he had made it to the Barcelona Olympics.

In the 3-meter final in Spain, in between dives, Lenzi listened to music of the rock group U2. The song: "I Still Haven't Found What I'm Looking For."

After five compulsory dives, the gold medal was coming down to three men: China's twenty-seven-year-old Tan Liangde, the silver medalist behind Louganis in 1984 and 1988; Germany's Albin Killat; and Lenzi. Killat slipped as he began his seventh dive, resulting in a belly flop that dropped him to last place. That left Lenzi and the favored Tan. By the end of the competition, Lenzi had the three highest scores of the competition and comfortably won by thirty-one points.

Before his final dive, a reverse 3½ that was his specialty, the Hoosier had essentially secured gold. Not that he knew. He had not looked at the scoreboard once.

"I don't want to know," he said. "That's a pressure I don't need. I just want to worry about me. It doesn't matter what anybody else does.

"Before my last dive, I went to Kimball and said, 'What do I need here?' He said, 'Do what you do every single day in practice.' I got myself calm, really relaxed, and said, 'God, let me hit this dive.' The Lord blessed me and let me have a great performance."

The aftermath of the Olympics was more difficult than learning new dives.

Oh, there were some high points, including participation in celebrity and charity events. Lenzi competed in ABC's *Superstars* competition in Cancun, Mexico, and finished first in the 50-yard freestyle swimming race. He posed with President Bush in the White House and appeared on *The Tonight Show with Jay Leno*. Lenzi was one of ten finalists for the AAU's Sullivan Award, which goes to the nation's outstanding amateur athlete.

Yet post-Olympic depression seized him. He once told Billingsley that winning the gold medal was the worst thing that ever happened to him. Lenzi acknowledged that he harmed his health with drinking and junk food. He suggested using his

Olympic medal as collateral for a loan to become a professional pilot. At one point, he could not get a job as a pizza delivery man in Bloomington.

Publicity about Lenzi's plight resulted in a 1994 appearance on ABC's *Good Morning America*. That gave him new opportunities. He signed as national spokesman for the National Air Transportation Association, whose headquarters are in Washington, and the Aviation Career Academy in Lakeland, Florida. It was a fit for Lenzi, son of a navy physicist. He had been around military aircraft all his life and called *Top Gun* his favorite movie.

He was lambasted, too, especially in his hometown newspaper. The Fredricksburg (Virginia) *Free Lance-Star* reported he was looking for a handout and did not know the value of his gold medal.

"If anybody understands what my medal's worth, it's me," Lenzi responded. "I'm the one that put in all the work it took to do it. I never wanted to sell my medal; I wanted to use it as collateral to get a low-interest loan."

Lenzi did eventually earn his pilot's license, but he was not through with diving yet. He returned to the sport in 1995, reuniting with Billingsley, who had intended to retire from coaching in 1989. Lenzi twice bettered Louganis's unofficial world record for an eleven-dive score. The diver trained diligently but could not stay healthy. He hurt his shoulder and pulled a stomach muscle.

At the Olympic Trials in Indianapolis, he was one dive away from not making the US team. But in vintage Lenzi fashion, he pulled it out with his second 100-point score on a reverse 3½ somersault. That pulled him into second place behind Scott Donie and qualified him for the Atlanta Olympics.

"He's amazing," Louganis said. "He's so tough. He's more of a competitor than I was. I had to learn to be a competitor."

Although Lenzi was defending gold medalist, he was not the favorite in 1996. There were moments in which Billingsley wondered if Lenzi should be in Atlanta at all. In a training camp in Lexington, Kentucky, Lenzi looked anything but ready for an Olympics . . . until reeling off a sequence of crisp dives in an exhibition.

"He didn't show a thing in practice, but when the lights came on, he was unbelievable," Billingsley said. "The tougher the competition, the better he would dive."

Lenzi resolved to enjoy his second Olympics. Barcelona was "the greatest Olympics I never saw," he said, and he reveled in the environment of competing in his home country. Yet the new attitude did nothing to douse the fire in the old Lenzi.

Gold and silver medals were won by two Chinese divers: Xiong Ni, who had won platform medals in 1988 and 1992 before injuries diverted him to springboard, and Yu Zhuocheng, the reigning world champion. Battle for bronze came down to the two Americans. Lenzi faltered on a couple of dives, acknowledging afterward that he was nervous.

Then he scored 92.40, highest of any score in the finals, on the last dive of his career—the reverse 3½ somersault. When it mattered, Billingsley said, he always hit that dive. Lenzi returned to the medal podium, edging Donie by 1.57 points.

"At Barcelona I was younger and on top of my game," Lenzi said. "The gold medal will always be a highlight. But I actually have to say the bronze medal means more to me right now because of all the injuries. I shouldn't even be here."

As the 2020 Tokyo Olympics approached, no American diver had won an individual Olympic medal on springboard since Lenzi. After Atlanta, he dabbled in various careers but ultimately came back to diving as a coach. He coached at Clemson, Indiana (junior team), and East Carolina.

He was inducted into the International Swimming Hall of Fame in 2003 but was just as thrilled to join the IU Hall of Fame in 2001.

"I dreamed about it when I first arrived on campus and saw all of the legends in Assembly Hall," Lenzi said. "Little did I know that one day I would have the honor of being included with this very prestigious group. I was so overcome with emotion at the ceremony that I almost broke down."

On March 28, 2012, Lenzi suffered fainting spells and was taken to Vidant Medical Center in Greenville, North Carolina, because of low blood pressure. According to his mother, he had been taking medication for a heart ailment. He died on April 9 at the age of forty-three. Lenzi was survived by his wife, Dorothy, mother, Ellie, and three siblings. His father, Bill, had died of a heart attack in 2007.

The Olympics are rich with stories of achievement amid unusual circumstances, but Lenzi's is as extraordinary as any. No one watches TV, tells himself he could win a gold medal, and then goes out and does so. Yet that is exactly what he did.

"The diving world has never seen anything like him, and probably never will," Donie said. "He came from out of nowhere and in three years he was World Cup champion. That's unheard of. And within six years, he won the Olympics. It was unbelievable."

Cynthia Potter
1972, 1976

America's Most Decorated Female Diver

CYNTHIA POTTER DID NOT RECEIVE A VARSITY LETTER FROM INDIANA UNIversity until 1997, twenty-five years after she represented the Hoosiers in diving. That was not the letter that changed her life, though. A letter from Hobie Billingsley did.

When she was thirteen, Potter, a Houston resident, was sent a letter by Billingsley asking her to come to IU. Except she never received it. Four years later, as the diver was about to enroll in college, her local coach gave the seventeen-year-old that letter. Potter immediately called the Indiana coach.

"He told me he was working with athletes in preparation for the Olympic Trials and suggested I come right away," Potter said. "I was so thrilled, I packed my bags."

Swim coach Doc Counsilman reasoned Indiana could accept up to three female divers without detracting from time spent coaching the men. She did not follow through on her plan to enroll at the University of Texas.

"So I told my mother that I was going to Indiana, and she looked at me like I was an alien," Potter recalled. "She said, 'You're going to Texas.' I said, 'I'm going to Indiana, and I'm going to dive there.' She must have thought I had gotten into the liquor cabinet."

Potter's decision was fateful. By the end of summer, she had become national champion and finished fourth at the trials, making her an alternate for the Mexico City Olympics.

She went on to win twenty-eight national titles, most ever by a female American diver. She made three Olympic teams, won a bronze medal on 3-meter springboard at Montreal in 1976, and was a three-time world diver of the year.

She became a television analyst for diving and has been part of NBC's broadcast team at every Olympic Games since 1992. Potter was a coach at Southern Methodist

Cynthia Potter, 1976.
IU Archives P0029417.

University, the University of Arizona, and clubs in Tucson and Atlanta, and she contributed to the sport as a judge, ambassador, and fund-raiser.

She was born August 27, 1950, in Houston. She began diving at the Shamrock Hilton pool, which in the late 1940s started one of Houston's first swimming teams, and at the indoor Tropicana Pool near Hobby Airport. Potter competed for the girls swimming team at Lamar High School because there was no diving program.

It was an era before Title IX, the civil rights law prohibiting gender discrimination at educational institutions. Female athletes persevered with little support.

"There were no scholarships—just girls that Hobie said could dive with the men's team," Potter said. "We didn't have access to any kind of facilities. We weren't allowed in the weight room. We didn't have a training room for medical attention. I knew the men were on scholarship and could dive during the NCAA season and ride on the school plane. We would pile into a station wagon and drive to an AAU meet if there was one nearby. But we didn't feel denied. We had a coach who was coaching us after high school. I thought I had died and gone to heaven."

In her first major international meet, at age twenty, she won two medals in the 1970 World University Games at Turin, Italy—gold on 3-meter and silver on 10-meter platform.

In 1972, Potter won Big Ten titles on 1- and 3-meter—and in the 400-yard freestyle relay, an occurrence unimaginable today for a diver. She subsequently qualified for the Munich Olympics but knocked herself out of contention there, literally and figuratively.

"I stayed up late. I visited all the athletes who had enthralled me for years," she said. "The bottom line—I was distracted and lost perspective."

Even worse, she hit her foot in a practice dive off the tower and was so badly bruised that she had to be carried to and from the *schwimmhalle*. She competed while medicated, finishing seventh on 3-meter and twenty-first on 10-meter. At the time, she said, she thought it was the worst thing in the world.

"Then I thought the worst thing was when President Carter ordered us to boycott the '80 Olympics Games, which were going to be my last hurrah," Potter said. "Now I realize both experiences resulted in other opportunities. That's something all of us can keep in mind, whatever our disappointments."

Diving off tower took a toll on her body, and she eventually discontinued that. She had elbow tendinitis, a wrenched arm, pulled shoulder muscles, and torn back ligaments. She took an eight-month layoff in the mid-1970s, during which she studied ballet in attempt to become more graceful in diving.

Sandwiched around her Olympic bronze medal were a bronze in the 1975 Pan American Games at Mexico City and silver in the 1978 World Championships at West Berlin. She won the last of her national titles in 1979, off 1-meter, and would have competed at Moscow if not for the 1980 boycott.

Moving into coaching was a natural progression, but her entry into TV came about because of her Hoosier connections. IU diver Ken Sitzberger was going to work for ABC at the 1984 Los Angeles Olympics, and the network wanted an analyst for women's diving. Sitzberger suggested Potter.

She auditioned and got the job. Sitzberger died before the Olympics, so ABC asked her to cover men's diving too. She has been a TV fixture ever since.

That once required triple duty. During an NCAA Championships at Indianapolis, she was a CBS commentator while also coaching one male and one female diver.

Awarding of an IU letter was belated but welcomed by Potter, who was honored along with other women in a 1997 ceremony on campus. When she competed, she said, she never thought about getting a letter.

"I am thrilled and grateful for all the blessings that have come my way, and there is no resentment over any "slights" of the time. You can't compare then to now.
... We never thought about scholarships, never thought about things now on all athletes' minds, not just young men like then. We didn't think about disparity. There weren't the words there are now to compare.

But that doesn't mean I don't think there should be comparisons or Title IX. We just didn't think about it. I think it's great that both genders now realize the importance of sport for women and men, and that sport doesn't inhibit a women's development but enhances it."

Potter is married to TV producer Peter Lasser and relocated to Atlanta. Besides her diving, coaching, and TV careers, Potter was a trustee for the US Diving Foundation, a Special Olympics volunteer, and a member of the USA Diving and International Swimming Hall of Fame boards of directors. She was inducted into the International Swimming Hall of Fame in 1987.

Lesley Bush, 1966.
IU Archives P0028247.

Lesley Bush
1964, 1968

A Gold Medal No One Could Believe

IT MIGHT HAVE BEEN THE GREATEST UPSET IN THE HISTORY OF DIVING. Indiana University coach Hobie Billingsley said it was.

In a span of six months in 1964, Lesley Bush went from afterthought to Olympic champion. Her parents were so incredulous that when an Associated Press reporter's transoceanic phone call came at 5:00 a.m. to deliver the news, they did not believe him.

"A miracle," Billingsley said. It seems more so with benefit of more than a half century of hindsight.

Bush was born September 17, 1947, in Orange, New Jersey. She started diving at about age nine in Mountain Lakes, New Jersey. Facilities were less than ideal. Practice was sporadic. She also trained at the Dick Smith Swim Gym when her family lived in Phoenix. Her high school in Princeton, New Jersey, did not have a diving team.

"My parents said if I worked hard and was nice to my brother, I could do it," she recalled.

At the beginning of 1964, she was not on any list of Olympic hopefuls. She said classmates at her high school didn't know who she was. After she finished eleventh in the national AAU Championships in April, she trained that summer under Billingsley. He told her, "There's an outside, outside, outside chance you could make the Olympic team."

The Olympic Trials were at Astoria, New York, about fifty miles from Bush's home. She finished fourth on 3-meter springboard, one spot away from making the team going to Tokyo. This was to be her first competition ever on 10-meter platform, an event that scares beginners because the thirty-three-foot tower is the height of three-story building.

Linda Cooper, twenty, of San Bernardino, California, won the trials with a score of 531.90. Barbara McAllister Talmage, twenty-three, of Phoenix was second with 514.45. Bush, then sixteen, was third with 497.95 to make the team.

It would have been more appropriate for Bush to be a tourist than an athlete in Tokyo. Indeed, there is an archived photo of her wearing a kimono in what is believed to be the Olympic village.

The prohibitive favorite on 10-meter was East Germany's Ingrid Kramer, twenty-one, who swept the gold medals at Rome in 1960 and won a third gold on 3-meter at Tokyo. One more gold would match the record for diving held by the United States' Pat McCormick.

"I was the darkest of darkhorses," Bush said.

On her opening dive in Tokyo, she earned 9s from the judges to seize a lead that she never relinquished. The 7s she received on her last dive were enough to beat Kramer by 1.35 points for gold, 99.80 to 99.45. Cooper finished fourth. Asked afterward what she thought when realizing she could upset Kramer, the seventeen-year-old replied, "It was sort of scary, but gee, gosh, it was great."

The reporter who first contacted Bush's parents assured them he was serious. Donald and Margaret Bush were convinced when their daughter called an hour later.

"We were glad she called," her mother said, "because we still couldn't believe it. We thought someone was fooling us."

She said she and her husband could not stop giggling. Everyone in Princeton knew who their daughter was now.

Bush left Japan before closing ceremonies and was welcomed home by a crowd of more than 2,500 in a half-mile-long parade down Nassau Street in Princeton. She sat atop a thirty-foot float, wearing the official uniform of the US Olympic team. There were signs and banners all around town. Elizabeth Hughes, wife of New Jersey governor Richard J. Hughes, presented the gold medalist with a china bowl bearing the state seal in a ceremony at the Princeton YMCA. Gold medalists were invited to the White House, where Bush shook hands with President Lyndon Johnson.

"He said I had a pretty smile," Bush said, "so everything he did after that was all right with me."

After high school graduation, she enrolled at Indiana—without an athletic scholarship because there were none for women—and continued diving. She won five AAU national titles: platform, 1965, 1967, 1968; 1-meter, 1967; and 3-meter, 1968. She won the Lawrence J. Johnson Award as diver of the year in 1967, when she won a gold medal on platform in the Pan American Games at Winnipeg, Manitoba.

She returned to the Olympics in 1968 at Mexico City. Unlike Tokyo, her first dive was a poor one, dropping her out of contention. She finished twentieth.

She retired from the sport thereafter. Her brother, Dave Bush, represented the United States at the 1972 Olympics and finished twentieth on 3-meter. Their father had fought in World War II in Europe and expected to be sent to Japan afterward. Coincidentally, his children competed in Olympics in Germany and Japan.

"I can't say I was thinking about that at the time," Lesley Bush said. "When I was in Japan, they didn't take us around to a lot of places. I know we had been to war with Japan, but that was not my Olympic experience. Mine was one of sportsmanship and camaraderie."

Bush, a 1970 IU graduate, was a science teacher for many years. She was once married to IU swimmer Charlie Hickox, who won three gold medals and a silver in 1968, but they divorced. She later married another schoolteacher, David Makepeace, while living in the Florida Keys.

Schoolchildren would ask Bush about the Olympics, and many touched her gold medal or wore it around their necks. Even after formal retirement, she continued to teach, tutoring students in Fort Myers, Florida.

"I get to help them in math, English, and science," she said. "I also get to share my story with them. I dived because I loved diving. I didn't do it for anyone else's pleasure but mine, and it took me all the way to the Olympics! I want these children to know that they should do something they love."

She was inducted into the International Swimming Hall of Fame in 1986 and became the first woman inducted into IU's Hall of Fame a year later. The NCAA honored her with a Silver Anniversary Award as part of the class of 1995.

Ken Sitzberger (*left*), 1965. Also pictured is Coach Hobie Billingsley.
IU Archives P0031079.

Ken Sitzberger
1964

Precise and Prophetic

VISUALIZATION IS A TRENDY TECHNIQUE INTRODUCED TO MODERN ATHletes by sports psychologists. It was not prevalent in the 1960s, but Ken Sitzberger did not need to learn any such mental tricks. He had his own.

After the 1964 US Olympic Trials on 3-meter springboard, he and longtime coach Jerry Darda went out for a sandwich. Sitzberger said flat out, "I will win the gold medal." Darda said he didn't want to ruin Sitzberger's confidence, but the diver had barely made the team, narrowly beating fourth place.

"But Kenny had analyzed the whole thing, the strengths and weaknesses of the other divers who were ranked one, two, three in the world—they were his competition—and he knew they'd all be going to training camp for a few weeks before the Olympics," Darda recalled. "He told me, 'Those guys are going to see me in training camp, and that's going to help me. They're going to feel a lot of extra pressure after they see me dive every day. They're going to realize I just don't miss.'"

He did not.

Sitzberger, then nineteen, was coming off his first year at Indiana University, and freshmen were not eligible for college competition. But he had already won national titles while in high school in suburban Chicago.

For most of the Olympic competition, Sitzberger's prophecy was preposterous. In preliminaries, he finished third behind teammates Frank Gorman and Larry Andreasen. In the finals, Gorman, a navy lieutenant, outscored Sitzberger on each of the first eight dives (out of ten). After the eighth dive, Sitzberger came to coach Hobie Billingsley and told him Gorman's lead was too large to overcome. Billingsley pleaded with the diver, explaining Gorman still had a difficult somersault dive on his list.

Gorman missed badly on that ninth dive, and Sitzberger overtook him. After the tenth, Sitzberger held on to win the gold medal, just as he forecast—even though

Gorman had beaten him on nine of ten dives. The Hoosier led a 1–2–3 American finish, the last such sweep because rules changed, limiting each country to two divers.

"He had the best attitude about himself," Billingsley said. "He was very competitive. He could take pressure pretty well. Was he cocky? I'd call it controlled confidence. He was able to communicate well. He once talked a cop out of giving us a ticket. I couldn't have done that."

Kenneth Robert Sitzberger was born in Cedar Rapids, Iowa, on February 13, 1945. He grew up in River Forest, Illinois, and even as a youngster attracted Billingsley's attention. Simply put, the kid was a pest.

Over several summers when he was at Chicago pools, Billingsley recalled:

"Every summer, this little kid would come up and say, 'Hi, Mr. Billingsley. I'm Kenny Sitzberger, do you remember me? Would you please watch my dives?'

"Then one day when he was still in high school, he just wiped out all our divers in the nationals. I said, 'Hi, Mr. Sitzberger. I'm Hobie Billingsley. Do you remember me?'"

And that's how the diver became a Hoosier.

At Fenwick High School in Oak Park, Illinois, he was a member of the National Honor Society, German Club, and dance committee. As a high school senior, he won a bronze medal in the 1963 Pan American Games at São Paulo, Brazil. By the time he graduated, he was a six-time national finalist.

Before those 1964 trials, Sitzberger was listening to Billingsley talk about who had the best chances among his training group of making it to Tokyo. The coach began by mentioning Rick Gilbert (who did not make the team but did so in 1968). "And I named a couple of others when Ken Sitzberger popped up and said, 'Hey, how about me?'" the Indiana coach recalled.

> I casually replied that he would make the team, and proceeded to name a couple others when he interrupted me and said, "Wait a minute, that's not good enough. ... How do you know I will make the team?" I again replied, "Because I just know."
>
> Again, he got into my face and said, "That's not good enough ... I want proof!" Getting a little exasperated, I said, "OK, if I prove it to you, will you stop bothering me?" With that remark, I took three coins out of my pocket and gave one coin to Rick Gilbert, one to Ken, and I kept the third coin. I then told him that we were going to flip the three coins, only once, and the odd man will win, which will be you. I again reminded him that the coins would only be flipped once ... period.
>
> We flipped the coins and Gilbert and I had heads and Ken had tails. He sort of went into shock, as did I. He just stared at me as he said, "You really do know," then walked away. I don't think I need mention that I never tried that again.

The coin trick might have been luck. Sitzberger's Olympic gold resulted from skill. He was perhaps better thereafter, winning five NCAA and four Big Ten championships in three IU seasons.

During the days leading up to competition in Tokyo, he dated his future wife, Jeanne Collier, who won a silver medal on springboard. They wed in 1966 and had four children. When Sitzberger graduated in 1967, he was nominated to be a Rhodes Scholar and Indiana's recipient of the Big Ten Medal of Honor, awarded by each school for excellence in academics and athletics.

He continued to be involved in the sport as a commentator for ABC Sports. He went into business with his father and later started his own business, working in real estate in Utah and insurance in California. Friends said he made a fortune and lost it. He was scheduled to work for ABC at the Los Angeles Olympics in 1984 but died on January 2 of that year at Coronado, California. He was thirty-eight.

An autopsy report described cause of death as a traumatic head injury. Authorities were told he fell and struck his head on a table at a New Year's party in his home. According to court documents, he was soon to have been a federal witness in a case of cocaine trafficking. Sitzberger's death was ruled to be accidental and unrelated to the drug investigation.

He belongs to the International Swimming and IU Halls of Fame.

Brian Maisonneuve
IU Archives P0070261.

Brian Maisonneuve
1996

Longtime Pro Has "Wow" Memory of Olympics

BRIAN MAISONNEUVE PERFORMED ON SOCCER'S BIGGEST STAGE, THE WORLD Cup, and twice played in the College Cup for the Indiana Hoosiers. Yet when it comes to can-you-believe-it moments, nothing tops the 1996 Olympic Games.

"Talking about it now, I get goosebumps," he said. "It's an amazing feeling to represent your country."

The midfielder—nicknamed Maze—did not compete in Atlanta or attend the opening ceremony because men's soccer was held at five cities spread across the Southeast. The Americans played their opener against Argentina in Birmingham, Alabama, where a Legion Field record crowd of 83,183 turned out. There was a separate opening ceremony there, and teams had to warm up in a parking lot. The first time players saw the crowd was when they walked onto the Olympic pitch.

"It was one of those moments when I remember being on the field going, 'Wow,'" Maisonneuve said.

He said there was no comparison between rosters because the United States mostly featured players in college or just out of college, and the Argentines were pros. The United States seized a 1–0 lead before losing 3–1.

"You don't get eighty thousand people cheering for your country," Maisonneuve said. "To be able to feel that passion, that excitement of representing your country in the US in the Olympics when you're hosting it, was about as special as it can get."

In the next game, Maisonneuve scored the Americans' second goal in a 2–0 victory over Tunisia before 45,687 at Birmingham. He scored again—a tap-in at the back post—in a 1–1 tie with Portugal before 58,012 at RFK Stadium in Washington, DC.

The Americans needed to beat Portugal to advance to the quarterfinals, so they were eliminated.

"We did everything but score to beat them," Maisonneuve said. "Their coach said, 'That was a quality team, and they gave us everything we could handle.'"

He was born June 28, 1973, in Warren, Michigan, about twenty miles north of Detroit. He grew up playing not only soccer but also baseball, basketball, and hockey. He became a *Parade* magazine All-American at De La Salle Collegiate High School.

He was not difficult for the Hoosiers to recruit. If Indiana coach Jerry Yeagley came calling, he said, you looked into it. Maisonneuve visited campus, and the deal was done.

"It's the best decision I could have made in terms of my growth and development," he said. "Not only on the field, but off the field."

He formed a close bond with Yeagley's son, Todd, and the two remained linked for years. They were freshmen in 1991 when the Hoosiers, in their first year of Big Ten competition, won the conference tournament by beating Wisconsin 2–0. Coincidentally, Wisconsin had won 1–0 earlier to stop the Hoosiers' sixty-eight-game unbeaten streak against Big Ten opponents.

Indiana beat SMU on penalty kicks to reach the College Cup. A 19-3-2 season ended with a 2–0 loss to Santa Clara in an NCAA semifinal.

The Hoosiers did not return to the College Cup until Maisonneuve was a senior. Indiana, top-ranked most of the year, beat UCLA 4–1 in a 1994 semifinal but lost to Virginia 1–0 for the championship. That ended a 23–3 season and Maisonneuve's college career.

"We were probably one of those teams that should have won a national championship, and didn't," he said. "But I wouldn't change my experience for anything."

Indiana was 73–15–7 during Maisonneuve's college years, and he won the 1994 Hermann Trophy as national player of the year in addition to twice being Big Ten player of the year. He scored forty-four goals in four years.

Not until he arrived at Indiana did he start getting call-ups to national team camps. He was selected for the under-23s—essentially what became the Olympic team—late in his college career. In nineteen games (eleven starts) for the U23s during 1994 and 1995, he had three goals and four assists.

Two days before the start of the Pan American Games in Argentina in March 1995, he tore ligaments and cartilage in his right knee. Less than six months later, he returned to play in four of Team USA's five games at the World University Games in Japan.

"I came back a little too quick," he conceded.

He played his entire pro career, 172 games, with the Columbus Crew of Major League Soccer. He would have played past 2004 but endured thirteen surgeries, mostly on his ankles. He and Todd Yeagley were Crew teammates for seven years.

In 1996, Maisonneuve was allocated to the Crew in the first year of MLS. He missed seventeen games while with the Olympic team and, in fact, scored the winning goal against the Crew in an exhibition at Ohio Stadium.

After returning from the Olympics, he helped the Crew reach the MLS playoffs. In a September 7 game at Kansas City, he became the first Crew player ever to score three goals in one game.

Maisonneuve was on Team USA again for the 1998 World Cup in France. He played in each of the Americans' three games, all losses—to Germany 2–0, Iran 2–1 and Yugoslavia 1–0. The World Cup in no way resembled college soccer. "The game is so much faster and the players are so much stronger," Maisonneuve said.

He was a three-time all-star in MLS (1998, 1999, 2002). He returned from serious ankle injuries that sidelined him for the entire 2000 season to post career highs in goals (eight) and points (twenty-one) in 2001. He finished second in voting for MLS comeback player of the year.

"In the big picture it might have been the best thing to ever happen to me," Maisonneuve said of his lost season. "It made me really appreciate things I hadn't before. It gave me a different perspective on life and what's important and how lucky I was."

He helped the Crew win the US Open Cup in 2002. When he retired at age thirty-one, he was one of two players to have played for a single MLS club. He finished his pro career with twenty-three goals and thirty-seven assists.

"Without what I learned at IU, there's no way I would have handled the things thrown at me in my pro career," Maisonneuve said.

He began his coaching career as an assistant with the US U17 team, spending four years there and two at the University of Louisville. Maisonneuve returned to IU in 2010 as an assistant to Todd Yeagley, who followed his father as head coach. In eight years, the Hoosiers had a 102–42–34 record and won the NCAA championship in 2012.

In April 2018, Maisonneuve came back to Columbus to become head coach at Ohio State.

Steve Snow (*right*).
Courtesy of Indiana University Athletics.

Steve Snow
1992

Mr. Nasty Was Tough on Defenses and Coaches

STEVE SNOW COULD NOT BE PLACED AMONG INDIANA UNIVERSITY'S OR US soccer's all-time greats.
When clicking, though, he was as great as any Hoosier or American has been in the sport.
"He was nasty. He was mean," former Indiana coach Jerry Yeagley said. "He had an edge. Strikers, many of them, do have that. He was tough and mean when he played the game—within the rules. Most defenders were the tough guys. He would dominate a defender with his physicality and toughness."
Snow was a dynamo at five foot eight, 165 pounds. He is perhaps best remembered for clashing with US coach Luther Osiander, who once called him "a cocky little twerp," at the 1992 Olympic Games. In the Barcelona opener, Osiander benched Snow, who publicly rebuked the coach after a 2–1 loss to Italy.
"He sits out his best player, and he expects me to carry the team the next two games, like I always have. That's so ridiculous," Snow said.
Osiander insisted Snow apologize before he would be reinstated, and Snow did. Snow scored eighty-fifth-minute goals in each of the next two games, a 3–1 victory over Kuwait and 2–2 tie with Poland, but the United States did not advance out of group play.
Snow did not always endear himself to teammates, either. His roommate was Alexi Lalas, who was injured during the Olympics.
"If he thinks he could have come in and dribbled by himself through five Italian players, he's sorely mistaken," Lalas said at the time. "If scoring points gets you on the field, then Steve Snow should have been on the field. But if attitude and support of your teammates is the concern, then Steve shouldn't just sit on the bench, he should be back in the United States."

The squabble contributed to Osiander's firing after the Olympics. It inevitably harmed Snow's career, too, although early retirement was largely due to a knee injury.

Snow was on the same Olympic team with future stars such as Lalas, Cobi Jones, Chris Henderson, Brad Friedel, Claudio Reyna, and Joe-Max Moore. Snow was the Americans' top scorer, though, with ten goals in ten Olympic qualifying games. His three goals lifted Team USA over Honduras 4–3 at St. Louis. Those were his only three shots of the game.

"I can play bad for eighty-nine minutes," he once said, "but if I score in the ninetieth minute, it will be a good game for me."

He is the second-youngest ever to play for the senior national team, having been seventeen when he came on as a second-half substitute in a June 14, 1988, victory over Costa Rica. The only younger American to play for the senior team was Freddy Adu, at sixteen, in 2006.

Snow led the United States to a best-ever fourth place at the under-20 World Cup in Saudi Arabia in 1989. In qualification, he scored five of the team's eleven goals. He scored three more in the U20 World Cup, including the goal in a 2–1 semifinal loss to Nigeria. That U20 tournament prefaced his lone season at Indiana.

Snow was born March 2, 1971, in Schaumburg, Illinois. At Hoffman Estates High School, he set a state record by scoring in forty-nine consecutive games, two more than his older brother Ken. The two practiced skills on a backyard goal, "just challenging each other," Yeagley said. Steve scored 111 goals in four seasons and was *Parade* magazine's high school player of the year in 1988.

"In our area, everyone knew who Steve was and how good he was. He was unstoppable," said former national team star Brian McBride, who attended nearby Buffalo Grove. "He had great feet in tight spaces, and in that day and age, he had the quickest release of anyone I'd see. And he was deadly."

At Indiana, Steve Snow was overshadowed by Ken, the Hoosiers' first four-time All-American and winner of the Hermann Trophy as national player of the year in 1988 and 1990.

In 1989, the Snow brothers helped Indiana's defending NCAA champions reach another College Cup. The Hoosiers had an eighteen-game unbeaten streak until losing to Santa Clara 4–2 in a national semifinal. Ken finished the season with twenty goals and ten assists, Steve thirteen goals and ten assists. Steve was top scorer in that NCAA tournament with four goals and one assist.

Yeagley called Ken a "creative finisher" and the best forward he ever coached. Steve was a "tank forward" who caused defenders to bounce off him.

"Very honestly, he was a challenge," Yeagley said. "Many strikers, many goal-scorers, can be a bit temperamental."

Steve Snow left Indiana after his freshman year and signed a pro contract with Standard Liege in Belgium. He led the U23 national team to a gold medal in the 1991 Pan American Games at Havana, Cuba, scoring four goals in five games. That team, too, was coached by Osiander.

After the 1992 Olympics, a knee injury required two surgeries. Snow scored thirty goals in forty-three games for the Chicago Power of the indoor National Professional Soccer League over two seasons, 1994 and 1995, but retired at age twenty-four. A genuine US outdoor league, Major League Soccer, made its debut in 1996. It was too late for Steve Snow.

He opened a restaurant, Roselli's Pizza, in the College Park area of Indianapolis and later relocated it to suburban Carmel, Indiana. He essentially cut himself off from soccer. He declined to be interviewed for this book.

"It was hard to leave the game," he said in 2000 interview with *Soccer America*. "Soccer was all I cared about my whole life, and that ended quickly. All my friends were still playing while I spent two and a half years struggling to build a successful restaurant. Those two and a half years were hard."

The MLS website caught up with Snow in 2014 and published a 4,400-word story on his brilliant, albeit brief, career. Much of the story focused on the feud between Snow and Osiander.

"Barcelona wouldn't have mattered at all if I hadn't gotten injured afterward," he told MLS.com. "But when I got hurt, anything I had ever done that was negative came out as a reason for them to pass me over. And if the national team says you're done, you're done. There was nothing else I could do."

Eventually, he concentrated on family—he has two daughters—and threw himself into the restaurant business. It was the same zeal he exhibited on a soccer pitch.

"It was all I had," he said. "Everything else had been taken away from me. The restaurant had to work."

John Stollmeyer
IU Archives P0070276.

John Stollmeyer
1988

"The Hub" in the Middle of Hoosier Dynasty

JOHN STOLLMEYER COULD HAVE GONE PRO RIGHT OUT OF HIGH SCHOOL. Instead, he enrolled at Indiana University, played for the Hoosiers' first two NCAA championship soccer teams, and was on US national teams for ten years. According to Stollmeyer himself, it was not because he was such a great athlete. His nickname was "The Hub" because he was in the middle of everything.

"I don't have the speed or the skill of most of the other players," he once said. "But I let the other team know I'm out there."

He let his own team know it, too. As much as any player the Hoosiers have had, Stollmeyer led by force of personality.

"No one cheated on effort when John was out there," Indiana coach Jerry Yeagley said.

Stollmeyer represented the United States at the 1981 World Youth Championship in Australia, the 1987 Pan American Games in Indianapolis and World University Games in Croatia, the 1988 Olympic Games in South Korea, and the 1990 World Cup in Italy. He earned thirty-one caps with the senior national team.

Stollmeyer was born October 25, 1962, in Pittsburgh. His father, Michael, who played soccer at Penn State, said he realized his son "was different" by the way he kicked a ball at age five. Sometimes the father wondered if he was pushing his son too much.

"But then I noticed he would work out even if I wasn't around," Michael Stollmeyer said.

The son attended Thomas Jefferson High School in Annandale, Virginia, and was selected by the Tampa Bay Rowdies in the first round of the North American Soccer League draft in December 1980. He was national amateur soccer athlete of the year for 1981. Instead of signing with the Rowdies, the nation's top recruit headed for Bloomington.

Stollmeyer, a center midfielder, became a three-time All-American and member of *Soccer America*'s all-decade team of the 1980s. In four years, he had twenty-seven goals and what was then a school-record thirty-nine assists. The Hoosiers were 76–15–8 in that span, winning NCAA championships in 1982 and 1983. They had a forty-six-game unbeaten streak over 1983–84, and lost to Clemson 2–1 in the 1984 national title game.

"He would just tear the heart out of an opposing team," Yeagley said. "Rock-hard tackles. He had no fear. Playing fair, but he would put his body in harm's way."

Eventually, Yeagley said, those on the other team did not even want to touch the ball if Stollmeyer was nearby. His strength was such that the Hoosiers had him take their goal kicks, rather than the goalkeeper. Stollmeyer could strike from distance in a way most strikers could not.

In 1985, he was drafted by the Cleveland Force of the Major Indoor Soccer League, and he was rookie of the year for 1986–87. His second season in Cleveland was his last because the team folded thereafter. He played for two other pro teams, the Arizona Condors and Washington Stars, and they also folded.

It was too late for the NASL, and Major League Soccer was years away. Stollmeyer considered offers from European clubs but eventually declined.

"It wasn't like it is now where you could make a real living by going to Europe," he said. "If you come out of college now, there's a future in the game and you can play for five or ten years as long as that league continues to hang in there. If you're good enough, you can go overseas for a couple of years, make some good money, come back, and still have something here."

Such pro disappointments did not keep him off the national team. The United States was 1–1–1 at the 1987 Pan Am Games but did not advance out of group play. In a qualifying match for the 1988 Olympics, Stollmeyer scored what proved to be the winning goal in a 4–1 victory over Trinidad and Tobago at Fenton, Missouri. At twenty-five, he was the oldest US player in the sixteen-team tournament at Seoul. The United States tied Argentina 1–1 and South Korea 0–0 but lost to the Soviet Union 4–2, again failing to advance out of group play.

Perhaps the most memorable match of his career was one in which he did not start. In a World Cup qualifier in November 1989 at Port of Spain, Trinidad, he was surprisingly replaced by Paul Caligiuri. The Americans tried to slip into the city unnoticed, arriving on a late-night flight, but were greeted by thousands of islanders, steel bands, and calypso music. US players slept wearing earplugs that night. Stollmeyer's father was from Trinidad, and one of his ancestors had built a Scottish-style castle on one side of Port of Spain's biggest park.

"I grew up with those records around the house," he said. "To me, it was almost like a normal sound."

It was awkward for Caligiuri, whose roommate on the trip was Stollmeyer. They talked it out before the game. Caligiuri was to mark Trinidad & Tobago playmaker Russell Latapy and specifically instructed not to go forward and risk counterattack. But when Caligiuri saw an opening in the thirtieth minute, he took it, shot with topspin, and the ball dipped into the net for a 1–0 lead. The Americans protected their one-goal lead, clinching their first World Cup berth in forty years.

"I remember going to the locker room, and we were just in there singing," Stollmeyer said. "All of us were completely exhausted. You're trying to drink water in as well as celebrate with champagne and beer. It was just pure elation in that aspect of it."

At twenty-seven, he was again the oldest player on the team. Emotion was not the same in Italy as it had been in Trinidad. The Americans were 0–3 at the World Cup, losing to Czechoslovakia 5–1, Italy 1–0 and Austria 2–1. On the other hand, US players won the respect of Italian fans, who thought their side should have won by more than one goal at Rome's Olympic Stadium. Stollmeyer said:

> When I was on the field and we were pressing, the crowd had actually changed who they were rooting for. Not that they wanted Italy to truly lose, but they were so upset that they were only beating us by one goal and not trouncing us like Czechoslovakia. They cheered for us as we went off. We weren't being booed. That experience, to be able to walk away from the World Cup like that, was kind of cool.
>
> The World Cup is what, I say, any one of us would have, and still would, trade our careers for and do it again, even knowing we would get beat. It was the one thing that you went after in your career. If you had the ability to make it that far and play in a World Cup, that was the peak and nobody could take that away from you.

Stollmeyer had four ankle surgeries, and he retired after the World Cup. He was an assistant coach at Notre Dame before beginning a career in investments.

He coached his son, Jake, at Hamilton Southeastern High School in Fishers, Indiana. Stollmeyer and his wife, Jill, an anesthesiologist, adopted three children from Russia—biological brothers Victor and Vanya along with a girl, Cassidy. All had been living in orphanages.

Angelo DiBernardo, 1978.
IU Archives P0090008.

Angelo DiBernardo
1984

Hoosiers' First Soccer Superstar

INDIANA HAS BEEN A NATIONAL POWER IN SOCCER FOR SO LONG, IT IS EASY to forget that was not always so. Jerry Yeagley coached the Hoosiers for ten years as a club team before they had varsity status.

What the coach needed was a superstar striker to make Indiana relevant. He found one—an Argentinian—on the Chicago playgrounds. Angelo DiBernardo went on to play with Pele and other greats of the sport, but he became the Hoosiers' Pele soon after he arrived on campus. It was 1976, and Indiana was in its fourth season as an authentic college program.

As a freshman, on October 10, 1976, DiBernardo scored all five goals in a 5–1 victory over St. Louis—the St. Louis that won a record ten NCAA titles between 1959 and 1973. It was the fifth victory of what became a sixteen-game winning streak that did not end until the Hoosiers' first appearance in an NCAA championship.

Yeagley said DiBernardo "put us on the map" with that spree against St. Louis. He and the Hoosiers were featured in *Sports Illustrated*.

"Angelo was blessed with an extra gear," Yeagley said. "You thought he was running all out, and he was like the roadrunner. He'd run away from you. He was explosive."

DiBernardo was born May 16, 1956, in Buenos Aires. He grew up in a family of Italian ancestry before moving from Argentina to the United States when he was sixteen. There was no soccer team at Morton West High School in nearby Berwyn, Illinois. So he played for the Sparta club team with what he called "a bunch of Czechoslovakians and Argentinians" in Cicero, Illinois. That team was coached by the father of prize IU recruit Charlie Fajkus, who recommended that Yeagley try to recruit DiBernardo.

"He was one of those needles-in-a-haystack, diamond-in-the-rough guys," Yeagley said. "He learned on the streets like Pele did in Brazil, like our best basketball players do on the playground. That's something we don't have enough of."

In DiBernardo's freshman season, he scored twenty goals and led the Hoosiers to their first College Cup. He scored both goals in a 2–1 semifinal win over Hartwick, extending their record to 18–0-1. So months after the Hoosiers won an NCAA title in basketball with an unbeaten record, they were poised to do the same in soccer. That ambition ended in a 1–0 loss to San Francisco.

DiBernardo became an All-American in each of his final two years, scoring fifteen goals in 1977 and nineteen in 1978. Indiana climbed to number one in the national rankings in 1978, largely because of a 2–1 victory over San Francisco. But in a rematch for the NCAA championship, San Francisco won 2–0.

Nevertheless, DiBernardo was Indiana's first Hermann Trophy winner as national player of the year in 1978. He scored fifty-four goals in three seasons, during which the Hoosiers were 53–5-2.

"He could take the team on his shoulder and carry the team, and yet not be egotistical," Yeagley said. "He was team player. A very good passer as well. He was one of the few guys that I coached who individually could break down a defense and create a goal."

DiBernardo was honored—along with Indiana's Ken Snow and Armando Betancourt—on *Soccer America*'s college team of the twentieth century. After college, DiBernardo was drafted by the Los Angeles Aztecs of the North American Soccer League and later traded to the New York Cosmos, who featured players such as Pele, Franz Beckenbauer, and Johann Cruyff.

DiBernardo earned his first cap for the national team in 1979 and was chosen the next year to be on the Olympic team. He did not play at the Moscow Olympics because of the US boycott or in the 1982 World Cup because the United States failed to qualify. The Cosmos were NASL champions in 1980 and 1982, although he played just one game in 1982 because of injury. When DiBernardo was asked to take a pay cut in May 1984, he refused and was placed on waivers.

Thereafter, he concentrated on the buildup to the Los Angeles Olympics. The Americans beat Costa Rica 3–0, lost to Italy 1–0, tied Egypt 1–1, and were eliminated. DiBernardo went on to play indoor soccer with the Kansas City Comets and St. Louis Steamers before retiring at age thirty-two in 1988.

He became a Spanish teacher and coach at Waubonsie Valley High School in Aurora, Illinois. In twenty-three seasons there, his teams were 334–148–55 (.673), including a third-place finish in the 2000 state tournament.

DiBernardo's younger brother, Paul, also became an All-American for the Hoosiers and played for NCAA championship teams in 1982 and 1983. Paul was chosen college player of the year by *Soccer America* in 1984. Angelo's daughter, Vanessa, played soccer for the University of Illinois and was on the US team that won the under-20 Women's World Cup in 2012.

Gregg Thompson, 1980.
IU Archives P0021908.

Gregg Thompson
1984

From running for touchdowns to kicking for goals

GREGG THOMPSON HAD THE STRENGTH AND SPEED OF A RUNNING BACK, which he was. He had the explosiveness of a long jumper, which he was. Fortunately for Indiana, he had the endurance of a marathoner, too.

In college soccer's 1982 championship game at Fort Lauderdale, Florida, the Hoosiers, riding a twenty-game winning streak, faced off against Duke. The teams were tied 1–1 through regulation play. They remained tied through one fifteen-minute overtime period, then two. Then it was on a third OT . . . and four, then five. Then eight.

Finally, with forty-four seconds left in the eighth overtime, Thompson was awarded a direct free kick from twenty yards after he was tripped by Duke sweeper Joe Ulrich. Thompson kicked the ball on the inside of his right foot, around the wall of defenders, and inside the right goalpost. Fifteen minutes before the stroke of midnight, the Hoosiers won 2–1 for their first NCAA soccer championship. Rules about overtime have changed, so it will forever remain the longest such title game ever played.

"I didn't know if I even had the energy to kick the ball, but I figured it was my last college game, so I would make the most of it," Thompson said of his goal in the 159th minute.

He made the most of a soccer career that just as easily could have been a football career. Coincidentally, Thompson finished second in balloting for the Hermann Trophy as 1982 college player of the year—behind Ulrich.

Thompson was born August 4, 1960, in San Jose, California. He spent his youth in California before his family moved to Stillwater, Minnesota, about twenty-five miles east of Minneapolis, when he was fourteen. He acquired the nickname

"Thumper" not because of the way he kicked a soccer ball but because he could run like the rabbit of the same name from Bambi. The 165-pound Thompson could run forty yards in 4.4 seconds and bench-press 350 pounds.

He played soccer with local youth clubs but and was a star running back in football. He rushed for 1,500 yards in ten games as a senior, leaped twenty-two feet in the long jump, and was chosen to be the Minnesota athlete of the year. In a state semifinal against Columbia Heights, he kicked a game-winning field goal from 37 yards, had the kick annulled by penalty, then made it again from 42 yards in a 16–14 victory. He had torn his anterior cruciate ligament on the fifth play of the game but still threw a touchdown pass and rushed for 125 yards. He received football scholarship offers from Colorado, Minnesota, Wisconsin, and Iowa, among others, but he chose Indiana for soccer.

"It was the toughest decision of my life," Thompson said.

Indiana coach Jerry Yeagley once called him the best athlete he ever coached. "He could stop anybody," the coach said of Thompson.

Yet Thompson was an average player when he arrived on campus, Yeagley said, because he had played very little elite soccer. In the midfield, everything was coming at Thompson from all directions.

"He struggled a bit. He almost left," Yeagley said. "He was going to play football. Teams still wanted him. 'Hey, Greg, let's move you to defensive back.' We moved him to wide defensive position where the game was in front of him. It was like the light bulb went on."

In Thompson's senior season, 1982, he was sidelined for five weeks with knee and thigh injuries. Then he scored both goals in the climactic victory over Duke.

Thompson was top pick of both the Los Angeles Lazers, of Major Indoor Soccer League, and Tampa Bay Rowdies, of the North American Soccer League. He played thirty games for the Rowdies and was NASL's rookie of the year in 1983, one season before the league folded. At the end of the pro season, he joined the US team in preparation for the 1984 Olympics.

In Los Angeles, the Americans beat Costa Rica 3–0, lost to Italy 1–0, tied Egypt 1–1, and were eliminated. Thompson scored the US goal in the eighth minute of the tie with Egypt before a crowd of 54,973 at Stanford Stadium. He went on to play twelve times for the national team in 1984 and 1985, including qualification matches for the 1986 World Cup. His last game with the national team came in a 1985 loss to Costa Rica that eliminated the Americans.

After collapse of the NASL, Thompson went back to Minnesota with the Strikers of MISL. He retired after 1988.

Two of his sons, Tanner and Tommy, played soccer for the Hoosiers. Tanner was a three-time All-American (2014, 2015, and 2016) and was the Big Ten midfielder of the year twice. He later played for the Indy Eleven of NASL. Tommy played one season, 2013, when he was Big Ten freshman of the year. He then went to the

San Jose Earthquakes of Major League Soccer. Another son, Ty, was an All-Pac-12 midfielder for the team that won Stanford's first-ever NCAA title in 2015.

"My dad is the most modest guy I've ever met," Tommy said. "There's still stories that are being told that are amazing stories that I didn't know."

Thompson became a partner in a real estate group in Roseville, California, and coached youth soccer.

Michelle Venturella, 1994.
Photo by Guy Zimmer.
IU Archives P0035187.

Michelle Venturella
Softball
2000

An Olympics on the Brink Ended Gloriously

HOW DOES A SLOW-PITCH, LEFT-HANDED FIRST BASEMAN BECAME A GOLD medal-winning softball catcher?
That is what Michelle Venturella did. She had belief, talent, and perseverance. She was surrounded by like-minded players on a US team that was on the brink of elimination in five successive games at the 2000 Sydney Olympics.
"Our group was not going to let that happen," Venturella said. "In a very short amount of time, you had to turn it around."
Team USA arrived in Sydney with a 112-game winning streak in international softball, then started the tournament 2–0. But after the Americans lost three in a row during round-robin play—which had never happened in the thirty-five-year history of the program—they beat New Zealand 2–0 and Italy 6–0 to reach the medal round.
In turn, the Americans proceeded to beat all the teams that had beaten them: China 3–0, Australia 1–0, and Japan 1–0 in eight innings. Venturella played a total of ten innings in two games, but she said it was worth it. Worth more than gold.
"That whole process was just amazing," she said. "I had a chance to be around such successful women. It taught me a different mind-set. It taught me how these true champions thought, how they did things. To walk into the Olympic Games, knowing what we had been through, some of the best players ever to play the game, is something I absolutely cherish."
Venturella was born May 11, 1973, in Gary Indiana, and grew up in Chicago's south suburbs. Their family moved to South Holland, Illinois, when she was eight. She began playing slow-pitch softball in a rec league, and, unconventionally, did not play fast-pitch until her freshman year at Thornwood High School.

"Now, if you're not traveling all over the world by the time you're ten, you're behind," she said.

Venturella followed her sister into softball, and because a friend played volleyball, she did that sport. Then basketball. Turns out she was more than a slow-pitch first baseman who batted and threw left-handed.

Thornwood's softball coach, Gary Lagesse, was ambitious. He told players they would win a state championship at a time Thornwood had endured previous disappointment. The Thunderbirds had finished third in the state in 1986.

"He just had everyone believing that that was going to happen," Venturella said. "We had four-hour practices. We practiced at night. It was crazy, but we were into it. He was extremely positive."

The Thunderbirds finished fourth in the state in 1989, which was her sophomore year, then went 35–5 and 33–8 in winning back-to-back state championships. Making it sweeter is that Thornwood, led by future major leaguer Cliff Floyd, won a state baseball title on the same 1991 night.

Venturella said she was lightly recruited, with offers mostly from colleges in the state. Illinois did not then offer softball, so that was not a Big Ten option. Indiana University made what Venturella said was her worst scholarship offer, but she loved her visit to the Bloomington campus. Her parents promised they would work it out.

"You look back, that was an incredibly big decision in my life," Venturella said.

Indiana coach Diane Stephenson was not bound by convention, and she was the one who transformed the five-foot-ten Venturella into a left-handed catcher in her sophomore season. Dizzyingly, she was trying out for the US Olympic team as a catcher three years later.

As a junior, she was Big Ten player of the year and second-team All-American in leading the Hoosiers to a 1994 conference championship (23–5 in Big Ten games). She batted .418 and set IU records with sixteen home runs, sixty-five runs batted in, fifty-six walks, and an .819 slugging percentage. In Big Ten play, her .486 average, sixty-nine total bases and thirty-three RBI all set conference records. Her total bases record lasted until 2015.

As a senior, she batted .377 with nine home runs and fifty-one RBI, repeated as All-Big Ten and was third-team All-American. She won IU's Big Ten Medal of Honor for athletics and academics.

Venturella made the 1995 national team and traveled with Team USA to Atlanta for the 1996 Atlanta Olympics. She was one of the last players cut, and did not play in those Olympics, in which women's softball was introduced. There was always 2000.

"After that, I realized I could do it. I think I could make the team," she said.

She continued with the national team in an era in which pro softball was not at a viable option. She was a full-time ballplayer, if not a highly paid one. She traveled to South America, Europe, Asia, and Australia.

Venturella was on the US team that won the 1998 world championship in Japan. In 1999, the national team was split into number one and two teams, and she was relegated to the second team.

"Being on the second team, I played all the time," she said. "It gave me an opportunity to show what I could do."

That showcase allowed her, at age twenty-seven, to make the 2000 team heading for Sydney. The pre-Olympics travel, both in 1996 and 2000, was "absolutely exhausting," she said. But USA Softball scheduled the games to keep the players sharp and to promote the team.

The Americans' comeback was breathtaking—they overcame a one-run deficit to beat Japan for the gold—especially to their backup catcher.

"I couldn't believe it," Venturella wrote in a diary for the *Indianapolis Star*.

> I ran out there and was celebrating with my teammates, but it didn't really sink in. It wasn't until we started jogging around the field with our flag that everything hit me all at once.
>
> We started running from right field to left field, and by the time we got to center, I had to stop because I felt like couldn't breathe. I was so overcome by my emotions, I could barely keep up with my teammates. I looked up and saw all of the cheering fans and kept on moving. There were so many hugs exchanged between all of us, along with many tears. It was a big relief that it was finally over!

Being a role player instead of a starter prepared Venturella for her next career: coaching. She said she learned to do whatever the team needed.

She had coached briefly during her playing career, as a Northern Illinois University assistant and as an IU volunteer. After the Olympics, she accepted a job at Iowa, where she was associate head coach for four years. She became head coach at Illinois-Chicago for eight years. At UIC, she led the Flames to four Horizon League regular-season championships, plus a league tournament title and NCAA Tournament appearance in 2011.

In July 2016, she took over as head coach at Washington University, an academically rigorous NCAA Division III school located in St. Louis. She and her wife, Beth, have two children.

Mickey Morandini, 1985.
IU Archives P0025181.

Mickey Morandini
Baseball
1988

Major Leagues Delayed for an Olympic Dream

BASEBALL WAS A DEMONSTRATION SPORT AT THE 1988 SEOUL OLYMPICS, BUT Mickey Morandini was indifferent to that technicality. It was the Olympic Games, and he wanted to be there.

So the Indiana University shortstop, after selection by Pittsburgh in the seventh round of the 1987 amateur draft, turned down the hometown Pirates' contract offer in order to keep a dream alive. He made an imprint all over the Hoosier record book, played eleven major league seasons and appeared in a World Series and All-Star Game. Nothing topped the Olympics.

"It was the greatest experience of my life," Morandini said. "It was a long summer. It was the first time many of us were overseas or away from home for that long a time, and to finish it with a gold medal was great."

Morandini was born April 22, 1966, at Kittanning, Pennsylvania. He was a high-scoring basketball guard at Leechburg, a Pittsburgh suburb, but his future was in baseball. Morandini, five foot eleven and 170 pounds, threw right-handed but batted left-handed.

At Indiana, he started as a center fielder, then moved to third base and eventually shortstop. He remains the lone three-time, first-team All-Big Ten player in school history. Thirty years later, he still holds the Hoosiers' career records for runs scored (277), stolen bases (127), and triples (29). Through 2020, his career batting average of .392 and 221 runs batted in both ranked third.

Statistically, Morandini's best college season came as a sophomore in 1986, when he batted .422 and had a slugging percentage of .844, which remains the school record. (The NCAA adopted new rules for aluminum bats before the 1999 season.) His ninety runs in 1986 remain the Big Ten record.

Morandini was the lone American all-star in the 1987 Intercontinental Cup, a tournament at Havana, Cuba. In thirteen games, he hit .404 and led the team in doubles (eight), runs (sixteen), and RBI (thirteen). Team USA won the silver medal. In his senior college season, Morandini earned second-team All-America honors from the American Baseball Coaches Association.

Sixty candidates reported to Millington, Tennessee, in the months before the Olympics. The roster was trimmed to twenty-five and later twenty. After the Intercontinental Cup, Morandini reasoned he had a good shot to make it to Seoul because the manager, Stanford coach Mark Marquess, would also lead the Olympic team.

"The special moment was seeing the final roster and seeing your name on that," Morandini said.

Seoul marked the sixth time baseball was a demonstration or exhibition sport, more often than any sport in Olympic history. Baseball became a medal sport in 1992 but was dropped after the 2008 Beijing Olympics. Baseball was reinstated for the 2020 Tokyo Olympics.

Three-fourths of the US roster in 1988 would go on to play in the major leagues, including Morandini, Tito Martinez, Robin Ventura, Ed Sprague, Tom Goodwin, and pitchers Jim Abbott, Andy Benes, Ben McDonald, and Charles Nagy.

The United States beat Puerto Rico 7–2 in a semifinal, then Japan 5–3 for the gold medal. Martinez hit two home runs in the final, and Abbot pitched a complete game. Morandini played in just one game, but that did not detract from the experience. The Americans ran around the stadium holding an Olympic flag to celebrate. The environment differed little from a World Series.

"The stadium was jam-packed," Morandini said. "It was very competitive when you go internationally."

Afterward, Morandini returned to Leechburg for a parade and spoke to schools about the Olympics. He had been selected by the Philadelphia Phillies in the fifth round of the 1988 draft and began his pro career the next year. He hit .351 in 188 at-bats for Class AA Reading and won the Paul Owens Award as the top position player in the Phillies' minor league organization. Morandini made twenty-two errors in his first pro season as a shortstop, and he was shifted to second base, which became his major league position. As a second baseman, he went on to set records for best fielding percentage.

He spent most of 1990 with AAA Scranton/Wilkes-Barre but made his major debut that season, batting .241 in twenty-five games for the Phillies. Morandini played eleven years for the Phillies, Chicago Cubs, and Toronto Blue Jays, earning $10.85 million. On September 20, 1992, against the Pirates, he turned the first unassisted triple play in the National League since 1927, and was the first second baseman ever to do so.

In 1993, he batted second in the order for the Phillies, who lost the World Series to the Blue Jays 4–2. Morandini was third in the National League that year with nine triples. In 1995, he was the first former IU player to appear in an All-Star Game since Ted Kluszewski nearly forty years before. Morandini had his highest batting average, .297, with the Phillies in 1997.

He was traded after the season to the Cubs and, at age thirty-two, had his best season in 1998. He set career highs for batting (.296), hits (172), runs (ninety-three), home runs (eight), RBI (53), and wins above replacement value (3.9). He made his only appearance in Most Valuable Player voting, finishing twenty-fourth. The Cubs made it to the divisional series but lost 3–0 to the Atlanta Braves.

After a contract dispute with the Cubs, he became a free agent in 2000. He signed with the Montreal Expos but had his rights purchased by the Phillies. He was traded in August to the Blue Jays, batted .271 in thirty-five games, and that was it. His playing career was over. When he retired, his fielding percentage of .989 was a major league record for second baseman playing a thousand or more games.

Morandini went on to coach baseball at Valparaiso High School and later coached in the Phillies' minor league organization. He spent the 2017 season as the Phillies' first-base coach. He and his wife, Peg, have three sons.

Dick Voliva
Wrestling
1936

Bloomington Native Is the Only IU Wrestling Medalist

THE LONE WRESTLING MEDALIST PRODUCED BY INDIANA UNIVERSITY WAS not supposed to be in the so-called 1936 Nazi Olympics.

Dick Voliva made the team as an alternate, but his form was so good in a pre-Olympics training camp that he was chosen to compete in Berlin by US coach Billy Thom, who was also the Indiana coach. Voliva won six successive matches before being pinned by France's Emile Poilve in the gold-medal final of the 174-pound freestyle class. The Hoosier was one of four US medalists on the team coached by Thom.

Richard Lawrence Voliva was born October 18, 1912, in Bloomington. Under coach Harold Mumby, Bloomington High School won six of the first thirteen state titles, and Voliva contributed to that dynasty. He won two state titles and had one runner-up finish. It was a natural progression to stay in town and compete for Thom's Hoosiers. Voliva also played for the football team, winning a special award as a senior.

He was a sophomore on the team that won the 1932 NCAA wrestling championship—first by a Big Ten school and the only one in Hoosier history. Individually, he was NCAA runner-up at 175 pounds in 1933. He was NCAA champion in 1934, led Indiana to a third straight Big Ten title, and finished with a 48–4 collegiate record.

After graduation, he served two years as an Ohio State graduate assistant coach. He finished third in the AAU national tournament in 1935 and was champion in 1936.

The Depression left the US Olympic Committee so tight on funds that it was unsure about sending wrestlers to Berlin. Thom was not about to allow that. While coaching, he continued to wrestle professionally. He won the world middleweight

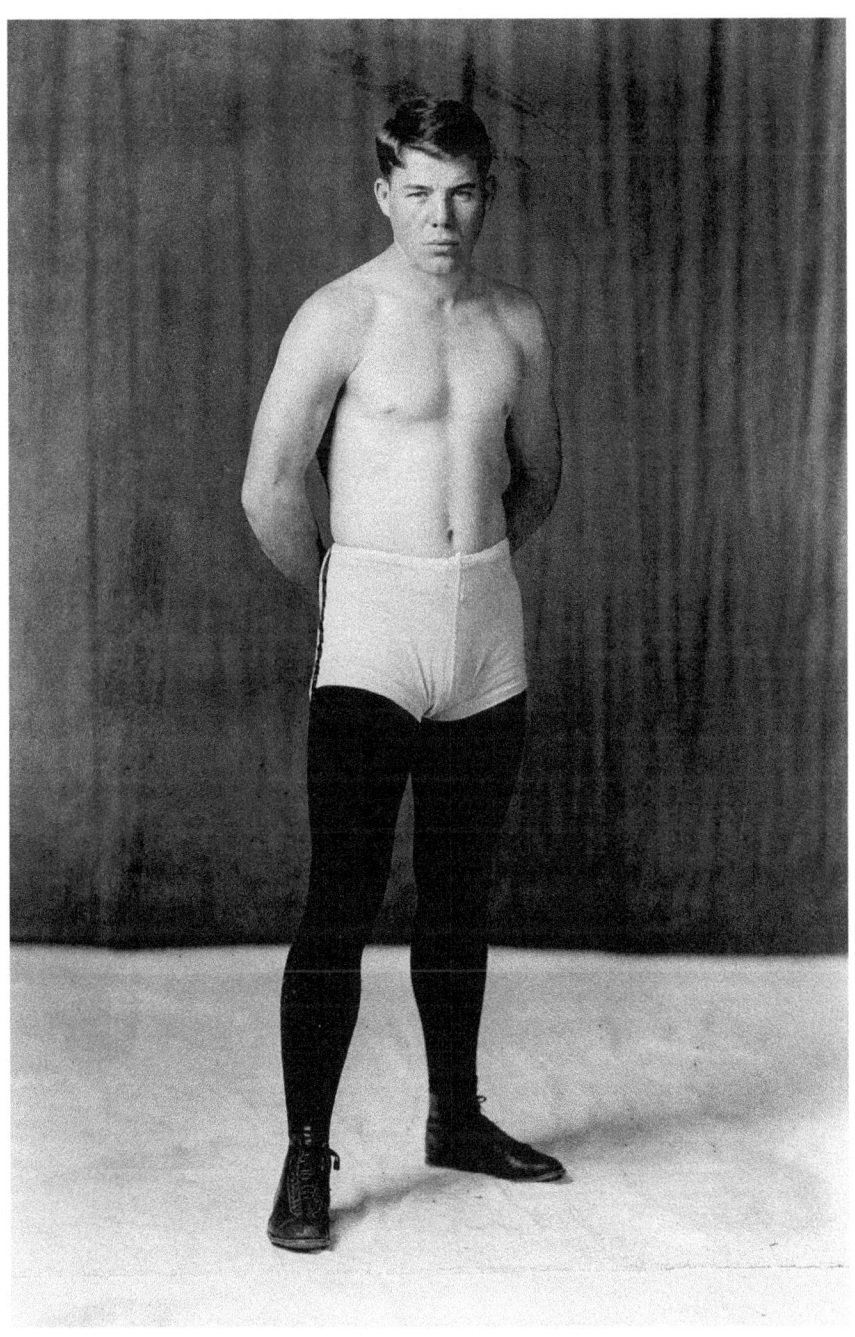

Dick Voliva, 1932.
From the 1932 Wrestling Manager's Book.
IU Archives P0027326.

title in 1928 and held it through 1937, retiring unbeaten. He participated in two pre-Olympic exhibition matches in Bloomington, raising $360. That helped send Voliva and two other Hoosier wrestlers, alternates Charley McDaniel and Willard Duffy, to Berlin.

Then came the silver medal. It was a defining moment not only for Voliva, but for his coach.

"A boy I had seen grow up in Bloomington and had coached to a Big Ten championship, an NCAA championship, a national AAU championship, and then the Olympic team . . . if I were to pick one incident as my greatest thrill, that would be it," Thom said.

On Voliva's return from the Olympics, he took a teaching job at Montclair State and, in 1938, started a wrestling program at the New Jersey school. Then he served in the army. He had been commissioned a second lieutenant on graduation in 1934, and during active duty, he rose in rank to lieutenant colonel.

Voliva returned to New Jersey and became wrestling coach at Rutgers in 1946, lasting twenty-three seasons. His Rutgers record was 142–71–7. He spent five years on the NCAA rules committee, two as chairman, and was president of the Eastern Intercollegiate Wrestling Association and National Wrestling Coaches Association. He was inducted as a Distinguished Member of the National Wrestling Hall of Fame in 1984. He died November 2, 1999, in Northampton, Massachusetts, at eighty-seven.

SOURCES

SPORTS HISTORIANS

Marshall Goss
Bob Hammel
Bill Mallon

BOOKS

All-Time World List (end 1958), by Association of Track and Field Statisticians
A Banner Year at Indiana, by Bob Hammel
Best Runs, by Joe Henderson
The Best That I Can Be, by Rafer Johnson
The Complete Book of the Olympic Games, by David Wallechinsky and Jaime Loucky
For the Glory of Old IU, by Bob Hammel and Kit Klingelhoffer
The Four-Minute Mile, by Roger Bannister
Glory Days Illinois: Legends of Illinois High School Basketball, by Taylor Bell
High School Track, by Jack Shepard
History of Olympics Track and Field Athletics, by Mel Watman
History of the Olympic Trials, by Richard Hymans
How They Train, by Fred Wilt
Indiana High School Basketball's 20 Most Dominant Players, by Dave Krider
Indiana's Best, by Jim Brandyberry
The Iron Man from Indiana, by Don Lash
The Longest Leap, by Greg Bell
Marathon: The Ultimate Training Guide, by Hal Higdon
Mark Spitz: The Extraordinary Life of an Olympic Champion, by Richard J. Foster
The Olympians, by Roy Tomizama
Olympic Track and Field Athletics Guide, by Mel Watman
Playing for Knight, by Steve Alford (with John Garrity)
Rome 1960: The Olympics That Changed the World, by David Maraniss

Unknown, Untold and Unbelievable Stories of IU Sports, by John C. Decker, Pete DiPrimio, and Doug Wilson

A World History of the One-Lap Race, by Roberto Quercetani

NEWSPAPERS, MAGAZINES, WIRE SERVICES

Arizona Republic
Associated Press
Bloomington Herald-Times
Brazil (IN) Times
Chicago Tribune
Daily Hampshire Gazette
East Bay Times
Evansville Journal and Courier
Fort Myers (FL) Daily News
Fortune
Free Lance-Star (Fredericksburg, VA)
Gary (IN) Post-Tribune
Honolulu Star-Bulletin
Houston Chronicle
Indianapolis News
Indianapolis Star
Jackson (MS) Clarion-Ledger
Kokomo (IN) Tribune
Los Angeles Examiner
Los Angeles Times
Midland (TX) Reporter-Telegram
Newark (NJ) Star-Ledger
New York Times
Orange County Register
Pharos-Tribune (Logansport, IN)
Philadelphia Inquirer
Princeton (NJ) Patch
Reno Journal-Gazette
Runner's World
San Diego Union-Tribune
Sandusky (OH) Register
Soccer America
Sports Illustrated
Swimming World
Terre Haute (IN) Tribune-Star
Times of Northwest Indiana
Toledo Blade

SOURCES

Track & Field News
United Press International
USA Today
Washington Post

OTHER WEBSITES

ESPN.com
Findagrave.com
Fourfourtwo.com
Gold56.org
Massivereportdata.com
NBCOlympics.com
Olympic Channel
RunBlogRun
Sports-reference.com\Olympics
SwimSwam.com
Therealxc.com
Tf-stats.com
Upclosed.com
Velonews.com
Wikipedia.com
Yahoo!Sports
Yanks-abroad.com

SPORTS GOVERNING BODIES, ORGANIZATIONS, AND COLLEGES

Association of Track and Field Statisticians (ATFS)
Athletics Canada
Atlanta Hawks
Ball State University
Baseball Almanac
Big Ten Conference (bigten.org)
Eastern Intercollegiate Wrestling Association
Federation of American Statisticians of Track (FAST)
Illinois High School Association
Indiana High School Athletic Association
Indiana Track and Field Hall of Fame
Indiana University
International Swimming Hall of Fame
Major League Baseball (MLB.com)
Major League Soccer (MLS.com)
Mississippi Sports Hall of Fame and Museum
Naismith Basketball Hall of Fame

National Basketball Association (NBA.com)
Ohio High School Athletic Association
TeamUSA.org
University of Michigan
University of New Mexico
USA Basketball
USA Diving
USA Swimming
USA Track & Field
USA Wrestling
US Soccer
US Masters Swimming
Wabash College
World Athletics (formerly International Association of Athletics Federations/ IAAF)

TELEVISION AND VIDEO SITES

KITV, Honolulu
WTHR, Indianapolis
YouTube

OTHER

Fenwick High School, Oak Park, Illinois
Historical Society of Princeton
Princeton, New Jersey, Public Library
Shell Point Retirement Community

INDIANA UNIVERSITY OLYMPIANS

1904 ST. LOUIS
Leroy Samse, track and field/pole vault, silver
Thad Shideler, track and field/110-meter hurdles, silver

1932 LOS ANGELES
Ivan Fuqua, track and field/4×400 relay, gold
Charles Hornbostel, track and field/800 meters, sixth

1936 BERLIN
Tom Deckard, track and field/5,000 meters, twenty-sixth
Charles Hornbostel, track and field/800 meters, fifth
Don Lash, track and field/10,000 meters, eighth; 5,000 meters, thirteenth
Dick Voliva, wrestling/147 pounds, silver

1948 LONDON
Roy Cochran, track and field/400-meter hurdles, gold; 4×400 relay, gold
Fred Wilt, track and field/10,000 meters, eleventh

1952 HELSINKI
Milt Campbell, track and field/decathlon, silver
Judy Roberts Thomas, swimming/100-meter freestyle, seventh in semifinal
Fred Wilt, track and field/10,000 meters, twenty-first
Bill Woolsey, swimming/1,500 freestyle; 4×200 freestyle relay, gold

1956 MELBOURNE
Greg Bell, track and field/long jump, gold
Milt Campbell, track and field/decathlon, gold
Frank McKinney, swimming/100 backstroke, bronze
Richard Tanabe, swimming/4×200 freestyle relay, reserve
Bill Woolsey, swimming/100 freestyle, sixth; 400 freestyle, fourth in heat; 4×200 freestyle relay, silver
Verle Wright Jr., shooting/rifle, three-positions, fourteenth; prone, thirty-sixth

1960 ROME
Walt Bellamy, basketball, gold
George Breen, swimming/1,500 freestyle, bronze
Willie May, track and field/110-meter hurdles, silver
Frank McKinney, swimming/100 backstroke, silver; 4×100 medley relay, gold
Alan Somers, swimming/400 freestyle, fifth; 1,500 freestyle, seventh
Mike Troy, swimming/200 butterfly, gold; 4×200 freestyle relay, gold

1964 TOKYO
Kevin Berry (Australia), swimming/200 butterfly, gold
Lesley Bush, diving/10-meter platform, gold
Tom Dinsley (Canada), diving/3-meter springboard, eighteenth; 10-meter platform, twenty-fourth
Kathy Ellis, swimming/100 freestyle, bronze; 100 butterfly, bronze; 4×100 freestyle relay, gold; 4×100 medley relay, gold
Chat Jastremski, swimming/200 breaststroke, bronze
Bob Loh (Hong Kong), swimming/100, 400, and 1,500 freestyles
Luis Nino de Rivera (Mexico), diving/3-meter springboard, twelfth; 10-meter platform, tenth
Inge Pertmayr (Austria), diving/3-meter springboard, sixteenth; 10-meter platform, sixth
Fred Schmidt, swimming/200 butterfly, bronze; 4×100 medley relay, gold
Lary Schulhof, swimming/4×100 freestyle relay, prelims
Ken Sitzberger, diving/3-meter springboard, gold
Terri Stickles, swimming/400 freestyle, bronze
Tom Trethewey, swimming/200 breaststroke, ninth
Bob Windle (Australia), swimming/1,500 freestyle, gold; 4×100 freestyle relay, bronze

1968 MEXICO CITY
Larry Barbiere, swimming/100 backstroke, fourth
Wes Brooker (Canada), track and field/400-meter hurdles, fifth in heat; 4×400 relay, seventh in heat
Lesley Bush, diving/10-meter platform, twentieth
Santiago Esteva (Spain), swimming/100 and 200 backstrokes; 4×200 freestyle relay; 4×100 medley relay, eighth
Rick Gilbert, diving/10-meter platform, seventeenth
Gary Hall, swimming/200 backstroke, fourth; 400 individual medley, silver
Jim Henry, diving/3-meter springboard, bronze
Charlie Hickox, swimming/100 backstroke, silver; 200 individual medley, gold; 400 individual medley, gold; 4×100 medley relay, gold
Jack Horsleyn, swimming/200 backstroke, bronze
Ron Jacks (Canada), swimming/400 freestyle; 100 and 200 butterfly; 4×200 freestyle relay, seventh
Chet Jastremski, swimming/4×100 medley relay, prelims

John Kinsella, swimming/1,500 freestyle, silver
Andy Loh (Hong Kong), swimming/400 freestyle, 100 butterfly
Bob Loh (Hong Kong), swimming/200 and 400 freestyle, 100 butterfly
Don McKenzie, swimming/100 breaststroke, gold; 4×100 medley relay, gold
Luis Nino de Rivera (Mexico), diving; 3-meter springboard, fourth; 10-meter platform, seventh
Dave Perkowski, swimming/100 breaststroke, third in semifinal
Inge Pertmayr (Austria), diving/10-meter platform, ninth
George Smith (Canada), swimming/200 individual medley, fifth; 400 individual medley, tenth; 4×100 freestyle relay, seventh; 4×200 freestyle relay, fourth
Mark Spitz, swimming/100 freestyle, bronze; 100 butterfly, silver; 200 butterfly, eighth; 4×100 freestyle relay, gold; 4×200 freestyle relay, gold
Bob Windle (Australia), swimming/100 freestyle, eleventh; 200 freestyle, sixth; 4×100 freestyle relay, bronze; 4×200 freestyle relay, silver
Win Young, diving/10-meter platform, bronze

1972 MUNICH

Romulo Arantes (Brazil), swimming/4×100 medley relay, fifth
Gary Conelly, swimming/4×100 and 4×200 freestyle relays, prelims
Scott Cranham (Canada), diving/3-meter springboard, fourteenth; 10-meter platform, twenty-seventh
Rick Earley, diving/10-meter platform, sixth
Gary Hall, swimming/200 butterfly, silver; 200 individual medley, silver; 400 individual medley, fifth
John Kinsella, swimming/4×200 freestyle relay, gold
John Murphy, swimming/100 freestyle, fourth; 100 backstroke, bronze; 4×100 freestyle relay, gold
Inge Pertmayr (Austria), diving/10-meter platform, eighth
Cynthia Potter, diving/3-meter springboard, seventh
Charles Richards, modern pentathlon/individual, ninth; team, fourth
Niki Stajkovic (Austria), diving/10-meter platform, eighteenth
Mark Spitz, swimming/100 and 200 freestyle, golds; 100 and 200 butterfly, golds; 4×100 freestyle, 4×200 freestyle, and 4×100 medley relays, all gold
Mike Stamm, swimming/100 and 200 backstrokes, silvers; 4×100 medley relay, gold
Wayne Stetina, cycling/team time trial, fifteenth
Fred Tyler, swimming/200 freestyle, fifth; 4×200 freestyle relay, gold

1976 MONTREAL

Romulo Arantes (Brazil), swimming/100 backstroke, eleventh; 200 backstroke, eleventh
Pedro Balcells (Spain), swimming/100 breaststroke, twenty-first; 4×100 medley relay, ninth
Quinn Buckner, basketball, gold
Scott Cranham (Canada), diving/3-meter springboard, sixteenth; 10-meter platform, seventeenth

Santiago Esteva (Spain), swimming/100 backstroke, fifteenth; 200 backstroke, seventeenth; 4×200 freestyle relay, twelfth; 4×100 medley relay, ninth
Gary Hall, swimming/100 butterfly, bronze
Jennifer Hooker, swimming/200 freestyle, sixth; 4×100 relay, prelims
Charles Keating, swimming/200 breaststroke, fifth
Mark Kerry (Australia), swimming/100 backstroke, seventh; 200 backstroke, fifth; 4×100 medley relay, sixth
Wendy Lee (Canada), swimming/400 freestyle, eleventh
Scott May, basketball, gold
Djan Madruga (Brazil), swimming; 400 freestyle, fourth; 1,500 freestyle, fourth
Jim Montgomery, swimming/100 freestyle, gold; 4×200 and 4×100 medley relays, golds
Cynthia Potter, diving/3-meter springboard, bronze
Niki Stajkovic (Austria), diving/10-meter platform, twelfth
Wayne Stetina, cycling/team time trial, nineteenth

1980 MOSCOW
(Boycotted by United States)
Mark Kerry (Australia), swimming/100 backstroke, ninth; 200 backstroke, bronze; 4×100 medley relay, gold
Djan Madruga (Brazil) swimming/400 freestyle, fourth; 1,500 freestyle, fourteenth; 400 individual medley, fifth; 4×200 freestyle relay, bronze
Niki Stajkovic (Austria), diving/3-meter springboard, twelfth; 10 meter platform, eighth
Claus Thomsen (Denmark), diving/10-meter platform, tenth
Juan Carlos Vallejo (Spain), swimming, 4×200 freestyle relay

LOS ANGELES 1984
Steve Alford, basketball, gold
Uwe Blab (West Germany), basketball, eighth
Linda Cunningham (Canada), basketball, fourth
Angelo DiBernardo, soccer, ninth
Mark Kerry (Australia), swimming/100 backstroke, fifth; 4×100 medley relay, bronze
Deryck Marks (Jamaica), swimming/100 freestyle; 100 butterfly; 4×100 freestyle and 4×100 medley relays
Sunder Nix, track and field/400 meters, fifth; 4×400 relay, gold
Rotimi Peters (Nigeria), track and field/4×400 relay, bronze
John Robert Plankenhorn, canoe/Canadian singles, 500 meters, fourth in heat; Canadian doubles, 1,000 meters, fifth.
Jim Spivey, track and field/1,500 meters, fifth
Gregg Thompson, soccer, ninth
Juan Carlos Vallejo (Spain), swimming/200 freestyle, tenth; 4×200 freestyle relay, eleventh

1988 SEOUL

Vilma Aguielera (Puerto Rico), swimming
Terry Brahm, track and field/5,000 meters, fifteenth in semifinal
Robert Cannon, track and field/triple jump, twenty-ninth
Eoin Collins (Ireland), tennis/doubles, seventeenth
Mark Deady, track and field, 1,500 meters, eighth in semifinal
Mark Lenzi, diving/3-meter springboard, gold
Sergio Lopez (Spain), swimming/200 breaststroke, bronze
Mickey Morandini, baseball, gold
Albert Robinson, track and field/4×100 relay, disqualified
John Stollmeyer, soccer, thirteenth

1992 BARCELONA

Uwe Blab (Germany), basketball, seventh
Eoin Collins (Ireland), tennis/doubles, ninth
Bob Kennedy, track and field/5,000 meters, twelfth
Mark Lenzi, diving/3-meter springboard, gold
Sergio Lopez (Spain), swimming/100 breaststroke, twenty-third; 200 breaststroke, bronze; 200 individual medley, ninth
Steve Snow, soccer, ninth
Jim Spivey, track and field/1,500 meters, eighth
Niki Stajkovic (Austria), diving/3-meter springboard, twenty-second
Dave Volz, track and field/pole vault, fifth

1996 ATLANTA

Bob Kennedy, track and field/5,000 meters, sixth
Mark Lenzi, diving/3-meter springboard, bronze
Brian Maisonneuve, soccer, tenth
Jim Spivey, track and field, 5,000 meters, thirteenth in semifinal

2000 SYDNEY

DeDee Nathan, track and field/heptathlon, ninth
Sara Reiling, diving/10-meter platform, thirteenth
Michelle Venturella, softball, gold

2004 ATHENS

Cassandra Cardinell, diving/synchronized 10-meter platform, seventh
Sara Reiling, diving/10-meter platform, tenth; synchro 10-meter platform, seventh
Rose Richmond, track and field/long jump, nineteenth
Kimiko (Hirai) Soldati, diving/3-meter springboard, twenty-first
Vasili Spanos (Greece), baseball, seventh
Phil Trinter, sailing/two-person keelboat, fifth
Kate Zubkova (Ukraine), swimming/100 butterfly, thirtieth; 4×100 medley relay, tenth

2008 BEIJING

Bader Al-Muhana (Saudi Arabia) swimming/100 butterfly, sixty-first
Kayla Bashore, field hockey, eighth
Mariangee Bogado (Venezuela), softball, seventh
Sergiy Fesenko (Ukraine), swimming/400 freestyle, sixteenth; 1,500 freestyle, twenty-third
Christina Loukas, diving/3-meter springboard, ninth
David Neville, track and field/400 meters, bronze; 4×400 relay, gold
Aarik Wilson, track and field/triple jump, thirty-third
Kate Zubkova (Ukraine), swimming/100 backstroke, twenty-first; 100 butterfly, twenty-fourth

2012 LONDON

Kayla Bashore, field hockey, twelfth
Derek Drouin (Canada), track and field/high jump, bronze
Margaux Farrell (France), swimming/4×200 freestyle relay, bronze
Christina Loukas, diving/3-meter springboard, eighth
Nicholas Schwab (Dominican Republic), swimming/200 freestyle, thirty-seventh
Dorina Szekeres (Hungary), swimming/200 backstroke, thirty-fifth
Oriancia Velasquez (Colombia), soccer, eleventh

2016 RIO DE JANEIRO

Kelsie Ahbe (Canada), track and field/pole vault, twelfth
James Connor (Australia), diving/10-meter platform, fifteenth
Amy Cozad, diving/synchronized 10-meter platform, seventh
Derek Drouin (Canada), track and field/high jump, gold
Marwan El-Kamash (Egypt), swimming/200 freestyle, twenty-fourth; 400 freestyle, sixteenth
Kennedy Goss (Canada), swimming/4×200 freestyle relay, bronze
Michael Hixon, diving/3-meter springboard, tenth; synchronized 3-meter springboard, silver
Ali Khalafalla (Egypt), swimming/50 freestyle, twenty-third
Lilly King, swimming/100 breaststroke, gold; 200 breaststroke, twelfth; 4×100 medley relay, gold
Cody Miller, swimming/100 breaststroke, bronze; 4×100 medley relay, gold
Olu Olamigoke (Nigeria), track and field/triple jump, thirty-second
Jessica Parratto, diving/10-meter platform, tenth; synchronized 10-meter platform, seventh
Blake Pieroni, swimming/4×100 freestyle relay, gold
Anze Tavar (Slovenia), swimming/100 freestyle, thirty-sixth; 200 freestyle, thirty-ninth
Orianica Velasquez (Colombia), soccer, eleventh

DAVID WOODS caught the Olympic spirit early. He has been covering Olympians since 1972, when, as a naïve college kid, he covered the training camp of the American women's track and field team in Champaign, Illinois, for the *News-Gazette*. Woods's first Olympics were at Los Angeles in 1984. He has covered Olympic sports for the *Indianapolis Star* since 1994, reporting from every Summer Games from 1996 through 2016. He is the first four-time winner of the Jesse Abramson Award in journalism from Track and Field Writers of America and has won more than twenty-five national and state awards. This is his fourth book. The three others were about Butler University basketball. Woods, a native of Urbana, Illinois, lives in Indianapolis with his wife, Jan. They have two married daughters, Karen and Kathy.

www.ingramcontent.com/pod-product-compliance
Lightning Source LLC
Chambersburg PA
CBHW042129160426
43198CB00022B/2953